THE EVERYTHING.
GUIDE TO WRITING
A ROMANCE NOVEL

Dear Reader,

Everyone has a dream. If you've picked up this book, it's probably because you have a dream of writing a romance novel of your very own, much like those by JoAnn Ross, Linda Howard, Johanna Lindsey, and the reigning queen of romance herself, Nora Roberts.

We know the feeling. After all, from the time we were both little girls growing up in the South—Christie in Alabama and Faye in Mississippi—our individual dreams have been to write books that touch the hearts of readers. We've both been lucky enough to have fulfilled our dreams, and we're thrilled at being given an opportunity to help you fulfill yours by writing *The Everything® Guide to Writing a Romance Novel.*

And this book truly is everything we both know about the craft of writing. From plotting and characterization to adding sexual tension and conflict, we've tried our collective best to give you the tools and information you need to succeed in your dream of writing a romance novel.

Best of luck, and Happy Writing!

Christie Craig   *Faye Hughes*

Welcome to the EVERYTHING® Series!

These handy, accessible books give you all you need to tackle a difficult project, gain a new hobby, comprehend a fascinating topic, prepare for an exam, or even brush up on something you learned back in school but have since forgotten.

You can choose to read an *Everything®* book from cover to cover or just pick out the information you want from our four useful boxes: e-questions, e-facts, e-alerts, and e-ssentials.

We give you everything you need to know on the subject, but throw in a lot of fun stuff along the way, too.

We now have more than 400 *Everything®* books in print, spanning such wide-ranging categories as weddings, pregnancy, cooking, music instruction, foreign language, crafts, pets, New Age, and so much more. When you're done reading them all, you can finally say you know *Everything®*!

QUESTIONS?
Answers to
common questions

FACTS
Important snippets
of information

ALERTS!
Urgent
warnings

ESSENTIALS
Quick
handy tips

PUBLISHER Karen Cooper

DIRECTOR OF ACQUISITIONS AND INNOVATION Paula Munier

MANAGING EDITOR, EVERYTHING SERIES Lisa Laing

COPY CHIEF Casey Ebert

ACQUISITIONS EDITOR Lisa Laing

SENIOR DEVELOPMENT EDITOR Brett Palana-Shanahan

EDITORIAL ASSISTANT Hillary Thompson

Visit the entire Everything® series at *www.everything.com*

THE
EVERYTHING®
GUIDE TO WRITING A ROMANCE NOVEL

From writing the perfect love scene to
finding the right publisher—all you need
to fulfill your dreams

Christie Craig and Faye Hughes

Adamsmedia
Avon, Massachusetts

This book is dedicated to the romantic that lives inside every writer.

An Everything® Series Book.
Everything® and everything.com® are registered trademarks of F+W Publications, Inc.

Published by Adams Media, an F+W Publications Company
57 Littlefield Street, Avon, MA 02322 U.S.A.
www.adamsmedia.com

ISBN 10: 1-59869-537-1
ISBN 13: 978-1-59869-537-3

Printed in the United States of America.

J I H G F E D C B A

Library of Congress Cataloging-in-Publication Data
is available from the publisher.

This publication is designed to provide accurate and authoritative information with regard to the subject matter covered. It is sold with the understanding that the publisher is not engaged in rendering legal, accounting, or other professional advice. If legal advice or other expert assistance is required, the services of a competent professional person should be sought.

—From a *Declaration of Principles* jointly adopted by a Committee of the American Bar Association and a Committee of Publishers and Associations

Many of the designations used by manufacturers and sellers to distinguish their products are claimed as trademarks. Where those designations appear in this book and Adams Media was aware of a trademark claim, the designations have been printed with initial capital letters.

This book is available at quantity discounts for bulk purchases.
For information, please call 1-800-289-0963.

Contents

Acknowledgments

Our heartfelt appreciation to: Our agents, Kim Lionetti of BookEnds LLC and Caren Johnson of Caren Johnson Literary Agency; our editor Lisa Laing, without whose support this book wouldn't have been possible; to our families—Steve, Steven, Nina and Jason; to our friends—Stephen, Debbi, and Ray; to our critique partners—Teri, Nancy, Suzan, and Jody; and finally to Kathleen E. Woodiwiss who started it all with a little book called *The Flame and the Flower*.

We thank you all.

Top Ten Reasons to Write a Romance Novel

1. You believe in happy endings.

2. You've always wanted to write a novel.

3. You *enjoy* reading romance novels.

4. Romance novels speak the universal language of love conquering all.

5. You're up for a creative challenge.

6. More unpublished authors make a first sale in romance than in any other genre.

7. Romance readers are loyal and will follow a favorite author to a new genre.

8. More romances are sold every year than any other kind of novel.

9. The strategy has worked okay for Nora Roberts.

10. You know in your heart you could succeed if you only had the chance.

Introduction

▶ Most of you can probably remember the moment it happened—the instant when the idea of writing a romance novel first filled your heart with dreams and your head with characters. Life became grist for the writing mill. The hunky cop who gave you a ticket becomes inspiration for your hero. A trip to the doctor's office for your child's earache becomes a chance to ask about a disease you plan to write about. It's as if you are suddenly looking at life in 3-D, wanting to see more, know more, experience more, so you can write about it.

For some, this magical moment happened after you finished a heartwarming romance and marveled at the author's ability to write such a story. For others, it happened when you couldn't find the type of book you wanted to read, and decided to just write it yourself. And still others experienced the moment after throwing a book against the wall and declaring, "I could do better than that!"

Whatever inspired you to try your hand at romance writing, you should know that you are about to embark on a journey—a wild, sometimes exciting, sometimes not so exciting, voyage. Because writing is basically a solitary profession, a lot of the journey will be one of self-discovery. As you trek down the writing path, you'll learn what is truly important to you. You'll find yourself digging deep into your heart and soul, tapping into your most private experiences—some good, some not so good—to add richness to the stories you put on paper. However solitary writing may be, if you take the recommendations of this book and join writing groups, you will also find a world of new friends. People who think like you think—people who don't consider it strange to rush out to the bookstore to buy the book, *101 Ways to*

Kill Someone or to ask your lawyer . . . "If I think my child was swapped at birth, and I wanted to track down my daughter, who do I need to see first?"

These people will understand that when you hear voices in your head, you are happy your characters are talking to you, and not the least bit worried about your mental health. Yes . . . the people you meet will be a part of this journey that you'll not want to miss.

As you prepare to embark on this journey, you'll need some supplies. A first-aid kit is crucial. Few of you will complete the writing adventure without having your feelings hurt and egos bruised at least a little bit. That's why you'll also be bringing some chocolate and a suitcase full of perseverance—yes, perseverance. This journey could take a while. Believing your first attempt at writing will be a bestseller is almost as farfetched as believing a brain surgeon's first day of training will involve a knife and a live patient.

You'll also need an endless supply of hunger for knowledge. For while *The Everything® Guide to Writing a Romance Novel* is a good place to start your education, writing is a nonstop course on the lessons of being human and crafting words.

Also, make sure you pack plenty of attitude for your journey. You'll need ammunition for people who ignorantly believe a book about love is somehow trivial. Hold your head high. The romance genre isn't 55 percent of all mass market fiction sold today for no reason. Young girls don't spend hours dreaming of their first kiss, their first dance, or the day they walk down the aisle for trivial reasons.

This journey will not always be easy. The rejections will probably come, and it may be a long trek before you arrive at that wonderful place called publication. But the joys of writing are not just about the destination, but about the journey. Only a writer will know the elation of creating people, of falling in love with these people, and then having them fall in love with each other. And oh . . . the bliss of completing a book. Savor your accomplishments; nurture your passion for writing, for this is the key to sustaining perseverance. And as you make this trek, remember the lessons you are learning about falling in love will not only have the ability to make you a better romance author, but a better person.

Bon voyage!

CHAPTER 1

Why Write a Romance?

Do you have what it takes to write a romance novel? You might be surprised to discover that you do. But turning that dream of becoming a published romance novelist into reality takes talent, hard work, determination, and an insider's knowledge of how the industry works. Before you start typing "Chapter 1," you'll need to know who writes the books, who reads the books, and, most important of all, what makes these books such perennial favorites. In other words, you'll need to start with the basics.

History of the Romance Novel

Romance novels have been around for almost as long as published books have. Maybe even longer, since many scholars point to the oral traditions of telling stories about the power of love to conquer all as being early forms of romance fiction.

ESSENTIAL

Remember the fairytales you heard as a child? *Beauty and the Beast. Cinderella. Snow White and the Seven Dwarfs.* At the heart of each lies a classic romance plot that can still be found in modern love stories—granted, the hero might be the one who needs rescuing these days but the basic premise of the redemptive power of love remains the same.

As a literary form, the romance novel probably first appeared in the nineteenth century, as a class of popular literature known as "domestic fiction," which were novels written by women for women. The books, which featured a poor but feisty heroine and little emphasis on a hero, sold extremely well, although the critics usually panned them.

Another precursor of the modern romance novel is the gothic. Popularized by authors like Ann Radcliffe, gothics featured spooky castles with secret passageways, mad relatives locked away in attics, and the occasional vengeful ghost.

For most people, however, three novels stand out as classic early romances:

- *Pride and Prejudice* by Jane Austen
- *Wuthering Heights* by Emily Brontë
- *Jane Eyre* by Charlotte Brontë

The enigmatic Mr. Radcliffe. The brooding Heathcliff. The spunky Elizabeth Bennet. Who could forget these memorable characters? The work of Jane Austen and the Brontë sisters have stood the test of time and inspired many of the writers who came after them.

The Queen of Romance, Barbara Cartland

No discussion of the history of romance fiction could be complete without a mention of Barbara Cartland, who was as well known for her trademark pink outfits, large plumed hats, and ever-present Pekingese as she was for her romance novels. Her books—usually short, non–sexually explicit tales of a young, inexperienced woman and a worldly titled nobleman, who meet and fall in love amidst a tale of historical intrigue—thrilled generations of romance readers. At the height of her popularity during the 1980s, she wrote an average of twenty-three romance novels a year, almost all of them dictated to an assistant while Barbara reclined on a sofa.

FACT

Dame Barbara was the most prolific romance writer of the twentieth century. At the time of her death at age ninety-eight, she still had 160 romance novels completed and awaiting publication.

In 1991, Barbara Cartland received her highest career award when she was named a Dame of the British Empire for her literary contributions and volunteer work. Although she passed away in 2000, her legacy lives on in her 723 published books.

Then Along Came Harlequin . . .

Meanwhile, Mary Bonnycastle, the wife of Canadian publishing executive Richard Bonnycastle, had noticed a virtually untapped market for romance fiction and convinced her husband to turn their fledgling book publishing company, Harlequin Enterprises, in that direction in the late 1950s.

Until that time, Harlequin had been printing a mixture of genre fiction and nonfiction paperbacks. That changed, however, in the early 1960s, when they moved exclusively to printing romance fiction previously published in Great Britain by Mills and Boon. The staple of the Mills and Boon collection were medical romances.

Rather than just offer their romance novels for sale in bookstores, Harlequin bucked tradition by making their books available in the places where women shopped most often—supermarkets, department stores, and drugstores. It was a smart move, too.

Before long, sales of Harlequin's romances were skyrocketing. In fact, Harlequin romances, with their tales of an arrogant, older, and more financially stable male and a younger, virginal, and impoverished female—soon became synonymous with romance fiction itself.

The Heyday of Romance Fiction

While romance sales were hot, the books themselves got a whole lot hotter in the late 1970s with more sexually explicit fare such as *Sweet Savage Love* by Rosemary Rogers and *The Flame and the Flower* by Kathleen Woodiwiss. These steamier romances quickly climbed the bestseller charts and launched the careers of many talented new authors.

Harlequin Enterprises took the lead but soon publishers like Avon, New American Library, and Doubleday came on board with new lines for romance fiction. One of the most successful romance imprints of that time was Silhouette Books, an entity of Simon and Schuster. Harlequin Enterprises bought Silhouette in 1984 and it remains a strong component of the Harlequin romance empire today.

Oh, Fabio!

If you're like most people, when you think of a romance novel, you probably think of those historical romance covers from the 1980s and 1990s with handsome, muscular men and beautiful women in amorous—though mostly clothed—poses. Known in the industry as "the clinch," these covers were a staple of the genre, but the books inside them were what mattered to the readers.

All of that seemed to change when a male model named Fabio Lanzoni appeared on the scene in the mid-1980s. Tall and muscular with flowing blond hair and smoldering good looks, the Italian hunk quickly became the next big thing in romance fiction, often drawing larger crowds at author gatherings than the authors did. Soon, other male hunks claimed the spotlight, but none had the lasting power of the "Great Blond One."

But a romance reader's first love has always been the books themselves. Soon, the male cover models faded to the background as the emphasis again became focused on the stories inside.

QUESTION?

Who did the cover art?
The creation of a historical romance cover was a complicated affair. First, a photographer posed the models in period costumes and photographed them. Then artists, such as Elaine Duillo, would paint the covers. The process could take several weeks. Ironically, in the case of many new writers, the artists were often paid more for the covers than the authors were paid for the books themselves.

Evolution of the Romance Novel

As times changed, so did romance novels. Gone were the virginal heroines and the arrogant, more experienced heroes. In their place were modern men and women, facing modern problems. Alcoholism, infidelity, abusive relationships—all become fodder for the fertile imaginations of the modern romance novelist.

Rather than being just "those silly little books," romance novels had the financial clout needed to be taken seriously. Unfortunately, literary respect was another thing.

Getting Past the Negative Stereotype

For most people, a romance author is a Barbara Cartland clone—a matronly lady in pink, maybe even with a feather boa around her neck, who dictates her novels to a nearby assistant while she reclines on a silk brocade chaise lounge feeding liver snaps to her well-groomed lap dog. But while that image may have worked for Dame Barbara, it is far removed from the reality of a bestselling romance author in the twenty-first century.

Romance Writers of America (*www.rwanational.org*), the largest group of writers of romance fiction in the world with over 9,500 members strong, is committed to changing that misconception through their advocacy program.

ALERT!

RWA does more than educate the public about the romance genre. They also protect their members from signing bad publishing contracts and hiring shady literary agents. The organization screens publishing companies and literary agents before placing them on an approved list for use by their membership.

Today's romance novelists come from everywhere—they're physicians, lawyers, soldiers, scientists, mothers, fathers, teachers, secretaries, homemakers, and business executives. The one thing they all have in common is their talent, their perseverance, and a firm belief that love really can conquer all . . . at least on the pages of their books.

Separating Myth from Reality

One of the biggest myths about writing a romance is the same myth found in other genres of fiction. Namely, that since the books follow a formula—girl meets boy, girl loses boy, girl wins boy back—they must be easy to write.

They're not, of course.

In fact, a strong argument could be made that the opposite is closer to the truth.

The market is fiercely competitive. Most publishers no longer accept unsolicited work from unagented writers, and many unpublished authors find it difficult to find an agent to represent them. While the books do follow a loose formula, publishers require—and readers demand—freshness and variety. To succeed in romance fiction, a writer not only has to tell a good story that has a unique twist to a familiar formula, she must write a good book.

Financial Appeal of the Genre

So, can you make money writing romance novels? Absolutely!

As for how much, well, that depends. A quick check of recent deals at Publishers Marketplace (*www.publishersmarketplace.com*) will probably show several major deals (deals over $500,000) for new novels by bestselling romance writers within the past year.

But new writers rarely sign those kinds of contracts. Often, a first book contract will come with a modest advance against earnings. An average advance for a series romance runs around $3,000 to $4,000. For a single title, the advances are generally higher, though they can be less for smaller publishers.

FACT

When most writers sign a publishing contract, they are guaranteed an advance, which is a good-faith payment made in anticipation of future royalties. The size of an advance can vary, as will the terms of the contract. Generally, an author can keep the advance, even if the publisher decides to cancel the deal through no fault of the author.

It can take a new author several years to build a sales record strong enough to allow her to quit her day job and write full-time. Still, for those who have the ambition and the talent, the sky is the proverbial limit.

Publishing Statistics

So, just how popular is the romance genre? With over $1.4 billion in sales each year, romance novels easily outsell any other type of fiction in the United States.

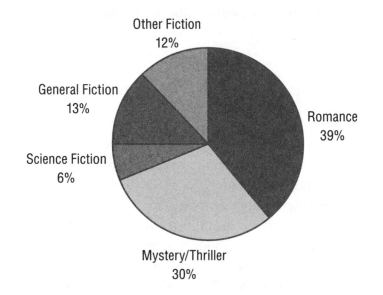

Romance Statistics

The majority of the sales are with mass-market paperback titles, though trade paperbacks and hardcovers are strong as well.

Understanding the Romance Reader

Who reads romance novels? A better question might be who doesn't read romance novels? According to statistics provided by Romance Writers of America, the average romance reader is female, married, and college educated. But fans of the genre can be of any age and any economic background. They could be your mother, your babysitter, your doctor . . . or even the father of one of your children's friends.

Yes, a steadily increasing number of romance readers are male. But regardless of gender, income, or career, the thing to understand about the romance reader is why they read this particular genre of fiction. They read it for the romance. They read it because they want to experience the emotion of falling in love.

Reading Is Recommended

Of course, one of the best ways to learn about romance novels is to read the work of those who are considered the best in the genre.

And who determines who is the best? Usually the readers who buy the books, the reviewers who rate the books, and the published membership of Romance Writers of America, who nominate them for the annual Rita award. RWA has several lists on their Web site—*www.rwanational.org*—of the current bestselling romance titles and award winners.

ALERT!

To get an edge on the competition, read the work of debut authors. Established romance writers can often break the rules of the genre but a new author trying to break in needs to make her manuscript rejection-proof. Reading a debut novel can give you valuable insight into the tastes of the acquiring editor for a particular publishing house.

Another great resource for finding a recommended reading list of current titles is to pick up a copy of *Romantic Times BOOKreviews* magazine (*www.romantictimes.com*), a leading monthly publication for fiction lovers of all genres, including romance. With over 250 reviews of current titles each month, as well as informative author interviews and writing tips for beginners, *RT* has been a staple of the romance community for years.

Famous Romance Novelists

So, who are the more renowned authors of modern romance fiction? The list is a long and varied one. Barbara Cartland, Danielle Steele, and Janet Dailey usually come to mind when thinking of popular romance authors from the twentieth century.

In recent years, though, several men have gained fame for their romance novels. Chief among them are Nicholas Sparks and James Patterson, who have both had romance titles at the top of the bestseller lists.

However, the most famous romance author working in the industry today is probably Nora Roberts, who sells more books each year than any other U.S. author.

CHAPTER 2

Understanding the Genre

More than half of all paperbacks sold in the United States are romance novels. But romances are far from just the girl-meets-boy, girl-loses-boy, girl-gets-boy-back formulas of the past. Some romances are sweet, even inspirational, while others are very, *very* spicy. Some are set in the present, others set in the past, and a few are even set in the distant future or in faraway galaxies. So, what makes a romance so appealing? You might be surprised to find that it's not what you think.

What Is a Romance Novel?

Defining a romance novel seems easy enough. It's a novel about two people who fall in love, right? Well, yes.

And no.

Margaret Mitchell's *Gone with the Wind* might be considered a romance but, technically speaking, it's not. The relationship between Scarlett and Rhett, while important, is not the central plot of that book. Scarlett's life journey is the focus of the novel.

Publishing professionals generally define a romance novel as a work of fiction with a love story that is essential to the plot and a Happily Ever After (HEA) type of ending. But what does that mean, really, when it comes time for you to write your novel?

Focus on the Romance!

Regardless of the type of romance, the one element they all have in common is that the romantic relationship between your two main characters is always front and center. Think about *Gone with the Wind*. If that book were truly a romance, the reader would have kept turning the pages to find out if Scarlett and Rhett would end up together, rather than to see what Scarlett would do next.

In other words, your subplots must support the central love story.

ESSENTIAL

It's hard to fill the pages of a 400-page book with only the romance of your main characters as the storyline. That's where the use of subplots and secondary characters come in. Whether they add humor or drama to your story, subplots and secondary characters can give your novel depth.

Readers keep reading a mystery novel to find out who done it. They read a romance novel because of the developing romantic relationship between your two main characters. Will the hero and heroine work through their inner conflicts and find a lasting happiness? That question fuels every romance novel's engine. Everything else—a war, a sudden illness of a child, a killer, family discord—is secondary to the main storyline.

The Payoff at the End

When they close the pages of your book, readers want their happy ending, too. Your main characters don't have to walk off into the sunset holding hands but the reader needs to know that their investment of time and emotion in your story was worth the price they paid for your novel.

It's the classic good-triumphing-over-evil premise. If your romance was done well, your main characters faced many obstacles on their path to a Happily Ever After and your reader expects—no, make that *demands*—their payoff at the end.

To put it another way, a good first chapter will sell that book . . . but a good last chapter will sell the next novel.

The Happily Ever After

Just how important is the Happily Ever After, or HEA for short, to the success of a romance novel? Very. Unlike some genres where the ending is just about tying up the remaining loose ends, the HEA in a romance novel needs to leave the reader feeling emotionally satisfied.

That doesn't mean that every romance novel must end with a marriage proposal. To the contrary, a romance reader will be happy as long as she feels the ending was positive and uplifting with a promise toward a future happiness.

The Role of the Hero and Heroine

Probably more so than in any other literary genre, the two main characters of a romance novel are the most important component of the book. If you choose the right characters to carry your story from the first page to the last, the readers will keep turning those pages. What's more, she'll probably recommend the book to her friends and place it on her "keeper" shelf.

But if you choose the wrong characters, well, there's a good chance your book may end up on the remainder table of your local bookseller.

The Heroine

She can be young and just falling in love for the first time. Or she can be older—widowed perhaps or divorced—and looking for someone to share the next chapter of her life. More than likely, however, the heroine of a romance novel is somewhere in the middle between the two extremes.

FACT

Modern romance heroines are usually strong, confident, and in charge of their own lives . . . although their love lives may be another story entirely. Romance heroines have been everything from cops to government assassins, and starship captains to Regency-era spies. But even if she's leading an ordinary life as a kindergarten teacher, she's the one who decides the course of her life.

More important than her age, however, is that she is someone with whom your reader can relate. Someone your reader can understand. While every character can and should be unique, romance heroines generally have two similar qualities:

1. The female reader can imagine herself as the heroine.
2. The heroine is the perfect match for the hero.

Other than those two similarities, your heroine is limited only by the plotline of your novel—and by the requirements of your intended market. (For more information about developing your heroine, refer to Chapter 10.)

The Hero

Much like the heroine, the hero of a romance novel can be of any age appropriate to the story, including being younger than his heroine. Most heroes, however, are in their thirties and have at least one failed romantic relationship in their past.

Just as it is true with the romance heroine, age isn't what defines a romance hero. It's his attitude. Whether an alpha male—the physically strong man of-action type—or the beta male—the emotionally strong, nurturing type—a romance hero knows how to win his heroine's heart. Regardless of what he may say in the beginning of the novel, he'll always step up to the challenge in the end, whether it's leading his troops into a battle he suspects they can never win or babysitting his sister's twin toddlers.

But all romance heroes do share two common traits:

1. The female reader can imagine herself falling in love with the hero.
2. The hero is the perfect match for the heroine.

The rest, however, is up to the author's imagination and talent. (For more information about developing your hero, refer to Chapter 10.)

Making your hero a multilayered character with emotional baggage is fine but try to avoid making him so complex that he's impossible to understand. After all, if your reader can't identify with why your heroine is falling in love with the hero, it's unlikely she'll care that much about finishing your novel . . . or buying your next one.

Sweet Versus Spicy

Romance novels can vary widely in terms of sexual content. Some readers like their romances to be less explicit when the temperature begins to rise between the hero and heroine. Other readers prefer a little more, well, spice in their reading materials, as evidenced by the popularity of erotic romances.

Luckily, romance novels can accommodate both tastes.

Sweet Romances

Sweet romances are those without graphic depictions of sex or sexual situations. Although they can have either contemporary or historical settings, the most common examples are short contemporaries, such as those published by Harlequin Enterprises through their Mills & Boon imprint in the United Kingdom and those published by smaller presses in the United States, such as Avalon Publishers.

A variation of the sweet romance is the inspirational romance, which has little if any sexual content and a strong emphasis on spiritual values. These, too, can either have a contemporary or historical setting.

When deciding how sexually explicit to make your romance, consider this: The plotline—and the main characters—of your romance novel, as well as your targeted publisher, should always determine the level of sensuality in your manuscript. A lot also depends upon your own comfort level. If writing sexually explicit love scenes makes you uncomfortable, it will show in your writing. Follow your instincts.

Spicy Romances

Spicy romances are those with sexual content—sometimes a little, sometimes a lot. Just as with the sweet romances, they can have either a historical or contemporary setting, as well as utilize elements of paranormal and science fiction/fantasy.

Just how sexy can they be? Well, that depends on the publisher, of course, and the type of romance. Generally speaking, though, they can be as sexy as you want to make them. *Romantic Times BOOKreviews* magazine (*www.romantictimes.com*) uses the following sensuality ratings scale in their reviews of historical, contemporary, and romantic suspense romance novels:

- Scorcher—Borders on erotic. Very graphic sex.
- Hot—Conventional lovemaking. Explicit sex.
- Mild—May or may not include lovemaking. No explicit sex.

Most modern romance novels fall within the middle sensuality rating of "Hot." Euphemisms are frequently used and the emphasis is on the buildup of sexual tension, rather than on the sex act itself, although these books can be, and often are, quite explicit. (For more detailed information on the use of sensuality in a romance novel, refer to Chapter 15.)

Series Versus Single Title

There are two distinct types of romance novels: single title and category. Category romances are short and fit into a publisher's clearly delineated grouping. Single-title romances are longer and do not fit into a publisher's standard category lines. The name *single title* can be misleading though as they are not always stand-alone titles and can be several interconnected books.

Series or "Category" Romance Novels

Category romances are the mainstay of the Harlequin Enterprises empire. These are shorter romances that have an easily recognizable cover brand, such as family and home for Silhouette Special Edition or mystery for Harlequin Intrigue. The books are part of a numbered series and the line publishes the same number of new titles each month. Most are carried in bookstores, and they're usually available through an in-house book club at substantial discounts, too, with each month's titles shipped to the reader as a single unit.

In 2007, Harlequin Enterprises released over 800 titles a month around the world from their various publishing operations. Their books are sold in ninety-four international markets, on six continents, and in twenty-five different languages. Is it any wonder that, on average, an imprint of Harlequin Enterprises purchases over two original works of fiction each day?

Levels of sensuality can vary from Mild to a full-out Scorcher, depending on the line. So can the size of the book, or word count. The lines generally range from a low of 50,000 words to a high of 85,000, although each book in the series is the same approximate number of pages.

To make the books uniform, word counts are especially important in category romances. Because each line has a general "theme" and a specific word count, the publishers offer editorial tip sheets, or guidelines, for writing the books. (For more information on writing series or category romances, please refer to Chapter 4.)

Single-Title Romance Novels

Single-title romances are longer books and encompass a wide range of subject matter. Harlequin Enterprises also publishes single-title romances, although the majority of these books are published through New York–based publishers, such as Berkley/Jove, Avon Romance, Kensington, Dorchester, Grand Central Publishing (formerly Hatchette Group), NAL, and Random House, among others. While these publishers generally do release new romance novels each month, there is no set number and can vary from month to month.

A single-title romance has more of everything—more plot, more characters, more romance. They can also tackle more complex and emotionally gripping conflicts, too, though that isn't always the case. The covers range from the traditional clinch to something with a more mainstream fiction feel. (For more specific information on writing single-title romances, refer to Chapter 5.)

The Romance Subgenres

Much like ice cream, romance novels come in a variety of flavors. From stories set in the past to stories set in the future, from the ones that make you laugh to the ones that make you cry, the romance genre has a little something for everyone.

QUESTION?

What is the most popular romance subgenre?
According to Romance Writers of America, of the 2,285 titles of romance fiction sold in North America in 2005, a full 64 percent were contemporary romance. The closest competitor was historical romances at 20 percent.

As reading tastes evolve, so do the subgenres of romance fiction, along with the subsets within those subgenres. Vampire romances may soar in popularity one year and plummet the next, as fast-paced romantic comedies become all the rage. The basic subgenres of romance, however, usually remain the same.

Contemporary Romance

As defined by Romance Writers of America, a contemporary romance is one that is set after the world wars. Most, however, are set in the present without a specific year mentioned in the text. (In fact, many publishers discourage the use of a time reference because it can date the novel and make future reprints harder sales.) Contemporary romances can be either a single title or a category in terms of size.

Historical Romance

Historical romances, by contrast, are romances set before the world wars. They are usually single-title releases, although a few are available in series-romance format. The word count, on average, for a historical romance is 100,000 words, or 400 manuscript pages. Rich with historical detail, these books transport the reader to another time and place.

ESSENTIAL

For up-to-the-minute information on market trends, your best resource by far is membership in Romance Writers of America. Members of the organization—both published and unpublished—have access to monthly market updates through *Romance Writers Report,* as well as the members' section of the RWA Web site (*www.rwanational.org*).

While historical romances can be set in any time period, some may be a harder sale than others, due to fluctuating reader preferences. Popular historical time periods include:

- Regency
- Medieval
- England or Scotland—
  Any time period
- American West
- Colonial America
- French Revolution

A quick review of the historical romances being sold at your local bookstore can give you a good idea of where the current market stands, although it may have little correlation to what type of books are being purchased right now by publishers.

A hot trend in historical romance could have already peaked by the time you see a book on the shelf of your local bookstore, since publishers usually sign the contracts with the author twelve months prior to the book's release date, if not longer.

Paranormal

Demons. Shapeshifters. Sword and sorcery epics. The colonization of faraway planets. They're all fair game in paranormal romances. Authors embrace an altered state of reality in a paranormal romance by creating new spins on existing folklore and legend, as well as complete new worlds. Connected books, or mini-series, are common in this subgenre. Popular types of paranormal romances include:

- Time travel
- Futuristic
- Fantasy
- Ghosts

- Witches and magic
- Vampires
- Shapeshifters
- Demons and the undead

But no matter the number of fairies, vampires, and alien life forms that populate these books, the romantic relationship between the hero and the heroine remains the central focus of the paranormal romance.

Romantic Suspense

According to a 2005 market survey conducted by Romance Writers of America, nearly half of all romance readers prefer their romances served with a side order of mystery. Romantic suspense blends the best of the genres of suspense and mystery within a solid romance plotline.

The tone of a romantic suspense can fluctuate between dark and edgy to something more lighthearted and humorous. With few exceptions, the mixture of romance to mystery is usually around 50/50.

Romantic Comedy

Romantic comedies are romances with a heavy emphasis on humor. They can have either a contemporary or a historical setting.

Multicultural

These are ethnically diverse romance novels that can have either a contemporary or a historical setting. In addition to the romance, the books usually contain elements unique to the characters' cultural background. Examples include African-American romances.

Alternative Lifestyles

These are romances with gay or lesbian main characters.

Inspirational

These are romances with spiritual themes, although usually the term *inspirational* refers to Christian romances.

Young Adult

Young adult romances are for the teen market, although a central love story is not a requirement of the plot.

Mainstream

Mainstream novels refer to women's fiction novels that may or may not contain a romantic element.

Erotic Romance

Erotic romances turn up the heat between the main characters to the boiling point. While inhibitions are often cast aside in an erotic romance, the central focus of the story never wavers from the romantic relationship between the two main characters.

Don't confuse an erotic romance with an erotica. Erotic romances are romance novels that contain a strong sexual content. An erotica, on the other hand, is a novel with strong sexual content that does not contain a central love story and a HEA.

Romance Hybrids

Sometimes a romance morphs with another genre and forms a hybrid with an even mix of romance to the other genre. Hybrids could include any variation of adding two unrelated romance subgenres and/or a non-romance genre, such as:

- Erotic paranormal historical romance
- Paranormal romantic mystery
- Romantic comedy suspense

The lines between genres often become blurred within the pages of a romance hybrid, as these books attempt to reach a wider audience than any single subgenre or genre could attain on its own.

Traditional Publishers Versus E-Publishers

In the mid-1990s, e-publishers, or electronic publishers, barely made a blip on the romance fiction radar screen. Ten years later, the story had changed as traditional print publishers began to offer their books in e-format. Much of the success of romance e-publishing can be attributed to e-publisher pioneers such as Ellora's Cave (*www.ellorascave.com*) who specialize in erotic paranormal romances, one of the new hybrids in romance fiction.

ESSENTIAL

Many e-publishers utilize Print On Demand technology, which allows them to print each book when an order has been received for it, rather than print a large number in advance of sales and store them in a warehouse.

As it became more difficult for new writers to break in, an increasing number of authors turned to e-publishers. Advances were low, if offered at all, but the higher royalty rates, frequent payment periods and creative freedom to write about subjects considered unmarketable by traditional publishers, made e-publishing an extremely attractive alternative.

Basic Structure of a Romance Novel

3

Forget the myth that writing a romance novel is easy. To the contrary, writing a compelling, saleable romance novel is just as difficult as writing any other form of fiction, maybe even more so since the romance market is so highly competitive. To succeed in the genre, you'll need to know the fundamentals of good novel writing—how to create hooks and plot points that grab your reader's attention. Then you'll need to know how to make your romance stand out from the crowd.

What Makes a Romance a Romance?

So, what makes a romance a romance? As you learned in Chapter 2, a romance novel requires two basic components: a central love story and a Happily Ever After (HEA) for the two main characters. But is it that simple? Well, yes. And no.

All forms of popular fiction will likely contain a romance for the main character. The difference, however, between a romance novel and other types of fiction is that the developing romantic relationship will always be front and center in a romance.

Romances are defined by their tone as well as by their focus. Imagine for a moment that you want to write a novel with the following story line:

A few days before an English Lit professor is to present a recently discovered handwritten first draft of a Pulitzer Prize–winning short story by a deceased American author at a literary symposium, the author's only child—who also happens to be the professor's ex-wife—appears on the scene with two bombshells. The first is that their quickie divorce in Costa Rica five years earlier wasn't quite legal. The second is that the manuscript purportedly written by her father is a fraud.

The basic plotline could work as a romance or as a mystery. What determines its type is its focus and tone.

Focus

Focus refers to the emphasis you place on certain details of your novel. For a romance novel, the focus would be on the romantic relationship between your two main characters. After all, romance novels can have a variety of subplots but these books are ultimately about the romance itself.

One of the biggest challenges facing a new author is in keeping the focus firmly placed on the romantic relationship between the main characters. An easy way to maintain that focus is to restrict your use of subplots to those that support the romantic conflict.

In the example given here, the novel becomes a romance when the focus of the story is placed on the renewed romance between the professor and his ex-wife—now, his current wife who wants them to get back together. Tension is heightened with the addition of a deadline—the heroine will only have a week or so to win back her hero before the arrival of the new divorce papers. The forged manuscript is relegated to a subplot that supports the romance. Because the hero authenticated the forged manuscript—and because the heroine will challenge that authentication once he makes an official announcement at the symposium—the potential for conflict in their romantic relationship is high.

Tone

Tone refers to the choice of language that you use to describe the events of your novel. All romance novels, regardless of their type and format, have a unique tone that sets them apart from other types of fiction. More specifically, romance novels inspire an emotional response in their readers, although the specific emotional response can vary. For example, some books may inspire laughter, while others may inspire sadness or fear. All, however, will inspire a sense of awe at the redemptive power of love.

Because romance readers want to experience every aspect of a romance novel as though it were happening to them, details matter. The key, however, is to filter those details through the eyes of the point-of-view (POV) character.

Remember the English Lit professor who discovers he has a wife and a possible fraudulent manuscript on his hands? Just as the focus on the romantic relationship between the two main characters defines the book as a romance, the novel's tone should also establish its genre. This tone is usually set within the book's opening lines. Here is the opening for the novel in question:

He still wanted her.

Justin Stone stood in the doorway of his office and stared at the raven-haired woman sitting on top of his desk. With the telephone receiver pressed to one ear, head tilted back, short leather skirt hugging her tanned thighs, she had all the self-consciousness of a cat sunning itself in a warm spot. And he wanted her with an ache of longing that cut straight through to his core, even though he knew such a desire was wrong. She belonged in his past, not in his present. And certainly not in his future.

They had both decided that a long time ago.

(—Faye Hughes, Can't Fight the Feeling*)*

Notice how word choices can convey poignancy, desire, longing, and regret. The specific language used here serves dual purposes. Not only does it establish mood and begin to tell the story of Justin and Morgan, it tells the reader that she is reading a romance novel, as opposed to a mystery or a science fiction novel, by establishing the tone.

Story Arcs

A story arc is the plot of your novel. More specifically, a story arc charts the trajectory of the events of your novel—the highs and lows, the conflicts and resolutions. They are called arcs because the path from point A (the beginning) to point B (the ending) is never a straight line. (And what fun would that be if they were?) Conflicts must arise during the course of your novel. Complications, too. What's more, when one set of conflicts or complications is resolved, a new set must arise to take their place.

When plotting your romance novel, try using poster board, a black marker, and a stack of sticky notes. Draw squares for each chapter of your book on the poster board. Write down an element of your story arc on one of the sticky notes—such as "first kiss"—and place the note inside a square. Move the notes around until you find the right fit.

Depending on its size and format, a romance novel can have multiple story arcs. One will be for the romance itself, the others would be for any subplot(s) that the novel may contain. The subplots must support the main romance plot—either by adding further conflict for your main characters or by adding more insight into their psyches.

Each story arc will have three main components:

1. Introduction of the plot/subplot
2. Development of the plot/subplot
3. Resolution of the plot/subplot

The number of manuscript pages needed for the introduction and resolution of your plot or subplot will likely be much fewer than the number needed for its development. Ideally, your subplot(s) will support your main plot, by not only strengthening it but by "filling in" when the action has slowed for your main plot.

QUESTION?

Does every scene have to support the romance?
Yes, although it may only do so indirectly. For example, if you have a suspense subplot and scenes from the villain's POV wherein he (or she) is plotting to kill the heroine, the danger the heroine faces is an obstacle to the romance with the hero.

The story arc for the romance between your two main characters will extend across the entire length of the book and will include every event, big and small, that contributes to the development of the romance and its Happily Ever After.

Story arcs for your subplots can be much shorter. Although they may only extend across several chapters, they will have the same components as your main plot. (For more information on story arcs, refer to Chapter 8.)

Plot Points

Plot points are the individual events that propel your story arcs forward. Ideally, they should change the status quo in some way. For example, when your two main characters share a first kiss, that event changes the course of their relationship because they now must acknowledge their romantic attraction. Or, when the worst thing that could happen to your main characters does indeed happen during the dark moment, it tears apart their relationship.

All romance novels will have the same basic plot points:

- Introduction, or cute meet
- First kiss/First acknowledgement of attraction
- First love scene/First acknowledgement of emotional commitment
- Dark moment
- Resolution, or HEA

As previously discussed, the subplot must support and advance the main story—the romance between your main characters. While a category, or series romance, may not have a subplot at all, a single-title romance could have several, although the integration of the different story arcs into the main plot should be just as seamless.

Although every romance novel may have the same basic plot points, each book is different. What makes a romance unique is the specific details of each plot point and how each point fits into the story arc of the novel.

Hooks

Much like a fisherman out to catch a trout will use a baited hook, a writer out to catch a reader must learn to do the same. In writing, authors use hooks—basically, a clever turn of a phrase, a unique twist on a classic plot, or a startling/alarming situation. A hook can be anything that catches the reader's attention and holds it. Authors use hooks in everything from their query letters to their opening and ending lines of their scenes. And for good reason. Hooks are what makes a reader—or an agent and editor—unable to put the book down.

ALERT!

Some new authors confuse a hook with a gimmick. True, they can both capture the reader's attention and get them to read, but a gimmick always rings false while a hook is a natural extension of your writer's voice and storyline.

Think back to the last romance novel you read and enjoyed. Chances are, it grabbed you from that opening page. The intriguing first line was a hook. The need to find out what happens next when you reach a scene or chapter end is another hook. Hooks keep the reader guessing . . . and they keep the reader turning pages.

Hooks as Opening Lines

Remember Justin, the English Lit professor with a newly discovered wife and a plagiarized manuscript in *Can't Fight the Feeling*? The opening line of the book—*He still wanted her*—is a good example of using a hook as a first line for a romance. Consider what those four words tell the reader. First, that he is thinking about a woman, a woman that he presumably no longer has but he still wants. Good hooks create questions in the reader's mind. After reading the opening lines for *Can't Fight the Feeling,* the reader will wonder, Why? What happened to end their relationship? More important, what will happen next?

Hooks as Ending Lines

Having a good ending line to your scene is just as important as having a good opening line. For many readers, the temptation to put down your book is strongest when they reach the ending of a scene or chapter. It's your job as a writer to make sure that doesn't happen.

In *Can't Fight the Feeling,* the first scene of Chapter 1 ended with the following lines:

Morgan was back.
By his estimation, for only five minutes or so.

But in that short period of time the old feelings had all come tumbling back. What did she want? he wondered.

And just how was he supposed to resist her this time?

Again, the reader is left to wonder what will happen next. Why had Morgan returned? Does she share Justin's feelings? *Can* he resist her this time?

Hooks as an Intriguing Premise

This type of hook is used primarily in query letters and in-person pitch sessions when meeting one-on-one with an agent or editor. They are the short descriptions of your book that demonstrate why your romance novel is different from the hundreds (if not, thousands) of other romance novels the editor or agent will likely receive that year.

FACT

Writers' conferences, such as the annual one sponsored by Romance Writers of America (*www.rwanational.org*), gives an unpublished author with a completed manuscript the chance to "pitch" her romance novel to an agent or editor. The sessions usually last seven to ten minutes and are designed to replace the traditional query letter.

Finding a good hook for a pitch session or a query letter is difficult, though. Some writers just focus on the unique plot twist for their novel. For example:

Mary Jane Stimmons is having the worst Monday of her life—her car breaks down on the freeway, gets hit from behind by a multitasking soccer mom and completely totaled. Then she arrives for work two hours late and everybody ignores her, probably because she missed an important meeting though that wasn't her fault. The only bright spot is the hunky guy in the kilt who keeps following her around. Too bad he's crazy because he thinks he's been dead for 500 years. What's more, he thinks she's dead, too—which if true means her Monday just got a whole lot worse.

Others compare their book to a couple of popular, though dissimilar movies, books, or television shows, such as "*Desperate Housewives* meets *The X-Files*" (for a light-hearted paranormal romance.) This method is known as the High Concept pitch, which is basically a story idea that can be reduced to a short, easily understood concept by comparing two existing products.

Scenes Versus Chapters

Every novel is broken down into chapters, with each chapter containing one or more scenes that propel the action forward or build characterization. What's the difference between the two? For some writers in today's market . . . not very much. Many successful romance novelists write short chapters, some only as long as a few paragraphs. But there is a difference between scenes and chapters.

Think of your novel as a photograph album that details your recent vacation to the Rocky Mountains. The album contains twenty pages, with each page holding eight pictures (front and back.) In this analogy, the pages of the album are chapters; the photos on each of the pages are a scene. Together, the scenes and chapters tell the story of your vacation.

Scenes

A scene describes one snapshot—this means the action of a scene usually takes place in a single location and over a specific space of time, although that isn't always the case. Scenes will have one or more of the following components:

- **Dialogue:** The characters will talk to each other.
- **Narrative:** This provides information that the reader needs to know about the current scene, such as a character's thoughts, but it doesn't interrupt the action.
- **Action:** Something will happen.
- **Description of setting:** This is filtered through the character's point of view.
- **Transition:** This announces a movement through time or space.

- **Exposition:** This provides information that the reader needs to know about previous events, such as backstory, which is a recapping of prior events, but it does not stop the action.

Scenes should begin—and end—with a hook, something that encourages the reader to keep reading. Usually, a scene is told through the point of view (POV) of a single character, although some writers can successfully combine several POVs in a single scene. (For more information on POV, refer to Chapter 12.)

The length of your scene dictates the pacing of your novel. Shorter scenes speed up pacing while longer scenes slow it down. Generally, most scenes run three to ten pages in length, with the average around four to five pages.

Ideally, each scene should lead into the next scene, much the way that one snapshot from a family vacation in the photo album leads to the next in sequence. That's not to say, however, that scenes must follow each other in chronological order. They don't. All that is necessary is that the scenes follow in a logical fashion that best tells the story.

When two or more scenes exist in a chapter, you should separate them by one of the following methods:

- A blank line with a pound sign (#), centered, either singly or in a group
- A blank line with an asterisk (*), centered, either singly or in a group
- A blank line with a dash (-), centered, either singly or in a group
- Four blank lines

Chapters

To continue the photograph album analogy, a chapter contains one or more snapshots, or scenes, that describe a series of events grouped together with a common theme. For example, a chapter might contain two scenes, one from the heroine's POV and one from the hero's POV. The first scene, in the heroine's point of view, might deal with a discussion of the subplot, while she fights against her attraction for the hero. The second scene in the hero's POV, several hours later, would continue the thread of the subplot and end with him kissing the heroine.

FACT

There is no standard length for a chapter in the romance genre, although some publishers may have a house style that dictates their preferred length, especially for some of the category lines. Generally, chapters can be as long—or as short—as an author wants them to be. On average, they run around twelve to eighteen manuscript pages.

Much like scenes, chapters must open and end with a hook, although the need to end with a hook is more critical for a chapter, since that is the point where most people will put down a book. Editors expect—and readers demand—a reason to keep reading. An easy way to make sure your chapter ends on the right note is to stop in the middle of an action scene. Make the reader wonder what will happen next. Make them feel they have no choice but to turn the next page of your book.

Importance of Setting

You've probably heard the old adage that in real estate, location is everything. It applies to romance novels also. From small towns to big cities, from barren, alien landscapes to lush tropical forests—the options for a setting for your book are endless. But it's *how* you use the setting that is important in a romance novel.

Remember, it's not paragraph after paragraph of dry information about your setting that the reader expects in a romance novel. It's the integration of that setting into the novel. Is your novel set in the tropics? If so, describe the warmth of the sand on the beach beneath the heroine's bare feet. Explain how the scent of the flowers growing in the garden outside her room reminds her of an event from her childhood—a good memory, perhaps, or a sad memory. Incorporate the setting into your novel and give the details an emotional impact, rather than simply provide a travelogue description. (For more information on using setting in a romance novel, refer to Chapter 13.)

Readers want to experience the romance novel as though its events were happening to them. Romance authors rely heavily on the use of the five senses—sight, sound, touch, taste, and smell—to make the story come alive.

Prologues

Where should you begin your novel? Why, in the beginning, of course. Or better yet, start it in the middle of action and then filter in the necessary elements like Who? and Why? as you go along. Sooner or later, however, every writer will work on a novel that has an important scene that occurs *before* the main story begins. And thus was born the prologue.

Prologues are backstory, usually concerning a dramatic event that occurred months or even years earlier. Their sole purpose is to set the stage for what happens in Chapter 1. Ideally prologues should be short, around two to three pages in length.

Many agents and editors profess a strong dislike for prologues in a romance novel, mostly because as a technique, they have been overdone. Often, information contained in a prologue could have been included in Chapter 1, or deleted altogether.

Epilogues

Much like prologues, an epilogue contains an important scene that occurs outside the normal course of the novel. In this case, after the story has ended. Some readers just aren't ready to say goodbye to their favorite characters when the book ends. Sometimes, they want confirmation that the

HEA really did come true. Hence, the use of an epilogue, which details events from months, even years into the future.

Some published authors have even written epilogues years after a book has been published and posted them on their Web sites because of reader requests to find out what happened next. Epilogues, much like prologues, should be used sparingly, if at all, and kept to a length of two to three pages.

Calculating Word Count

It may be hard to believe, but one of the most hotly debated issues among authors is how to determine the word count of a manuscript. On the surface, such a debate seems silly. After all, modern word processing programs list the word count for each document, so what is there to debate?

Plenty, actually.

Traditionally, some book publishers, especially those that release the same number of romance novels each month as part of an established line, have strict production guidelines that require manuscripts to fall within a preset number of pages. For them, the actual word count doesn't always give the projected page length of a novel, which is crucial to ensure the novel meets the production requirements for their books. After all, a 300-page manuscript with lots of snappy dialogue may have an actual word count of 55,000 words, while another 300-page manuscript with more narrative might contain 75,000 words. To compensate, these publishers use a formula to calculate word count that requires 12-point Courier font, double-spacing, and one-inch margins (top, bottom, left, and right.) With those settings, the publisher estimates each manuscript to contain:

- 25 lines each page
- 10 words each line
- 250 words each page (number of lines multiplied by number of words)

Other houses rely on the actual word count provided by the word processing program, so no such "guesstimations" about word count are necessary. Of course, as with all information about a publisher, always refer to their Web site or editorial tip sheets for specific information about how they calculate the word count of a manuscript.

CHAPTER 4

Writing the Category Romance

For many new romance writers, the path to publication often begins with a category romance, and for good reason, too. With their smaller page counts and a tighter focus on the core relationship, these books are perennial reader favorites. Many bestselling authors—Jennifer Crusie, Janet Evanovich, and even the reigning queen of romance herself, Nora Roberts—began their successful careers by writing category romances. Do you have what it takes to join their ranks?

Defining the Category Romance

Series or "category" romance is the mainstay of the romance industry. Harlequin Enterprises publishes most of the ones in the market today, which is why the name *Harlequin,* for many, is synonymous with romance fiction. So, what is a category romance? Generally, it's a shorter romance that is released as part of an established line. Each novel in the line, or series, is given a number, which is reflected on the spine of the book.

FACT

In an average month, Harlequin Enterprises in North America releases more than 115 novels. The majority of these books are "category" romances, such as Silhouette Desire, Harlequin Blaze, and Harlequin American.

Much like their single-title counterparts, series romance novels can cover a wide spectrum of subgenres. Paranormal elements, romantic suspense subplots, erotic overtones—if the subgenre is a hot seller in the romance market as a whole, it's a safe bet that it will be available in a category format.

Because of their need to keep pace with the tastes and interests of a worldwide romance readership, category lines are continually growing and changing. Lines that were popular one year may be discontinued the next and replaced with new ones. Older lines may be revamped and relaunched under a new name.

Generally, however, series romances have the following four distinct characteristics:

1. Books in the line have a specific word count.
2. The line releases the same number of titles each month.
3. The covers have a similar tone and style.
4. The publisher follows specific editorial guidelines for each line.

In addition to being available in a variety of retail and wholesale outlets, series romances are usually sold as part of an in-house book club that sends all titles for that month to a reader at substantial discounts and usually in advance of their bookstore placement.

Long Contemporaries

Long contemporaries are contemporary romance novels that are more than 70,000 words in length. The level of sensuality can vary widely, as can the type of subplots used.

Short Contemporaries

These contemporary romance novels are between 40,000 and 69,000 words in length. The level of sensuality can also vary, although many of the sexier, more sexually explicit titles fall into this category.

Historicals

Category historicals are romance novels set before the world wars. With varying levels of sensuality, these books are generally between 40,000 and 95,000 words in length.

A Little Something Different

These are romance novels that deviate from the traditional formula in some way, whether through their format or their subject matter. Examples include romance novels that focus on the entire life of the relationship rather than just the courtship phase, or the recent NASCAR-themed line of romances from Harlequin Enterprises.

Publishers are always on the lookout for the next hottest selling subgenre. Often, they get their inspiration for new category lines from popular television shows, movies, or bestselling fiction in non-romance genres.

Romance publishers also experiment with new formats, such as immediate e-book releases for erotic romances, as well as manga romances, which are romance novels packaged as graphic novels that utilize the popular Japanese manga (comics) style.

Advantages

Granted, writing category romance novels isn't for everyone. Contrary to what many people believe, writing a smaller book isn't easy. While larger books may include more characters and subplots, a category author must work at telling a concise story in fewer words. But for those who enjoy crafting a tightly plotted romance of between 200–360 pages, the rewards can be great . . . in terms of both the fairly consistent monetary compensation and reader appreciation.

ESSENTIAL

A new romance line offers an unpublished author one of the best shots at publication. But unless you know about the publisher's call for submissions, you won't be able to make that sale. That's why a membership in writers' organizations such as Romance Writers of America (*www.rwa national.org*) can be invaluable for new writers.

But easier-to-project sales figures and bags of glowing fan mail aren't the only advantages to writing series romance. Most category authors rarely have to promote their novels because their publishers have already done an excellent job of advertising the line. Plus, with the frequent creation of new lines, category publishers give romance authors multiple opportunities to experiment with fresh, innovative takes on the traditional romance. Is it any wonder then that many "working" romance authors—meaning those who support themselves solely from their writing income—often spend their entire careers writing these smaller books and never attempt to "break out" with a single title release?

Steadier Income

While single-title authors have the potential for making more money than their category romance sisters, the odds aren't in favor of a single-title author progressing much beyond the mid-list. When you factor in all the things that a writer can't control about her book—such as the cover art, the release month, etc.—it can be nearly impossible to project with any degree of certainty the earn-out on a new single-title romance novel.

Not so with a category romance.

Generally, the author of a series romance can predict the earn-out of a new title in an established line by using royalty statements from her previous titles. But be aware that some series lines perform better in foreign markets than others, just as some types of romances might do better than others in the same line. (For example, an American West–set contemporary romance might sell better in certain foreign markets than a New York City–set contemporary by the same author, for the same line.)

While the earn-out from a single category romance may not be enough to allow an author to quit her day job and write full-time, when added to the income produced from writing two or three of these books a year, such a step is possible.

Built-in Reader Base for New Authors

Perhaps the biggest benefit for category authors is the reduced need for author-funded promotion efforts. All the books in a particular series will have similar cover art—similar in terms of type of artwork used, its general tone, the font size and color scheme, etc.

QUESTION?

Do authors receive equal treatment in category romances?
Generally, yes. While some bestselling category romance authors will receive a larger print run and a larger font size for their name on the book cover, most authors are treated the same in terms of the size of their print runs and book placement in stores.

Some category authors do advertise their books. Generally, they target their efforts toward the promotion of their name, especially if they have several new releases coming out in a short period of time.

Editorial Guidelines—the Upside

Publishers of single-title romance novels will often suggest that new authors read their books to get a sense of the type of stories they release. It is good advice, since reading the romance novels of a publisher is the best way to research a market. But the publishers of series romances will usually offer editorial guidelines for their books.

Typically, these editorial guidelines, or tip sheets, will offer insight into the following:

- The tone and feel of the books in the line
- Acceptable/unacceptable subject matter
- Sensuality levels
- Expected word counts
- Manuscript formatting requirements
- Submission procedures

These editorial guidelines for each series line are generally available for download at the publisher's Web site.

Greater Flexibility in Subgenre

Many writers find that they get bored writing the same type of book year after year. For the authors of series romances, this boredom doesn't have to happen, thanks in large part to the myriad of subgenres reflected in the category lines.

FACT

A good resource for checking out the hottest new category lines is to visit Harlequin Enterprises (*www.eharlequin.com*) since they are the industry leader of series romances. In addition to informative articles about the romance industry at large, you'll find up-to-the-minute details on which of their category lines is currently acquiring.

This greater flexibility in subgenres in category romance gives authors the opportunity to experiment while still writing to their core readership.

Disadvantages

As previously mentioned, writing the category romance isn't for everybody. Some authors find the limited shelf life of the novels to be a deterrent, as well as the restrictions placed on them by a shorter word length and limitations of the story content. When you add to this list of disadvantages the limited number of publishers currently releasing category romances . . . well, it's clear that this is not a format for the faint of heart.

Editorial Guidelines—the Downside

While some people can flourish creatively when given specific guidelines under which to work, others cannot. In fact, some writers simply write books that are larger in scope or contain a storyline that would be inappropriate for a series romance.

Also, in the majority of series romance novels, the primary focus—sometimes, the *only* focus—is on the developing relationship between the two main characters. This means that there may often be little space for secondary characters or subplots.

Short Shelf Life

One of the biggest downsides to writing series romances is their reduced lifespan. Most category romances only remain on the bookshelf for four weeks. When the new crop of titles arrives in the bookstore, the old ones are removed to make space. Consider the consequences, therefore, if a natural disaster, such as a hurricane or earthquake, delayed a delivery of books. Or, as sometimes happens, a bookstore failed to put the books out in a timely fashion. With a short shelf life, sales for that particular title would be impacted. Perhaps irreparably.

Not all bookstores will remove last month's series romances to make room for the new stock. In fact, some "romance-friendly" booksellers will leave the series romances on the shelf for several months. Online book-sellers, such as Amazon (*www.amazon.com*), also continue to offer the books months after their release date.

Cap on Potential Earn-Out

Another disadvantage to the series romance is that their potential earn-out, or the money the books actually earn from sales, is capped. Unlike single-title romances, which can return for a second, a third, or even more printings if demand requires it, a series romance is rarely sent back for additional printings. This means that while booksellers can usually order additional copies during the book's four-week run, the book's potential earn-out is limited to the number of copies published during its initial print run.

Importance of Editorial Tip Sheets

Just because you regularly read the books in a particular series, doesn't mean you shouldn't also read the publisher's editorial tip sheets. For starters, you'll need to know how the publisher wants to receive submissions for that line. Perhaps even more important, you'll need to know if the editors are looking for a change in direction for the line.

Most publishers will have copies of their editorial guidelines posted on their Web site under a section called "Submission Guidelines." If you don't have Internet access, you can usually obtain a hard copy by mailing a stamped, self-addressed envelope to the publisher.

The editorial guidelines often give you additional insight that you might not get from reading the books. Interpreting the tip sheets, however can sometimes be a challenge.

Interpreting the Tip Sheets

Assume for a moment that the editorial guidelines for the Happily Ever After romance line at Big-Time Romance Publisher states the following:

The Happily Ever After line of romances releases four 60,000-word contemporary novels each month that focus on the magic of falling in love with that One Special Person. Sometimes humorous, sometimes dramatic, our stories are never predictable but always emotionally satisfying and have an ending that leaves little doubt the hero and heroine will live Happily Ever After. Levels of sensuality can vary; authors should write to their comfort level and to the requirements of their book's storyline. We will accept submissions from unagented writers but please query first.

What does the tip sheet tell you? Quite a lot, actually. First, it offers specific information about the line, such as the word count and manuscript submission procedures. Second, it offers general information about the tone of the novels in the line, which is information you should bear in mind while reading the books.

ALERT!

Think of the editorial tip sheets as general guidelines when it comes to things such as story content and tone. Always read the novels published by a specific imprint to get a general feel for the books, rather than rely solely upon the tip sheets.

What the Tip Sheets Don't Tell You

Sometimes the editorial tip sheets don't give a complete overview of the line, especially for what the publisher expects from a new author. To obtain this information, you'll need to read a sampling of the books. A good rule of thumb when choosing books to read for researching a line is to read all their releases within the last two months. Make a note of which selections were from new authors since that will give you a clearer idea of the type of new projects that work for the publisher in this line.

Assume that you have read all eight of the Happily Ever After romances released for the past two months. Of those books, three were from new authors, four were from authors who've sold two or more titles to the line, and one was from an author considered to be the line's top seller. Observe the tone of the four books written by the line's existing authors but pay close attention to the storyline in the three titles from new authors. How do those books differ from the others in the line? How are they the same?

Answering these questions correctly is often the key to selling your romance novel to the targeted publisher's line.

Pushing the Envelope

Some category romance authors like to take risks with their writing; others do not. For the latter group, they focus on writing a good, solid romance that adheres to the editorial guidelines. As for those risk-takers, they are the others who continually push the envelope, whether with explicit language, controversial storylines, or innovative storytelling techniques. Which path should you take?

How about trying for a little of both?

When It's Okay to Bend the Rules

Nothing will make a category romance editor or agent happier than to discover a new writer who pushes the boundaries of the line a little by finding an unusual twist or a fresh take on a familiar plotline.

When coming up with your own rule-bending idea for a series romance, bear in mind that the story must still fit within the framework of the series' editorial guidelines.

ALERT!

It's best to leave the truly shocking and controversial plot elements to more experienced writers in series romance. A slight bending of the rules is fine—a complete breaking of the rules is not, and it may result in an automatic rejection.

In the previous example given for the Happily Ever After romance line, consider how the following might push the envelope just enough to make things interesting:

- **Incorporate a comedic paranormal twist**—the heroine is a witch whose magic spells never work properly and the hero is a magician who doesn't believe in "real" magic.
- **Incorporate a dark mystery element**—the hero is a mob informant and the heroine is the contract killer sent to silence him.
- **Try an unconventional storyline**—the hero and heroine are a bitterly divorced couple who have to set aside their differences and join forces to find their missing daughter.
- **Try an unconventional approach to storytelling**—the book opens in the Darkest Moment when the hero is in surgery following an auto accident; the book is told in a series of flashbacks as the heroine waits for word on his condition.

If the story is still told in the tone and style of the series—and if the editorial department of that line is open to something new—these storylines might work well for the Happily Ever After line.

When You Should Play It Safe

Sometimes, however, it's wisest to play it safe rather than attempt to push the boundaries of convention in a series romance novel. As suggested previously, reading the books in the line to get a sense of what the editors like, especially from the debut novels of new authors, is the smartest move a new writer can make. If the other debut authors are playing it safe in the line, it might be wise for you to do the same . . . or to target a different line or publisher for your project.

Know When It's Time to Spread Your Wings

So, what happens when you find you're no longer able to fit your new story idea neatly into the framework of a series romance? You could set aside the story and work on something more category-friendly . . . or you could attempt to write a single-title romance.

FACT

When a successful category romance author crosses over into writing single-title romances, she has the potential for bringing along a loyal reader base. Promoting the new title to her fans is critical, as is writing a "bigger" book that is similar in tone to her series titles.

Making the leap into single-title romances isn't without its pitfalls, however, since success in one format doesn't necessarily guarantee success in another. For this reason, many category romance authors will only venture into single-title territory if they can maintain a presence in the series romance market, thereby maximizing their exposure to readers and minimizing the risks. (For more information on writing a single-title romance, refer to Chapter 5.)

Advances and Earnings Potential

Perhaps it's human nature. But all discussions about writing a romance novel of any format—as do discussions about any profession—will eventually turn to money. How much can you expect to receive as an advance? Better yet, how much can you expect to earn overall from the sale of the book?

- First book advance range: $1,000–$4,000
- First book earn-out range: $1,000–$11,000
- Subsequent books earn-out range: $1,000–$60,000

The amount of the advance for a first novel in a category line is often determined by the overall success of the line, as well as by house policy. (In other words, an agent isn't likely to get you a huge increase in terms of an advance for a series romance.)

ALERT!

Most authors are hesitant to discuss the amount of money they make. The Internet, however, can be an excellent source of such information, especially a Web site such as romance author Brenda Hiatt's Show Me the Money (*www.brendahiatt.com/id2.html*), which collects data on the average advances and earn-outs for romance fiction.

Naturally, some category lines sell better than others do. This means they have the potential for an even larger earn-out. As with most things in the publishing industry, however, the popularity of a series line fluctuates along with the popularity of its particular subgenre.

Do You Need an Agent?

One of the biggest questions asked by all new authors of category romance fiction concerns the need for a literary agent. Unlike single-title releases, however, most category lines will accept unagented submissions. Still, many category authors do have agents who handle their contracts.

Yes—and Here's Why

Many category romance authors also write for single-title houses—or plan to write for them, at any rate. A literary agent can make certain that the manuscript due dates are reasonable from the author's perspective. Even for those authors who write strictly in category lines, a literary agent might be able to negotiate better terms under the house's boilerplate contract, such as invitation-only submission opportunities for special lines.

No—and Here's Why

Generally, the contracts with a series romance publisher are very straightforward and have little "wiggle room" for the agents to negotiate. Royalty rates are fairly standard, as are advances. It's rare that an author could negotiate subsidiary rights, such as foreign sales, in her favor. Even if she were to do so, it might not be prudent because series romance publishers have more contacts in the international market and a broad system for sub-right sales already in place.

CHAPTER 5

Writing the Single-Title Romance

Okay, so, what happens if you can't tell your romance in 65,000 words or less? You move past the land of category romances and straight into the world of the single-title release. These longer books offer some advantages, but they can also prove more difficult to write for some new writers. Jumping straight into bigger novels, learning to balance subplots and secondary characters can be tricky, but armed with information, writers—even beginning writers—can plunge right into the big pool of single-title romance.

Defining the Single-Title Romance

Saying you are writing a single-title romance novel is as vague as saying you are baking a cake. The first question most people will ask is, "What kind?" Indeed, the single-title romance market includes an array of subgenres, and hybrids, as pointed out in Chapter 2. This said, there are some commonalities that make up single-title romances.

First, and probably the most important element, is the romance. No matter what's happening in your book, be it a serial killer who is stalking your hero, or the heroine who discovers she has a genie living in her perfume bottle, the relationship between your hero and heroine is going to be more important, or at least as important, as any other element in your story. Many writers have been known to stick notes to their computers that say, "Remember, it's a romance!"

FACT

One of the most common reasons for rejection of single-title romance novels is the lack of focus on the relationship between the two main characters. New writers need to make sure their love story remains the center focus of their book.

Another trait of single-title romances is they are what some people call the "bigger books." (The term probably stemmed from the comparison of single-title romance to category romance.) And yes, single titles are bigger books. Bigger in page length, bigger in the complexity of your characters, and with what most would call bigger-than-life plots.

Bigger in Page Length

While publishers' requirements vary on the word count of their novels, most single-title romances start at around 80,000 words. Some will accept manuscripts with as many as 150,000 words. However, the average single-title romance runs anywhere from 90,000 to 100,000 words. With approximately 250 words per page, the average single-title novel would run 375 to 400 manuscript pages. (For tips on how to calculate your word count, refer to Chapter 3.)

Some publishers put out novellas or novelettes in anthologies that have the feel and voice of single-title novels. While many of these books are reserved for the house's established writers, some are open to new writers. A good way to find out about these projects is to check out publishers' Web sites and be involved in different writers' organizations and groups.

Bigger in the Complexity of Your Characters

Single-title novels are filled with characters that have layer upon layer of issues to resolve. They are the innocent man accused of murdering his wife who served five years before the real killer stepped forward to confess or the single mom who realizes the child she has raised for the last five years was swapped at birth. As children, they might be the ones abandoned, kidnapped, or raised by circus clowns. They can be many things, but most of them are fabulously flawed due to some traumatic or bizarre circumstance. They are not so flawed that the reader find them sympathetic—just flawed enough that the reader finds them fascinating. What they seldom are is perfect. Unless they are perfectionists, and that, in itself, is their flaw.

Plainly put, perfect people are boring. Complex characters with internal angst intrigue readers and are essential to the romance genre. Readers want to see them struggle through life. Readers want to see them confront their demons and win. Ultimately, in these books readers want to see them overcome their hurdles and fall in love with that one perfect person.

This isn't to say that category characters don't have depth or issues. They must and they do. However, with almost twice the page count of most category books at their disposal, single-title writers have that many more words to explore a character's psyche. Most writers of longer books understand the more complex the character, the more likely a reader is to keep turning pages, even if those pages equal 400. (For more information on creating complex characters, see Chapter 10.)

Bigger-Than-Life Plots

While readers of single titles are going to expect fascinating characters to fill the pages of the books they read, they will also expect those characters to do something after a while, or the readers' interest will wane and they will stop reading. That action, a string of related events that drives the story forward, is called a plot. And in single-title novels, the plots are varied. Generally speaking, a common denominator between these plots is that they consist of things that could have been ripped from the newspaper's headlines.

A good way to start brainstorming plots is to listen to the news bites for the evening news and try to come up with story ideas for each. While these ideas may not actually become worthy story plots, the exercise will get you moving in the right direction.

While some writers start their stories with a plot and others start with characters, the truth is it isn't important which comes first. What is important is that the string of events that make up your single-title plot are created in such a way that the reader is entranced by what may or may not happen next. And one of the best ways to keep the reader guessing is to make sure the plot brings out the best—and the worst—in your issue-laden characters.

And don't forget, you have to make sure the love story is a central part of the plot. See the two examples below:

- The husband, who had been accused of killing his wife, finds a dead body in the trunk of his car. Can he go to the police and risk being accused of murder again? Can he trust the sexy, female homicide detective to believe him, when it was her testimony that landed him in jail the first time?

- The mom of the child who was swapped at birth learns that her real daughter died in a car accident and the child she has now needs a bone marrow transplant—from a blood-related donor. Will saving her child's life mean she loses the child? When she discovers that the child's real father is a big-wig family practice lawyer, and that he's widowed and just the type of man she could love, dare she hope he'll offer his bone marrow and leave her with his child? And what about her heart?

Can you see how the romance is linked to the plot and as the story evolves so does the relationship? Making sure the romance is closely connected to the external plot is one way of making sure the love story is always in the forefront. (For more tips on plotting, see Chapter 8.)

A single-title romance and a category romance can have very similar storylines. What distinguishes one from the other is how the author tells the story. Single-titles allow the author to get grittier or darker with the details.

Advantages

A quick look at the average advances and payouts garnered by some authors leaves little doubt that the possibility of receiving more money exists in the single-title market. This isn't to say that a couple of the single-title publishers don't pay advances below some of the averages for category romance lines. That is one of the many reasons you should research the markets and know as much as you can about the publishers to whom you are targeting your work.

ALERT!

Single-title romance books have a longer shelf life than series romances. Some publishers will keep books in print and available for readers for several years, which allows the authors to sell more copies. More copies sold results in more royalties earned by the authors.

While the possibility of earning more money is a nice advantage, the truth is that the financial benefits are seldom the reason an author decides to write single titles. Most writers target the single-title romance market because their plots, characters, and writing voice fits the more broadly focused genre of single title than the category lines.

In other words, single-title guidelines are less stringent and have larger word counts that allow authors more pages to explore their plots and characters. While the rules are constantly changing, category lines often frown upon things such as explicit language, multiple sex partners during the course of a book, and dark subjects such as rape or abuse issues. Also, stories with several subplots or secondary characters are not common in category lines.

Are all single-title publishers created equal?
No. Some single-title houses offer larger advances or larger print runs and are known for producing books that offer bigger earn-outs. Also, while the single-title market as a whole may offer a broader range in subject matter and word counts than category romance, each house has its own guidelines. Studying guidelines and understanding the business practices of a publisher before submitting is essential.

Disadvantages

As with everything in life, what some people see as advantages, others may see as disadvantages. Some writers are simply more comfortable writing the shorter category books. Their stories and voice lean more toward the shorter format; therefore, for them, having to meet a higher word count is considered a disadvantage. Others are more at ease with the stricter guidelines and find it easier to plot stories because of the boundaries. Most writers agree that complex stories with subplots and secondary characters are tricky to write. If writing were compared to juggling, it would be safe to say that adding subplots and more secondary characters is like adding more balls to your routine.

While it's hard to look at earning a higher advance and having a larger print run as a disadvantage, it's easy to understand that with the increase of money comes the increase of risk. A publisher who has invested $4,000 (in the way of an advance) is less likely to be as affected if the author doesn't make the expected sales than a publisher who has invested $50,000. Category will generally give an author several books to find an audience, while final sale numbers are a bigger deal for single-title publishers.

Probably because of the risk and worry over sale numbers, and because the single-title genre doesn't have the established readership of category romance lines, single-title writers often have to spend more of their time and money promoting themselves and their books. For some writers, the promotion needed to stay on top of the single-title game is viewed as a big disadvantage.

How much a publisher is willing to help a writer promote herself and her book is as important, if not more so, than the amount of the actual advance. Many writers have been quoted as saying, "A publisher's promotional support, or lack of, can make or break a writer's career."

The Importance of Subplots

It would be wrong to say that every longer-format book has a subplot. Some single-title authors rely on plot twists, layers, and complications to carry the story from beginning to end. However, many of today's bestselling single-title romance authors use subplots to add texture, depth, and a bigger-book feel to their novels. To comprehend the importance of subplots, you need to be able to recognize them and their contributions to your stories.

Will the Subplot Please Stand Up?

Subplots are often misunderstood, misidentified, and definitely unappreciated. The first thing to understand about subplots is that it is a plot. It is a story within itself. It has the same elements of your main plot: characters, goals, motivations, conflict, black moments, and resolutions. Subplots are not just complications that occur in your main plot. In the example of the husband accused of killing his wife, his finding the body would not be a subplot, but rather a complication.

Be careful that your subplot never outshines your main plot. One indicator of a dominating subplot is that your secondary stories and characters are occupying more pages than your main plot.

To give you an idea of what would be a subplot, let's use the example of the mother of the child who was swapped at birth. Let's say the father of the child, who is also the hero, is presently litigating a child custody battle over a twelve-year-old boy. The boy's grandparents, the hero's clients, are also family friends who claim their grandchild was abused by his recovering alcoholic mother.

The boy, living with his grandparents, has refused to talk about the case. Slowly, he befriends the hero and opens up. The child denies the allegations of abuse. The hero is torn between loyalty to his clients and doing what he now perceives to be the right thing.

What's the Subplot's Job?

Subplots have work to do and it isn't just to add more words. The sad thing is that when their job is well done, they seldom get credit. Why? Because a subplot's job isn't so much to draw attention to itself but to make your main plot stronger and more interesting. To do that, the subplot must be linked to your main story premise. Below are several ways that subplots do their thankless jobs:

- **By contrasting or reflecting the conflict or theme of the main plot.** In the example of the child custody battle, the pain of losing a child is present in both plots. The hero sees what the custody battle is doing to the boy and wonders if fighting for his daughter would not be detrimental to her.
- **By revealing the depth of the main characters.** As the hero starts to empathize with the boy involved with his case, he tries to step back. His need to distance himself shows his weakness of running away from emotional involvement.
- **By picking up the book's pace, adding or relieving tension, and contributing interest.** When you are in a quiet place with your main plot, you can keep the reader's interest by having action happening in your subplot. Or if something dramatic is happening in the main plot, your subplot can be less intense and allow the reader some emotional breathing room.

The link between the main plot and subplot is crucial and the sooner this is apparent to the reader the better. If the subplot can be removed without changing the outcome or the emotional impact of the main story, then the writer should question whether it belongs in the book.

The Importance of Secondary Characters

Imagine *Gone with the Wind* without Melanie Hamilton Wilkes. Or *Pride and Prejudice* without Jane Bennet. Novelists in every genre use secondary characters to build interest in their books, but in the longer formats, the secondary characters have bigger roles and authors have more space to develop them. As stated earlier, several of those characters even have their own plots. Think of the romance of Jane and Charles in *Pride and Prejudice*.

FACT

Make sure that the names of your characters are different enough that your readers don't get them confused. Names beginning with the same letters, sounds, or names that have the same amount of consonants—Katie and Kathy, Susie and Sarah—can create confusion for a reader.

It's true, the major characters deserve and will require most of the book's focus. They are the brides and the secondary characters are the bridesmaids. However, this doesn't mean that the secondary characters require less attention in their development. A well-crafted cast of characters not only enhances the role of the main characters but adds layers of interest to the novel. Here are some of the reasons that secondary characters deserve respect:

- Readers often fall in love with the main protagonists through the eyes, ears, and thoughts of the secondary characters. Human beings can have skewed views of their own strengths and weaknesses. Secondary characters can paint truer portraits of the protagonists than the protagonists themselves.
- Characters are judged by the company they keep. Whom a main character allows close and whom she attempts to push away will tell the reader a lot about her moral compass.
- People are problematic. Characters are tools in which to introduce problems/conflict into novels. And because secondary characters are not held to the same standards as the hero/heroine, the writer can give them less sympathetic and more outrageous traits.

- Secondary characters are great compare-and-contrast tools. A well-developed secondary character will bring out the best and the worst in the main protagonists.
- People talk. Dialogue is crucial to stories. Nothing can hurt a scene more than too much narrative. Creating a large cast of characters who know the right things to say and ask, and the wrong things to say and ask, will make a story come alive for the editors and the readers.
- Bridesmaids become brides and groomsmen become grooms. Lots of series have been developed accidentally because a secondary character grabbed the hearts and imagination of the readers and editors.

Contemporary Versus Historical

From ancient civilizations to some as recent as the Second World War, the readers of historical single-title romances want to be magically transported back in time. While historical single-title novels contain the same elements of their contemporary counterparts—bigger-than-life-plots, lots of secondary characters and subplots, and a richly textured love story—the backdrops and settings become even more important.

ESSENTIAL

Historical writers should always check the publisher's guidelines to know which houses publish which time periods and settings before sending out their work. Submitting a story for consideration that doesn't fit the publisher's guidelines is not only an unneeded expense and waste of the author's time, but will label the writer as unprofessional.

Should You Write Historical Fiction?

For most new writers, the decision to write either historical or contemporary fiction is pretty easy. Generally, that decision is based on what they love to read and whether or not the plots running amuck in their heads are set in this time period or in the past. However, there are other things to know and ask yourself before jumping into writing about the world of yesteryear.

Historical single titles have a tendency to run a little longer. Most authors in this genre feel the word count is needed to paint the scenes with the vivid details of the past. Yet for authors who prefer the shorter format, historical single-title romance might not be the best choice.

Does your voice lend itself to the historical tone? Just as an actress playing in a period film will present herself differently than she would in a film about a modern-day love story, a writer must pen her words and stories in a way that fits the time period of the book. For some writers, this comes easily; for others, it may be more difficult.

FACT

One way to understand the tonal difference between historical and contemporary fiction is to read aloud the first few pages of a historical and a contemporary. Note not only the difference in language, but the difference in sentence structure. Pay attention not only to the difference in descriptions, but to the importance of details.

Are you a fan of research? While every novel, be it contemporary or historical, will require an ample amount of the author's time checking and rechecking the accuracy of her facts, writing the historical romance novel brings to the table even more research requirements. For example, words have birthdays. To use a word before its time period is a no-no for historical writers. And it's not just the words. Every tool used, every piece of furniture sat upon, every article of clothing worn, must be period accurate.

Subgenres and Hybrids in Historical Romances

Just as subgenres and hybrids exist in contemporary romance, they also exist in the world of historical romances. Plots with paranormal elements, mystery elements, or historical plots that are in themselves romantic comedies are common in the market. Balancing different genre elements can be tricky, especially when you consider that in some cases the setting/time period is an element in itself. However, most editors agree that when two or more elements are blended seamlessly, it can amplify the quality of the work and make the story even more marketable.

Do You Need an Agent?

While some multipublished single-title authors manage to market and negotiate their own contracts, the single-title genre offers more difficulties to the nonagented writer than series romances.

First, unlike some of the category houses, single-title contracts tend to be more open for negotiation. That means, you have more to gain or lose in a deal during the negotiation process. A good agent should know what is and isn't negotiable and can bring the writer the best deal to the table.

Second, many of the single-title romance publishing houses limit their submissions to only agented writers. Their reasons can be varied. However, the most common reason is that by accepting only agented material, they are guaranteeing that the manuscripts landing on their desks have had at least one professional's (the agent's) stamp of approval. Yes, there are single-title houses that still accept unagented material, though their numbers are dwindling. However, do you really want to be limited in submitting your work? This doesn't mean there aren't ways for unagented writers to get their manuscripts in front of editors in some of the larger publishing houses. (Read Chapter 20 for some tips on how to market your own work.)

FACT

A good place to begin your search for an agent is through Romance Writers of America (*www.rwanational.org*). RWA keeps an updated list of RWA-approved agents for their members. This means that the agents listed have a documented sales history in the genre.

Most writers will tell you that getting an agent is as difficult, if not more difficult, than selling the actual manuscript. The process can be long and trying for even the most talented writer. Even some well-established authors find getting an agent a difficult process. However, the good news for writers is that without authors, an agent has no employment. Agents are eager and ready to discover new talent in the single-title romance market. (For more tips on finding an agent, read Chapter 20.)

CHAPTER 6

Before You Start Writing

Are you itching to put pen to paper, or rather fingertips to the keyboard? Are plots bouncing in your head? Or, are you feeling frightened of the process? Don't fret if the answer is . . . all of the above. The back and forth between fear and motivation is normal and possibly even needed. Motivation keeps you going. Fear, when not paralyzing, can encourage preparedness. Like with any plan of action, preplanning can save you headaches. This chapter helps you map your path to publication and avoid some of the more common pitfalls.

Choosing Your Targeted Market

You've read the chapters explaining the differences between category and single-title romances. Now it's time to start thinking about where you and your stories fit. The earlier chapters are great starting points for understanding the differences between the genres, but now it's time to read the books. You've read them, you say? Yes, you probably have. Most aspiring romance authors are romance readers themselves. But reading for pleasure and reading for research is different.

FACT

Becoming a writer can change the way you read. Great books become case studies. Knowledge of the most common writing mistakes makes you more aware of a book's flaws. While you may never go back to being the strictly-for-pleasure reader, most writers eventually learn to turn off the editing process and once again be swept away by the power of words.

Reading for pleasure is like being the passenger in a vehicle on a country drive. You enjoy the trip and appreciate the sights, but you came along only for the ride. Reading for research is like driving the car on that country drive. While you can still enjoy the trip, your focus never strays too far from your job of operating the vehicle. You are also more aware of the turns and twists you take because you are the navigator. So, grab a stack of books and move over into the driver's seat.

Reading for Research

Your job as you read is to get a feel for the different genres, categories, and the overall tones of books from certain lines and publishers. Then, you need to decide which houses and lines are most like the stories you want to write. To get a thorough overview, you'll need to read more than one from each line or genre—three or four is a good number. Make sure these are new releases and try to get a mix of books written by established and newer authors. This way, you'll have a better idea of most recent trends and the editor's expectations of new writers. (It is wise to remember that established authors may get away with pushing the envelope on genre expectations, while newer writers will probably adhere closer to the guidelines.)

Not all publishers offer guidelines for their romances. Some, especially some of the single-title houses, believe that the books themselves are the best way a writer can get an idea of what the publisher wants to see. However, checking out a publisher's Web site is always recommended.

You may not need to read books from each and every line. A quick review of the publisher's guidelines—when available—may help you narrow your focus. For example, you may know up front that the books you want to write will contain a certain amount of sexuality, and therefore you may be able to rule out the sweeter lines. If the idea of incorporating paranormal elements into your stories, or writing historical plots, isn't something you want to do, you can eliminate certain genres. However, before you start marking too many off your list, remember the bit of wisdom: Try it; you might like it.

You can't judge an entire subgenre by one or two books. Be aware that each author brings to the table her own voice, plot, and writing style. Your like or dislike of certain books may have nothing to do with how you feel about the genre itself.

How to Know When the Subgenre Feels Right

Enjoying a certain subgenre, or books from a particular publisher, while you are researching doesn't necessarily mean it's the subgenre or house you should target, but it could be a good sign. Discovering what kind of writer you want to be when you grow up isn't always easy. Here are some tips on how to know when a subgenre feels right.

- In addition to liking the types of books you've found in a certain line or subgenre, the plots and premises hold similar traits to the stories that you dream of writing (i.e., your ideas all have an element of suspense in them, or a similar premise of family and community, as does a particular line).
- There isn't any common element in the subgenre as a whole (e.g., explicit sexual scenes or graphic violence) that goes against your basic moral principles.
- Just reading these particular books sparks your imagination and you begin to come up with plots that are similar, but still different.
- The traits of the certain subgenre, such as word count and the number of characters and subplots, all fit with the type of stories you think you would feel comfortable writing.
- Check your "keeper" bookshelves for books that you loved. What stories started you thinking you might want to write? (All that past reading is going to come in handy.)

QUESTION?

Can't I just write the book of my heart?
Yes, you can. Many writers started their careers by doing just that. Some have even sold those books. However, the risk of writing a novel that doesn't fit any publisher's guidelines, or writing the book that requires major revisions, is greater than if you took the time to familiarize yourself with the market.

Still Unsure Where Your Stories Belong

Don't panic if you're still uncertain about your targeted market. Some writers have to start writing before they are certain where they belong. Some writers complete several books in different genres before they discover the right fit.

One thing that may help you discover your preferred path is to start coming up with different plots and see which ones intrigue you the most.

Brainstorming Ideas

One of the most common questions writers are asked is, "Where do you come up with your ideas?" Some writers can tell you exactly where an idea came from. They saw a news segment about the subject and started piecing things together. Others will tell you that they honestly don't know. They woke up one morning and it was as if the idea fairy came during the night and left a few ideas under their pillow. In other words, the ideas are a direct result of their imaginations.

FACT

A good book to help develop your stories and ideas is *The Fiction Writer's Silent Partner* by Martin Roth. The text offers thousands of facts, possibilities, and "what ifs" on topics ranging from characters and possible careers to unusual locales.

Jump-Starting Your Imagination

Prolific authors know that they can't sit around and wait for their imaginations to kick in. Sometimes imaginations, or muses as they are often called, need to be jump-started. Below are some tips to get your imagination fired up. (Remember to take notes as ideas come to you while following these tips.)

- **Read the newspapers.** Many novels read as if they were ripped from the headlines for a reason. Numerous plots and characters were inspired by newspaper articles.
- **Take your skeletons out of the closet and dance with them.** Think of all the secrets you don't want to talk about. Whispered secrets make good plot triggers.
- **Face your fears.** What are you the most afraid of? How can you turn that into a plot?
- **Make lists.** What are the top ten worst things that could happen to you? (e.g., Your house burns down. Your husband wants a sex

change operation.) Now, think about the people you know. What would make their top ten worst list?

- **Play the "what if" game.** What if you came home and found an unconscious man on your living-room floor? What if you walked into the bank while it was being held up? What if your mother told you that she kidnapped you from your real parents? What if you found out aliens really did exist?

- **Host a brainstorming party.** Invite some friends over to help you come up with unique story premises and plots. (They don't even have to be writers, just creative people.)

- **Join a writer's organization.** Inspiration is contagious. Nothing can get your brain working quicker, or help you learn faster, than surrounding yourself with other writers. To find a local writer's group, call the local libraries, check the Internet, or log onto RWA's Web site (*www.rwanational.org*) to find the closest chapter.

Taking Ideas to Possible Plots

Not all of your ideas will be usable. As a matter of fact, some of them may be downright laughable. And that's okay, because part of brainstorming is thinking outside the box. Some ideas may consist only of the seed of a character, others may be snippets of a situation. What's important is that you have some ideas, no matter how big or small, with which to work.

It is a good idea to keep a file of your brainstorming results. Make sure to include all of your ideas, even those that seemed too farfetched. On a new day, you may see this idea with fresh eyes and realize it has merit.

As you comb through your notes, notice any two ideas that share themes, or that convey similar emotions, and consider the possibility of combining them. Could one be the perfect subplot or perhaps a plot twist to another?

Next, find the one idea that excites you the most—the one that truly sparks your creative nature. (Remember, you will probably spend the next six to eight months—depending on how quickly you write—with this idea, so it has to thrill you.)

Fleshing Out Your Ideas

Once you think you have your chosen concept, it's time to flesh it out. If your ideas consist mainly of a character, it's time to put them in a situation that will cause the most tension and will test their abilities. If it is a situation, it's time to create characters in which the situation will have the most dramatic effect.

The ease or difficulty in which stories are born does not necessarily affect their outcome. Some great American novels came into being in a flash; others were labored over for years. If an idea continues to nip at your thoughts, even if it doesn't seem to work at first, don't disregard it. It may just need more time to gestate.

Don't forget, this is a romance. Linking the love story and love interest into the external plot and developing it early on is important. Most writers have a tendency to want to write the stories in the order in which the idea comes to them. Focusing on the romance angle as you brainstorm can save you from having to rewrite the beginning scenes. (For more on plotting, see Chapter 8. For more on creating characters, see Chapter 10.)

How Other Writers Write

Whether you're trying to write a book or build a house, it's human nature to study how others have succeeded and try to follow in their footsteps. Indeed, you can, and should, attempt to learn from the pros. However, it's wise to remember that when what you are trying to accomplish is of a creative nature (such as writing), individuals may follow their own unique path. This said, here are varying work habits and approaches to writing that different accomplished writers use to achieve success.

- **Character-driven versus plot-driven:** Character-driven writers generally come up with their characters first, and their stories zero in on more of the internal conflicts and character growth than what is happening in the story. Plot-driven writers mostly start with a situation and rely heavily on actions and events in the story to move the plot forward.

- **Pantsers versus plotters:** Pantsers write by the seat of their pants without always knowing what will come next. Plotters write outlines and have the novel all planned out before they begin.

- **Night writers versus day writers:** Night writers find that their creativity peaks in the late hours. Day writers need the alertness and the freshness of a new day to be creative.

- **Homebody writers versus coffee shop writers:** Homebody writers need to be in the same place with their own things surrounding them to write. Coffee shop writers believe the variety of settings inspires them.

- **Silent writers versus bring-on-the-noise writers:** Some writers need a soundless environment to produce pages—no music, no chatter. Bring-on-the-noise authors need the background sounds; some will purposely leave on the television in the next room.

- **Rough-draft writers versus polish-as-I-go writers:** Rough-draft authors write their copy and don't worry about getting it perfect the first go-round. Polish-as-I-go writers edit and proof as they write.

- **Fast writers versus slow writers:** For some fast writers, completing twenty or more pages a day is the norm. Slow writers know that they may be able to squeeze out five pages a day on their best days, with only three or four being the norm.

- **Under-pressure writers versus no-stress writers:** Some authors simply work better under pressure. The closer the deadline looms, the more productive they become. No-stress writers go blank in the face of pressure and therefore, they realize the importance of staying on course.

Discovering Your Own Writing Path

While modeling yourself after those who are successful is a great start, most writers need to find their own methods to reach their highest potential. Being creative in how you approach the writing process can help you discover your own recipe for success. Night writers, try getting up early to produce pages. Homebodies, try getting out.

Don't push yourself to be a highly prolific writer such as Nora Roberts because, well, you aren't Nora. Nothing is wrong with challenging yourself to write faster, or to write better drafts, or to shake up your normal routine. Give the schedule or new habit more than several tries before ruling it out. In time, you will know when something isn't working both by your gut instinct and by your productivity.

Your Writer's Voice

Just as your vocal cords create a recognizable sound, once you get comfortable with this craft, your writing will stand out from the work of other authors. Those who have read your work before will be able to pick up a book without looking at the cover and say . . . "Hey, I think I know who wrote this."

Just as an artist's brush stokes, color choices, and the methods in which he conveys mood are recognizable, a writer's voice also becomes detectable. While two authors may have similar voices, each author's style, word choice, and story selections are unique. In other words, it's okay to resonate the talent from other well-known authors, just make sure it has your own unique appeal.

Defining Voice

Voice is a combination of many elements. It isn't a genre; it is how you approach the genre. Jennifer Crusie's voice isn't humor; it's her own unique style of humor. Tami Hoag's voice isn't suspense; it's how she evokes suspense. Voice can also cross genres because it involves things such as word choices, sentence structures, and the mood and feel of a book. Tone is a strong indicator of voice. Some writing voices are said to be poetic, gritty, quirky, or sensual.

One method of understanding voice better is to read several books, back to back, by an established writer who is known to have a strong voice. As you read, study the common elements in the different novels. Read aloud and listen to how the stories sound, take note of how the stories make you feel, and how the words and sentences are put together to create images.

How to Find Your Voice

The best way to discover your voice is to write and keep writing. Try your hand at different genres and experiment with tones. Try to write passages in a very poetic voice, then attempt to be gritty and dark. If one seems to feel right, keep working on it. Many writers will note another author's voice before they will recognize their own.

While there may always be some recognizable qualities of an author's voice in everything she writes, writers can learn to improve and change the quality of their voice very much like singers can learn to control pitch and tone.

Create Your Writing Space

While some new writers have great offices, a designated room designed especially to help them produce wonderful books, the truth is that there are probably more writers who started out on a dining room table or a tiny desk tucked into a corner of an extra bedroom. The many how-I-began stories, from some of the more successful writers, prove that the desire to write is more important than where you write. This said, there are things you can do to make your space, be it a room of its own, or a stolen corner in another room, more writing friendly.

Make It Comfortable

Nothing can hinder your creative process more than a backache or a neck ache. Making sure your keyboard and screen are positioned correctly for your needs will help you be productive.

One of the most important pieces of office equipment is the chair. If the chair isn't a good fit, you will likely be constantly getting up and down—losing focus and losing time. Look for a chair that adjusts to your unique body, and that readjusts to accommodate the changes in the way you sit, type, or roll around your desk.

Ward Off Distractions

Many writers have completed bestselling novels while dealing with a houseful of toddlers that required constant attention. However, most writers have learned the importance of limiting distractions when possible. If you have teenagers who play loud music, attempt to set up your writing area on the opposite end of the home. If the sight of other family members coming in and out of the front door distracts you, choose a room away from the front-door entrance.

Keep Needed Tools Close and Organized

Most writers consider their writing time precious, but some unorganized souls spend more time looking for needed tools, from books to printer cartridges, than they do writing. Keeping all your tools within reach and organized will save you from spending time being a gofer and allow you to spend more time being a writer.

Build Your Writer's Toolbox

Every trade has a list of needed tools—imagine a photographer without a camera or a contractor without a hammer. Writing is no exception. While an imagination is sure to be the most required tool of a career novelist, you'll find several other items will help you achieve success. Having a stocked toolbox will aid and quicken your journey to publication.

The Computer and Printer

While some writers still prefer to write their first drafts in longhand, most agree that a reliable computer and a good printer are on the top of their must-have list. The price of computers can vary, but generally speaking, a basic system with a word processing program with spelling and grammar capabilities, will have all the bells and whistles required to fulfill your obligations as a writer.

> Don't forget to have some sort of backup system to save your work in case your computer crashes. Either a zip drive or an alternate backup drive will work. If not those, get an online e-mail account with file storage and forward copies of your work.

While the price of printers has come down tremendously, the acceptance of electronic submissions has made the need for the fastest letter-quality printers less of a priority for established writers. Most authors are printing out fewer completed manuscripts for submission purposes.

Internet Access

Your computer isn't just the tool to produce your work, it allows you to connect to all kinds of resources. The Internet provides a wealth of information on markets, publishers, and specific information about any subject you may need to research. Today, a lot of writers admit most of their research is done online. However, be aware that just because it's found online doesn't make it true. Facts still need to be checked. And then rechecked.

Times have changed. The cyber highway is now probably the preferred form of communication in the publishing industry. Without an Internet connection, e-mail is unavailable. The Internet also offers you access to all sorts of writing sources, including Web sites, writing organizations, chat rooms, and online courses.

Other Items

There are several reference books that you will want to have on hand. A good, up-to-date dictionary is the first on the list. (The smaller pocket dictionaries can prove to be lacking.) A thesaurus is equally important. While a lot of writers use the thesaurus on their word processing system, many do not compare to a quality book. Also found in many author's personal libraries are how-to-write books that offer quick helpful facts on everything from writing techniques to genre-specific information.

Also needed is some sort of a filing system. All your books will need to have their own files. You'll also have an idea file, a file for writing-related receipts, or possibly a file for each character. (You don't need to invest a lot in these items. Inexpensive file folders, or plastic file bins, can serve the purpose.)

FACT

Save all your receipts for any writing-related item for the Internal Revenue Service. Whether you show a profit or loss, your business expenses are still deductible. And even if you decide not to claim your deductions this year, you can do so next year since the IRS allows you to claim expenses from prior years.

The Value of a Critique Group

As you start planning to put words on paper, you might want to start thinking about joining a critique group. A critique group is two or more people who have joined forces and decided to support each other's writing career. Different groups set different guidelines, but most of them do the following: read each other's work and offer constructive feedback, help brainstorm ideas, share knowledge, and basically help each other through the writing process.

Writers are so often blind to their own strengths and weaknesses, while another writer can easily see weak areas and point out strengths. A critique group or partner can be tremendously helpful in helping you achieve success. While you may think a group needs someone with more experience, and that can be helpful, two people who are both learning and sharing knowledge can offer substantial benefits to each other. Basically, two heads are stronger than one. It also bears noting that each writer comes into the craft of writing with different strengths and weaknesses. Some people may be naturals at characterization, while others may excel at plotting.

How to Find a Critique Group

The best place to find a group is within a writing community. Join writers' organizations and don't neglect to look to the online groups. A lot of organizations offer monthly newsletters where you can post your interest in forming a group. Another good place to connect with other writers is in adult continuing-education writing classes.

ALERT!

Don't confuse a writer's organization and a critique group. A writer's organization usually offers speakers and advice at regular meeting intervals, but joining an organization such as Romance Writers of America does not automatically supply you with a critique partner.

Making Sure the Critique Group Is Right for You

It is best to start every critique group on a trial basis. Finding the right group is like buying a new pair of jeans. You might have to try on several different brands and styles before you find the one pair that feels right and fits your body shape.

Just as the right group can be tremendously helpful, the wrong one can be terribly harmful. One way to make sure a group is a good fit is to start off on the right foot by talking about expectations and setting critiquing guidelines and rules. Rule number one: treat your writing partners with the same respect you expect for yourself. Rule number two: respect every writer's right to agree or not agree with any criticism.

Criticism can be difficult to take, even when it's constructive, but dealt harshly, it can be detrimental to one's love of the craft. If a group doesn't feel right, bow out gracefully. And remember: just because one group didn't work, doesn't mean the perfect critique partner or group isn't out there.

CHAPTER 7

The Mechanics of Writing Well

Part of being a good writer is knowing how to write well. Sounds like a no-brainer, doesn't it? But often, new romance writers sabotage their fledgling careers with poor grammar choices, misspelled words, incorrect punctuation, and other mechanical faux pas. Does that mean you have to be a grammar whiz in order to write a romance novel? Of course not. But you do need to know the basics.

Why Good Grammar Matters

So, why does good grammar matter in a romance novel? After all, much like mysteries and other novels of popular fiction, people read these books for the stories inside them, not because of the grammar used to tell the story. Besides, if you used proper grammar in your novel, wouldn't that make your work seem stilted and awkward?

Actually . . . no. At least it shouldn't if you've done your job correctly.

> Rules of grammar exist for a reason, and the reason is to ensure that the words you put on paper make sense to the people who read them. Think of good grammar choices as just another tool in your writer's toolbox, much like a good word processing program or a dictionary.

Consider this: When a reader picks up your romance novel and starts to read, the only thing she should care about is the story you're describing. That won't be possible if she has to stop and reread passages because she isn't sure what you were trying to say. Luckily, you can easily solve this problem with a quick refresher course on the fundamentals of good grammar.

Proper Sentence Structure

Some writers are naturally adept at the mechanics of writing. Others have to work at it because their strength lies in the art of storytelling. Still, knowing how to write a grammatically correct sentence—and knowing when it's okay to bend or even break those grammar rules—is a necessary skill for an author . . . especially if she hopes to get published.

Back to the Basics

Before you can write a good romance novel, you need to know how to write a good sentence. Understanding what makes a sentence complete—and most important, what makes a sentence incomplete—is the first step.

A good reference book for learning the grammar basics is *The Only Grammar Book You'll Ever Need* by Susan Thurman. Written by an English teacher, it offers easy-to-understand tips for comprehending the complexities of using proper grammar.

Simply put, sentences are a word, or a string of words, that do one of the following three things:

1. Make a statement, such as *Mark kissed Helen.*
2. Ask a question, such as *Who kissed Helen?*
3. Issue a command or a wish, such as *Shut up and kiss me!*

For a sentence to be complete, it must have a subject and a predicate. The subject is a noun or pronoun that represents the person, place, or thing at the center of the sentence. The sentence also must have a predicate, which is a verb (the words in the sentence that describe existence, action, or occurrence) and its various modifiers. The subject performs the action described by the predicate. For example, in the sentence, *Mark kissed Helen*, *Mark* is the subject, *kissed* is the verb, and *Helen* is the object, or recipient, of Mark's kiss.

Not all complete sentences have to contain an object—or even a subject, for that matter. Short one- or two-word sentences with an action verb and/or an object are perfectly acceptable. *Run! Give me the pencil.* Both sentences imply "you" as the subject.

Subject-Verb Agreement

One of the most common grammar mistakes involves subject-verb agreement. This occurs when the verb tense being used doesn't match the subject. Grammar rules state that singular subjects require singular verbs. Conversely, plural subjects require plural verbs. Mistakes happen when a writer pairs a singular subject with a plural verb, or vice versa.

For example, *Tom walk down the hall* would be incorrect because the singular subject, Tom, requires a singular verb form of "walk," which in this case is *walks.* The correct sentence would be *Tom walks down the hall* or *The men walk down the hall.*

Usually, if the subject is a proper name or a pronoun, it's easy to choose the right verb form. (Tom is. He was.) Not so for a place or thing. Remember, places, such as cities and states, are singular but things can be either. To figure out whether your non-proper name subject needs a singular or plural verb, try substituting the words *he* or *she* for a singular subject and *they* for a plural subject. When you read the sentence aloud, the correct verb choice should be clear.

Your computer's word processing program can be your grammar coach, if you let it! Enable the grammar check option when you have the program check your spelling. It will alert you to common grammar errors and offer recommendations on how to fix them.

Using Adjectives and Adverbs

All writers want to make their work as vibrant as possible. Often, however, new romance writers will rely on the use of adverbs and adjectives to achieve their goal, rather than choose more descriptive nouns and verbs. As a result, the novel loses the very sense of vibrancy and strength that the writer hoped to accomplish.

The Role of Adjectives and Adverbs

Adjectives and adverbs are both modifiers, meaning they are the parts of speech that clarify or describe the subject and predicate. Adjectives modify nouns; adverbs perform the same function for verbs. To put it another way, think of adjectives and adverbs as the seasoning you'd add to a pot of soup. The core ingredients—vegetables, meat, pasta—are the nouns and verbs. Just as seasonings should enhance the natural flavor of the main ingredients and not overshadow them, so should adjectives and adverbs.

To see if you're overusing adverbs in your romance novel, have your word processing program search for all words ending in *ly*. While not all *ly* words are adverbs, the majority of them will be. Once you've identified an adverb, analyze the sentence to see if you could use a stronger verb instead.

Why Using Modifiers Can Be a Problem

Sometimes, problems arise from the use of adjectives and adverbs. Usually, this occurs when an author relies upon the modifiers to do the job of making their writing vivid when using more descriptive nouns and active verbs would have sufficed. For example,

- **Susan ran quickly down the hall:** The adverb *quickly* describes the verb *ran*; replacing the verb and adverb with a stronger, more active verb solves the problem; i.e., *Susan raced down the hall* or *Susan sprinted down the hall.*
- **The witch gave a harsh, sharp laugh:** The adjectives *harsh* and *sharp* describe the noun *laugh*; since a "harsh, sharp laugh" is a cackle, the sentence can be rewritten as, *The witch cackled.*

Of course, eliminating all adjectives and adverbs from your writing would be as big a mistake as overusing them. After all, modifiers serve a valuable function—they clarify meaning and add color to your writing. The key is to use them selectively.

Using Descriptive Verbs and Nouns

Just as poor word choices can make your writing weak, wise word choices can make your writing stronger. One of the most powerful weapons in a writer's arsenal is the language itself—using action verbs and more descriptive nouns make for more powerful writing because it forces you to be clear and precise in your word choices. It also gives your writing the sense of immediacy—the "active voice"—that it desperately needs to capture and keep the reader's attention.

Often a new writer of any genre will use twelve words to describe what could be adequately covered by three. Not only can choosing the right words make your work stronger, it can quicken the pace.

Choosing the Right Verbs

Verbs come in two types—linking verbs, such as *is, was,* and *are*—and action verbs, such as *run, walk, talk,* or *dance.* Of the two verb forms, action verbs support a more active writing voice. But not all action verbs are the same. Some depend on an adverb to clarify their meaning while others paint a more descriptive image in the reader's mind of the action being performed.

For example:

- Instead of *walked slowly and steadily,* use *trudged* or *plodded*
- Instead of *sat down heavily,* use *plopped* or *collapsed*
- Instead of *lifted the box with great effort,* use *hoisted the box*
- Instead of *cried uncontrollably,* use *sobbed*

When choosing an action verb, strive to find the one that best conveys the image you are trying to evoke. Be specific, rather than general.

FACT

Since your words paint a picture for the reader, choose action verbs that match your scene's emotional tone. For example, use verbs that convey an element of danger for suspense scenes and verbs that convey a sense of whimsy for humorous scenes.

Choosing the Right Nouns

Just as choosing the right verb can strengthen your writing, so can choosing the right noun. Nouns come in two basic types: concrete, meaning it has a physical existence or you can experience it with one of your five senses, and abstract, meaning you can't experience it, such as a concept or a place. Some concrete nouns may be proper nouns that refer specifically to a person or thing, while others just pack a powerful punch, much like strong action verbs. If possible, try to choose a noun that is vivid and descriptive in its own right, without the need for clarifying adjectives.

For example:

- Instead of *large, deciduous north temperate-zone tree,* use *elm*
- Instead of *the tall, dark-haired man who was Bob's best friend,* use *Fred*
- Instead of *harsh, discordant sound,* use *cacophony*
- Instead of *tall, powerful black-and-tan shorthaired dog,* use *rottweiler*

Using the right noun improves your writing because it gives the reader a clear, precise mental image of the subject being described.

Pronouns and Antecedents

Another potential source for grammar mishaps involves pronouns—the *he, she,* and *they* words—and their antecedents, the noun to which each pronoun refers. For a sentence to be grammatically correct, pronouns and antecedents must agree in three ways:

- **Person**—the pronoun must match the specific person being referenced; *Tom handed Bob the file. He smiled.* If the writer's intention is that Tom is the one who smiled, the sentence has a problem, since the pronoun *he* refers to the last masculine noun before it, namely *Bob.* Replacing the pronoun with *Tom* or changing the sentence to *Tom handed Bob the file and smiled* removes the problem.
- **Number**—the pronoun must match the specific number implied by the noun; *The man raced across the yard. They tripped over an exposed root and fell.* The pronoun *they* refers to the noun *man,* which is singular. Since *they* is incorrect, it should be replaced with *he.*
- **Gender**—the pronoun must match the gender implied by the noun; *Jennifer walked down the hall. He stopped.* The pronoun *he* refers to the noun *Jennifer,* which is incorrect. The correct pronoun should be *she.*

Making the pronoun agree with the antecedent when the pronoun refers to a person is probably one of the most common mistakes made by new writers. This is especially true in the romance genre since most novels are written in third person. Many writers hesitate to use the hero or heroine's given name when writing from their POV because it can distance the reader. As a result, authors rely heavily on the use of pronouns.

ESSENTIAL

> Making sure that all the *he* and *she* references in a romance novel are accurate can be especially tricky for scenes with more than one character of the same gender. One technique is to print out the chapter, then circle in red every pronoun you find and draw an arrow back to its implied antecedent to make certain it's correct.

While it's true that overuse of your character's given name, especially when writing from her POV, can distance the reader, having an incorrect pronoun-antecedent agreement is worse. After all, if a reader becomes confused while reading your novel, she may decide to put it aside . . . and never pick it back up again.

Rules of Punctuation

Once you've chosen the right verbs and nouns, trimmed the unneeded adverbs and adjectives from your sentences, and made sure your pronouns match their antecedents, you'll need to check for punctuation missteps.

Periods, Question Marks, and Exclamation Points

Most sentences end with one of the following three basic forms of punctuation:

1. **Periods:** Used at the end of declarative sentences, as well as at the end of sentences that ask indirect questions; no additional period is required if the last word in the sentence already has a period (as in an abbreviation).

a. *The dog crouched down and began to bark.*
b. *Tom wants to know who ate the ice cream.*
c. *"Shanna, if you don't hurry, you'll be late for P.E."*

2. **Question marks:** Used at the end of questions.
   a. *Will Samantha and Derek find true love?*
   b. *"Are you ready to go?"*

3. **Exclamation points:** Used at the end of sharply worded commands.
   a. *"Stop, thief!"*
   b. *"Fire!"*

Limit your use of exclamation points. Ideally, this type of punctuation should only be used for short, sharply worded commands or rebukes.

Quotation Marks

Quotation marks are used to identify direct quotations. Generally, the other punctuation marks will go inside them.

- *"Thanks," Martin said.*
- *"Are you sure you can trust him?" Jim asked.*
- *"Wait," Betty said, "I'm coming with you."*

When placing a second quotation inside a quote—e.g., *"Michael's exact words were, 'Tell her I'll be back.'"*—use a single quotation mark for the second quote.

Dialogue tags, such as *said* or *asked*, identify who is speaking. The comma is the most used punctuation with a dialogue tag—e.g., *"Okay," she said*—but the question mark can be used when a character asks a question. Because the tag is part of the main sentence, always place a single space between the dialogue and the dialogue tag.

Ellipses, Em Dashes, and Parentheses

Some punctuation marks can show a break in action or offer an aside comment to the reader. An ellipsis mark, which is " . . ." or three periods separated by three spaces, is used to show a pause or gradual fading away in thought or dialogue. Em dashes (—) or a long dash without spaces on either side of it, can be used in the place of commas, colons, semicolons, or parentheses. They can also be used to show an abrupt cessation of action. Parentheses, the two ( ) on your keyboard, show an aside comment, or offer additional information.

- *"Paul . . . I'm sorry," Mary said.*
- *"I had hoped that we . . ." Alyssa bit her lip and looked away.*
- *"What are you—?" Jessica screamed.*
- *They rode the Tilt-a-Whirl twice. (Three times but Jessie wasn't counting.)*

Semicolons and Colons

Semicolons and colons are rarely used in fiction. The semicolon (;) is used to separate two complete sentences that haven't been joined by a conjunction (*and, but, or*). The colon (:) is used at the end of a complete sentence to introduce a list of items, or between two strong clauses that reference each other.

- *I wrote the letter to my boss on Monday; I tore it up the following day.*
- *My goal was simple: Find the killer before the killer found me.*
- *I had a short to-do list: Pick up the cat from the vet's office, drop off the laundry, and pay the electric bill.*

Commas

Commas serve a variety of functions in fiction. They can separate lists, introduce clauses, and attribute a direct quotation to a speaker, among other things. The following general rules apply when using a comma:

1. Use a comma when your sentence starts with a subordinate clause, which is a clause that cannot stand on its own as a sentence.
   a. *As you know, Gregg moved to Cleveland.*
   b. *"Aside from the ending, what did you think of the movie?"*

2. Use a comma to separate two clauses joined by a conjunction.
   a. *Martin took the afternoon off to go fishing, and he didn't feel the least bit guilty.*
   b. *"I may have robbed the gas station, but I didn't kill nobody," Bobby said.*
3. Use a comma to separate lists or series.
   a. *Theresa, Mary, and Kathleen waited outside the church for Peter to arrive.*
   b. *We gave Paul a baseball, a bat, and a catcher's mitt for his birthday.*
4. Use a comma to introduce or pause during a direct quotation.
   a. *"Maybe," Jane said, "but I don't think so."*
   b. *"I'm ready to go whenever you are," Micki said.*

Commas can also be inserted to set off a direct address—e.g., *"I'm glad you could join us, Maxine"*—among other uses. Avoid comma mishaps, though, such as comma splices, which happen when you use a comma to connect two complete sentences. (A comma and a conjunction is the proper format in that instance, or a semicolon.)

Spelling Basics

When you submit your romance novel to a prospective agent or editor, you will want to make certain that it is as rejection-proof as possible. That means having a manuscript that is free from spelling errors. While your word processing program's spell checker will catch most spelling errors, you will still need to proof your manuscript carefully.

And while you proof the pages, you'll need to remember the spelling basics.

Plurals and Possessives

Many writers get confused about how to spell nouns when they change from singular to plural or where to place the apostrophe when indicating possession. Of the two, making a noun possessive is perhaps the easiest— you either add an apostrophe and an *s*, or an apostrophe after an existing *s*, such as *the man's tie* or *the two dogs' master.*

The rules for making a noun plural aren't as simple. If in doubt about the proper plural form of a noun, consult your dictionary. Your computer's word processing program has a built-in spell-checker program that can scan your document for misspellings. Also, many dictionaries are now available online, such as the Merriam-Webster Dictionary at *www.m-w.com*.

QUESTION?

Isn't it the job of the editor to catch the spelling errors?
Well, yes. Editors—or the copyeditors, as is the case for most publishers—will proofread your manuscript for typographical errors, misspelled words, and incorrect punctuation, but this only occurs after they've agreed to publish the novel. Manuscripts with numerous "writing mechanics" errors will likely never reach that stage.

Commonly Misspelled Words

Sometimes your spell-checker program won't identify a word as being misspelled because the word, while incorrect for its intended usage in the sentence, is spelled correctly. Words to watch out for include:

- **Your** (possessive)—**You're** (contraction of *You are*)
- **Their** (possessive)—**They're** (contraction of *They are*)—**There** (adverb)
- **Conscience** (a sense or right or wrong)—**Conscious** (a state of awareness)
- **Affect** (verb)—**Effect** (noun)
- **Accept** (verb, meaning *to agree*)—**Except** (preposition, meaning *to exclude*)
- **Advice** (noun)—**Advise** (verb)

Because your word processor's spell checker isn't likely to find these types of errors, make sure you proofread your manuscript. Some writers read their work aloud. Others will have their work read by a critique partner. Often, another set of eyes can catch things that you may have overlooked.

Passive Versus Active Voice

The most common piece of advice given to new writers of all genres is probably to show the action that occurs, rather than to tell the reader about it after the fact. This advice is especially important for a new romance novelist. "Telling" relies upon the use of passive voice, whereas "showing" uses active voice. What's the difference between the two?

Quite a bit, actually.

Passive voice is dependent upon the use of the "to be" verbs, which are forms of linking verbs such as *is, was, am, were,* and *has been.* No action is implied with the use of "to be" verbs; they merely relay information.

Not all uses of passive voice are wrong. Sometimes, an author will use this technique when describing a secondary character through the main character's POV. For example, *John was a tall, thin man whose hunched-over shoulders and sallow complexion had always reminded Mary of a large vulture.*

Active voice, on the other hand, uses action verbs, which show the action as it occurs. Notice the difference in the following examples:

- **The pizza was eaten by the football squad.** (passive)—*The football squad ate the pizza.* (active)
- **Julie was kissed on her neck by Robert.** (passive)—*Robert kissed Julie on her neck.* (active)

Using the active voice gives your writing immediacy and puts the reader into the middle of the action. Once the reader is involved in the action, it's more difficult for her to put down your book.

Finding Help When You Need It

If you've followed the suggestions for proper punctuation, spelling, and grammar in this chapter and feel you still need assistance, don't despair. Help is just a mouse click away. Whether you want to purchase punctuation and style handbooks (*www.amazon.com*) or research a prickly grammar question at a university's Web site (*http://owl.english.purdue.edu*), the Internet can be a tremendous resource.

Beware of ads for editorial services for fiction writers that you might find at some Web sites. While many such companies are legitimate, many others may be scams, especially when coupled with claims of "guaranteed publication" after using their services.

Another great resource is your local library or teachers at your local high school or community college's English Department. Often these professionals are happy to answer a specific question for a new writer.

Finally, if you feel your grammar skills really need more assistance than you can obtain from books and online research, consider taking a night course at your local community college.

CHAPTER 8

Plotting Your Romance Novel

Ask any two published romance authors how they plot their novels and you'll likely get two different answers. After all, some develop their plot as they write while others plot the entire novel before writing a single page. Either way, certain universal truths remain. Namely, to write a marketable romance novel, you'll need to come up with characters your readers will care about and a storyline that intrigues, along with great supporting subplots and secondary characters that will keep the readers turning pages, eager to find out what happens next.

Choosing Your Creative Method

Are you a pantser—meaning, you write by the seat of your pants—or are you more of a plotter? More specifically, are you the type of writer who creates the characters of a novel and then finds a plot to suit them? Or, do you create the plot first and then create the ideal characters to tell that particular story? Do you know? Better still, does it matter?

In the long run, the answer is probably no. After all, deciding *how* you will develop your plot—or even *when*—is far less important than actually developing a plot that is strong enough to sustain the reader's interest for the length of the novel.

Choosing Your Plotting Guideline

So, how do you create a strong romance plotline? Well, for starters, you'll need to make certain your romance is introduced, developed, and resolved in a believable and emotionally compelling way. Some authors prefer to follow the three-act paradigm, or structured theme, while others use the five-act method. And then there are the authors who focus on the hero's journey as the building blocks for their plot.

Three-Act Paradigm

This archetype is most commonly associated with screenwriting and is probably the most easily recognizable of all story formats. Essentially, it says that a romance novel, like all stories, will have three components: a beginning, a middle, and an end.

ALERT!

Many new writers find inspiration for plotting a can't-put-it-down romance novel by taking a screenwriting workshop that follows the three-act paradigm laid out by long-time Hollywood script doctor and screenwriting guru, Syd Field. To see what types of screenwriting workshops are available in your area, check your local library and/or community college.

The three acts are not divided evenly through the romance novel. In fact, the second act contains roughly one-half of the book's content, while the first and third acts contain the remainder. Included within the three-act method are two main plot points (or turning points), along with a mid-point that dramatically changes the direction of the story and a Dark Moment where all seems lost.

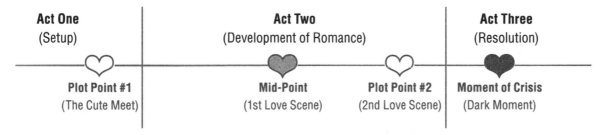

Act One	Act Two	Act Three
(Setup)	(Development of Romance)	(Resolution)
Plot Point #1	Mid-Point / Plot Point #2	Moment of Crisis
(The Cute Meet)	(1st Love Scene) / (2nd Love Scene)	(Dark Moment)

Three-Act Paradigm
This is the layout of a three-act paradigm. Notice that the Mid-Point and 2nd Plot Point are identified as love scenes; however, depending upon the type of a romance novel you're writing, the plot points could just as easily be an escalating development of the emotional commitment to the relationship.

The specifics of the three-act paradigm are as follows:

1. **Act One**—The Introduction or Setup
   a. The hero's and heroine's conflicts—external, internal, and romantic, if all are present—are introduced (or at least foreshadowed).
   b. Includes the first turning point (toward the end of the first act,) which will be the Cute Meet.
2. **Act Two**—The Development of the Romance
   a. The hero and heroine begin to fall in love.
   b. Secondary conflicts (such as external and internal) are confronted and resolved, while the primary conflict (such as the romantic) is not, although an inevitable confrontation is foreshadowed.
   c. Includes the mid-point, or major turning point, which is usually the first love scene, or the first scene of physical and/or emotional intimacy.
   d. Includes the second turning point (toward the end of the second act,) which raises the stakes of the romance while still foreshadowing the coming Dark Moment.

3. **Act Three**—The Resolution
   a. Includes the Dark Moment where the primary conflict explodes and the romance seems doomed.
   b. Includes the final resolution, also known as the Happily Ever After.

Because the three-act paradigm is the simplest of all plotting structures, it is a perfect choice for writing a shorter-format romance novel when the romance is the only plotline.

Five-Act Paradigm

The five-act structured theme is based upon the layout of a play, as interpreted by Gustav Freytag. Much like the three-act paradigm, this method has four main plot points that describe the introduction, development, and resolution of the romance. The primary difference is that in the five-act paradigm, the development phase is broken into three acts containing the rising action, the mid-way turning point, and the falling action.

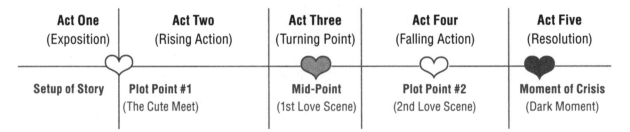

Act One	**Act Two**	**Act Three**	**Act Four**	**Act Five**
(Exposition)	(Rising Action)	(Turning Point)	(Falling Action)	(Resolution)
Setup of Story	**Plot Point #1**	**Mid-Point**	**Plot Point #2**	**Moment of Crisis**
	(The Cute Meet)	(1st Love Scene)	(2nd Love Scene)	(Dark Moment)

Five-Act Paradigm
This is the layout of a five-act paradigm. Notice that the first act is labeled as "exposition" or setup of the story, while the 1st Plot Point (The Cute Meet) seems to occur somewhere between Act One and Act Two. This is because a longer format romance may have additional subplots that might affect the timing of the Cute Meet.

The specifics of the five-act paradigm are as follows:

1. **Act One**—The Exposition or Setup
   a. The hero's and heroine's conflicts—external, internal, and romantic—are introduced (or at least foreshadowed).
   b. The primary subplot, such as a suspense element, is introduced.

c. May include the first plot point, which will be the Cute Meet. (This could be alternatively placed at the beginning of Act Two.)

2. **Act Two**—The Rising Action
   a. The hero and heroine begin to fall in love.
   b. Subplots and secondary characters are introduced (if not already done so) and the stakes rise.

3. **Act Three**—The Mid-Point
   a. Some secondary and supporting conflicts are confronted and resolved.
   b. Includes the mid-point, or major turning point, which is usually the first love scene, or the first scene of physical and/or emotional intimacy.
   c. Includes the major turning point for the primary subplot (such as the suspense element).

4. **Act Four**—The Falling Action
   a. Includes the confrontation and resolution of secondary conflicts, while foreshadowing the inevitable confrontation of the primary romantic and primary subplot conflicts.
   b. Includes the second turning point (toward the end of the fourth act), which raises the stakes of the romance while still foreshadowing the coming Dark Moment.

5. **Act Five**—The Resolution
   a. Includes the resolution of all remaining secondary conflicts involving secondary characters, as well as the resolution of the primary subplot.
   b. Includes the Dark Moment where the primary conflict explodes and the romance seems doomed (can be combined with the resolution of the primary subplot, especially if a romantic suspense).
   c. Includes the final resolution of the romantic conflict, also known as the HEA.

Since the five-act paradigm can support the inclusion of one or more subplots, it's a favorite among writers of larger-format romance novels.

The Hero's Journey

Another method employed by romance writers when plotting their novels is the use of the hero's journey paradigm. This structured theme is based on the work of another screenwriter, Christopher Vogler, whose book *The Writer's Journey: Mythic Structure for Writers* was in turn based upon his interpretation of the archetypes described by Joseph Campbell in his seminal work on mythology, *The Hero with a Thousand Faces*.

ESSENTIAL

There have been many great how-to books on writing that utilize Vogler's observations. One of the best is probably romance writer Debra Dixon's *Goal, Motivation, and Conflict.* Dixon's workshops on plotting have been must-attend events for many novice writers of all genres, romance especially.

Basically, Vogler suggested that all fictional heroes—whether in a novel or a screenplay—would follow a similar path during the course of the story. When Vogler's insights regarding the hero's journey are applied to the three-act paradigm for writing a romance novel, the result can flesh out the plot and give insight into character.

It can also ensure that you'll avoid the saggy middle and other plot pitfalls.

Specifically, the hero's journey paradigm includes:

1. **Act One**
   a. Ordinary World: The H/H (hero and heroine) are in their normal world before story begins.
   b. Call to Adventure: The H/H learn of the problem, receive a challenge or the call to adventure that can lead to their romance.
   c. Refusal of the Call: The hero or heroine (or both) refuses the call (due to their respective internal conflicts).
   d. Meeting with the Mentor: The H/H meet with a mentor who offers advice or training.

  e. Crossing the First Threshold: The H/H take the first step toward the romance (the first kiss, perhaps).

2. **Act Two**

  a. Tests, Allies, Enemies: The H/H face and resolve their numerous non-primary conflicts and meet the secondary characters who will hinder or help them on their path to true love.

  b. Approach to the Inmost Cave: The H/H encounter numerous obstacles while pursuing their primary goal (a HEA).

  c. Supreme Ordeal: A major plot point where an important secondary conflict seems to doom the romance (could also include the primary conflict peripherally, though not always).

  d. Reward: The H/H overcome their secondary conflict.

3. **Act Three**

  a. The Road Back: The H/H begin the return to their ordinary world, although the primary conflict is still unresolved.

  b. Resurrection: The Dark Moment where the H/H face the loss of their romance and must use every lesson they have learned along their journey to resurrect their love.

  c. Return with Elixir: The H/H return from their journey with the "elixir"—their HEA.

Many successful novelists—in all genres—believe that Vogler's paradigm provides the best setup for creating a rejection-proof plotline. The method can be especially useful when plotting a romance novel with a large cast of characters and plotlines.

Choosing Your Plot

Now that you understand the different archetypes for plotting that are available to you, it's time to develop the plot of your own romance novel. If you haven't already decided on the type and format of romance you wish to write—single title versus category, contemporary romantic suspense versus sexy Regency-set historical, etc.—now is the time to commit. After all, knowing the word count and subgenre—as well as the likelihood of a prospective market—before you plot out your novel will save you a lot of frustration and rewrites later. (For a quick refresher on your romance subgenre options, refer to Chapter 2.)

If, for example, you've decided to write a 100,000 word single-title paranormal romance, you'll know before you start writing that you must have a plot with enough story and conflict revolving around a paranormal premise to sustain a large word count.

While many romance authors end up writing the type of romance novels they enjoy reading, few will actively read in their chosen subgenre while they're writing a manuscript. Reasons vary, although fear of inadvertent plagiarism figures high. Reading, however, is still the best source of inspiration for a writer. Therefore, consider switching your for-pleasure reading preferences to another subgenre while writing your romance novel.

Your Characters' Goals, Motivations, and Conflicts

So, who are your characters? What are their goals, motivations, and conflicts? Best of all, how will your hero and heroine complement—or clash with—each other on the pages of your romance novel? As will be discussed in Chapter 10, a smart romance novelist strives to create believable characters with quirks, fears, and insecurities that a reader can easily understand. A smart writer will also make sure that their main characters' individual goals must be in direct conflict. For one to win, the other must lose.

Or seem to lose, anyway.

QUESTION?

Do I have to create my characters before I develop the plot?
No. In fact, some writers find it easier to create the plotline first and then develop the perfect characters to bring that story to life. Either approach is fine, as long as characterization, conflict, and plot are intrinsically linked in your novel. Find the method that works best for you and let your imagination fly.

With your characters and their conflicts in mind, choosing the right romance plotline becomes a matter of finding the scenario that would best exploit your hero's and heroine's weaknesses while playing up their strengths.

For your single-title paranormal romance, assume your characters include the following:

- **Heroine:** Lisa is an inept apprentice witch whose spells never work right, which is probably why she doubts herself and feels more at home with her dusty scrolls than with other people, especially men. Still, she is always willing to try and make things right when she makes a mistake.
- **Hero:** Darius is a by-the-book homicide detective who stopped believing in magic years ago, especially the kind that involves love. He only trusts what he can see, measure, analyze, and has little patience with those who believe otherwise.
- **Villain:** Mordecai is a demon bent on destroying the world.

With those types of characters in place, certain plot points are a given:

- The hero, heroine, and villain's lives will intercept.
- The hero's disbelief in magic will clash with the heroine's belief.
- The heroine must learn to believe in herself, and the hero must learn to trust things on faith alone.
- The hero and heroine must fall in love, vanquish the villain, and have their HEA.

The next step is to combine the characters' background with the anticipated plot points and a possible plot. For example:

When Lisa's translation of an ancient text inadvertently opens the gateway to hell, she realizes she may be an untalented witch but she has a gift for slaying demons. Good thing, too, since there is a particularly nasty one running amok, thanks to her. She can vanquish him, but how can she explain her new calling to hunky homicide detective Darius? (Especially since he thinks she's a beautiful distraction—if not an outright nut job—who is disrupting his search for a twisted serial killer.) Soon, though, it becomes apparent that they need each other to achieve their goals, although both realize they'll ultimately end up in direct opposition—Darius wants to bring the killer to justice while

Lisa knows the only solution is to kill the demon. Falling in love is something neither anticipated.

Once the bare bones of a plot are in place, you can build the story by using one of the previously mentioned paradigms.

The Cute Meet

How do your hero and heroine meet? Will it be funny? Dramatic? Or just plain "cute"? The best way to choose your Cute Meet, which is usually the precipitating event in a romance novel, is to make it an integral part of the novel's natural progression.

Always bear in mind the tone of your romance novel when crafting your Cute Meet. After all, the term *Cute Meet* doesn't mean that the meeting itself has to be cute, or even funny. The first meeting could be gritty and dramatic if the storyline required it. The important thing is that it sets the romance in motion and sets up the conflicts of your story.

For the romance between Lisa and Darius, the "Cute Meet" might occur when Darius interrupts Lisa's attempt to vanquish the demon after he'd just committed a murder and she has to explain to a very skeptical cop just what she'd been trying to accomplish with a plastic bag filled with strange-smelling herbs and an ornate dagger. Not to mention the dead guy on the pavement.

How do *your* hero and heroine meet? How could it kick-start your romance?

The Dark Moment

The Dark Moment is when the worst thing imaginable finally happens to your hero and heroine. The key to choosing the right moment of crisis for a romance is to make sure that it relates to the main romantic conflict. Meaning, if the romantic conflict has always been the hero's inability to trust, the Dark Moment would come when the hero must trust the heroine . . . and fails. Naturally, having the Dark Moment be linked to secondary conflicts—for example, a suspense subplot—is fine also, but the primary focus must be on the romantic conflict.

Because romance novels are designed to elicit an emotional response from the reader, your Dark Moment should be as emotionally gripping as possible while still remaining faithful to the story premise. In other words, even a rollicking comedy could benefit from a tug of the heartstrings during the Dark Moment.

For Lisa and Darius, their Dark Moment might be when their romance ends after Lisa realizes Darius will not bend on his vow to bring the "killer," aka the demon, to justice, rather than allow her to vanquish him.

Fleshing Out Your Major Plot Points

The final step will be to flesh out your major plot points, which are the points in your novel when the action turns in a new direction. Again, use the characters' conflicts, goals, and motivations to find what will work best for your romance.

Incorporating a Subplot and Secondary Characters

Subplots and secondary characters can add richness and texture to your romance novel. As will be discussed in Chapters 10 and 11, secondary characters can have their own internal conflicts, just as your hero and heroine could have additional conflicts of their own. All characters and subplots must follow the same rules set in place for the primary characters and plotline. Meaning, subplots must have an introduction, development, and resolution and support the main plotline in some way; secondary characters must be well thought out and increase the reader's understanding of the main characters.

What type of subplot or secondary characters do you need to make your novel complete?

Better yet, how can you tie your subplots and secondary characters to your main storyline? As you create your main plot, don't forget to think about the subplot and secondary characters. Find a way to weave all the elements together, by either having their goals meet or by making them part of each other's internal conflict.

Don't get carried away with your use of subplots and secondary characters, especially when you're trying to write a "bigger" romance novel. Having a large cast of supporting characters is fine—so is having more than one subplot. But if you add too many, the story becomes convoluted and the reader will quickly lose interest.

Trying Something Different

Figuring out your romance novel's plot doesn't have to result in hours—if not, days—of frustration while you consider and reject plot points and paradigm methods. If the traditional methods of plotting aren't working for you, maybe you should try a different, more creative, approach to connect with your inner muse.

Making a Collage

Many authors find that making a collage that represents their romance novel frees their creativity and gives them insight into their book and characters. To create one, you'll need scissors, a glue stick, a piece of poster board, and a stack of magazines.

While thinking about your book, flip through the magazines and cut out the images that grab you or reflect your novel's theme. Then, arrange the images on the poster board. Feel free to move things around until you get the right "look." When you have the arrangement set in your mind, apply some glue to the images and attach them to the poster board.

Making a Video

Another fun way of brainstorming story ideas is to create a book video—think of it as one of the movie previews you see on television, only for a romance novel. All you need to get started is a piece of software that creates home videos or presentations, some stock photos and music, and a few ideas.

Most new computers come pre-installed with Windows Movie Maker or I-Movie for Mac. Both applications are easy to use and involve the creation of a timeline (a storyboard) and allow you to insert stock photos, sound clips, and text.

If you don't feel you're up to tackling a movie trailer with video-editing software, you can achieve similar results by creating a presentation with Microsoft PowerPoint or another type of presentation software. The goal is to get in touch with your creative side, experiment with images and sound, and inspire yourself to create.

There are dozens of Internet Web sites that offer royalty-free stock photos for use in digital presentations at a low cost, such as iStockphoto (*www.istockphoto.com*). There are also several Web sites that provide music downloads for a nominal fee.

Find photos that describe your story's theme, its location, your hero and heroine, even your subplots and secondary characters. Then find a piece of music that echoes the theme. Combine them with text using your computer's video-making application and voilà! Instant book video.

Keep the Reader Guessing

If you want to keep the reader turning the pages of your romance novel, you'll need to avoid being predictable. After all, if your reader can figure out what will happen next long before she turns the page, she'll soon become bored.

And a bored reader is a reader who will likely put down your novel.

Keep her guessing. Find new twists on classic plotlines. Push the boundaries of your creative limits. Don't be afraid to try something new.

But most of all, have fun!

CHAPTER 9

Openings—Why First Impressions Count

Ask any author, regardless of genre, what the hardest part about writing a novel is and you'll likely get the same answer. Namely, that it's writing the very first page. While it's true that finding the perfect first line or crafting a great hook to end your first chapter is hard work, it doesn't have to be a stressful experience. In fact, creating a great opening should be as much fun for you to write as it is for the reader to enjoy.

Find Your Opening

If you're not sure where to begin your romance novel, you're not alone. Most authors will rewrite their first chapter multiple times. The reasoning is simple. Professional writers know the importance of getting their opening right. After all, editors and agents—much like potential readers browsing through new releases in a bookstore—will often gauge their interest in the book based on the strength of its opening pages.

ALERT!

Do you want to make your manuscript rejection-proof by readers and publishing professionals alike? If so, make sure your opening is the best that it can be. Great first lines—and great opening scenes—are the fastest way to get your manuscript out of the slush pile and onto the Must-Be-Read stack.

As covered in Chapter 2, romance novels come in a variety of subgenres, so there is no standard type of opening that will work for every book. For example, some may open with a prologue while others start with Chapter 1. Some may focus on narrative and characterization; others will concentrate on dialogue and action.

At one time, it was common to open a romance novel with a travel scene, such as the heroine traveling by train to a new city and a potential new life. Her thoughts would swirl around her as the miles flew past. Modern readers, however, demand more immediacy from their romances, which translates into less introspection and more action in an opening.

The romance genre offers its authors a great deal of flexibility when it comes to how to introduce the reader to the book's main characters and plotline. However, most romance novels will utilize one or more of the following elements in the opening pages:

- The hero introduces the conflict, through either the intriguing premise or precipitating event, such as the Cute Meet.
- The heroine introduces the conflict, through either the intriguing premise or precipitating event, such as the Cute Meet.

- The villain introduces the threat of danger or other major subplot that serves as the external conflict.

There are exceptions, of course. Established authors with a faithful following can successfully deviate from these guidelines, but it's rare that a new writer will be allowed to do so. After all, romance readers know what they want to read in their favorite books—namely, a romance. More specifically, though, readers want an opening in the point of view (POV) of a main character. They also want a hint of what the story is about in those first few pages, such as the conflict. Opening in a secondary character's POV or leading with a long, beautifully written description of the weather is more of a recipe for rejection than it is for success.

Ideally, a romance novel should open with the first meeting between the hero and heroine, aka the Cute Meet. Of course, that isn't always practical, especially in larger-format romance novels. Still, most authors try to have the first meeting between their hero and heroine as close to Chapter 1 as possible.

Finding the right way to open your romance novel can be perplexing, even to the most experienced writer. Should you open with dialogue or an internal thought? Should you go with a prologue or dive right into the first chapter? These are all decisions that you must make before starting page 1. But, more important, you need to have a good hook—something that will grab the reader's attention and make her want to read your book ahead of any other book presented to her.

Hooking the Reader

So, how do you hook a romance reader? It depends upon both your writing style and the type of romance you are writing, of course. Generally, however, you can grab a reader's interest with one of two techniques: the intriguing premise or the precipitating event.

The Intriguing Premise

An intriguing premise is the bare bones of the plot, the concept behind the novel that intrigues and sparks the reader's curiosity. It's what makes your romance seem different from the hundreds of other romance novels for sale in the market in any given month. It could be an unusual situation, a previously unexplored character type, or a familiar story that is presented in a fresh, new way. It is always linked to one or both of the main characters' conflicts.

For example:

In 1880, the last thing ex–Texas Ranger Jack MacBride needs complicating his life is having to escort his new boss's fiancée to California for their wedding—not only is Lady Sarah Banks an untouched English beauty, she's a spoiled brat. But Sarah's not quite what she seems. In fact, Sarah's not even Sarah—she's really Samantha St. James, a spy for Her Majesty in search of a master criminal . . . and she'll stop at nothing to achieve her goal, including seducing Jack MacBride.

If you want to keep your reader hooked beyond the first page of your romance novel, you'll need to engage her emotions. Make her laugh. Make her cry. Most of all, make her care about what will happen to your characters.

The Precipitating Event

Many writers refer to the precipitating event as the initial moment of crisis or moment of change. Also linked to the main characters' conflicts, this scene shakes up the world of your hero or heroine and launches your plot. For most romances, it would be the Cute Meet, although it could just as easily be the introduction of a major subplot, such as the mystery element in a romantic suspense. Much like the intriguing premise, the precipitating event's purpose is to grab the reader's attention and make her want to read the book to find out what happens next.

Finding Your Hook

So, where should you open your romance novel? The short answer is, you should open it at the place where things begin to get interesting, when the conflict arises due to either the intriguing premise or the precipitating event. To help you choose the right hook—and therefore, the right opening—ask yourself the following questions:

1. What is your intriguing premise?
2. What is your precipitating event?
3. Which is the stronger element of the two?

Naturally, you'll want to lead with your strongest element. Once you've chosen your approach, you're ready to open your novel with a first line that will play off your hook and keep the reader turning those pages.

Good First Lines

As previously discussed, a good first line in a romance novel is one that immediately grabs the reader's interest and compels her to keep reading. Ideally, it should describe or comment on an action associated with the precipitating event, the unique premise, or its underlying conflict.

ALERT!

If you're unable to start your book because you can't find the perfect opening line, go with a temporary one to get you started. Consider using something like *Once upon a time <the precipitating event> occurred* or *Once upon a time, there was <an intriguing premise>*—with your elements inserted in the appropriate spaces, of course.

The opening line should match the tone of your novel. It should also be a natural extension of your intriguing premise or precipitating event, rather than a line that you tacked on for its shock value. After all, gimmicky openings, while initially successful, will quickly alienate your reader when they realize they've been duped.

In the following examples, notice how the opening lines serve as a springboard for the launching of the plot:

- **Of all the sins Harry Spencer, the Twelfth Earl of Chestershire, had committed, it hardly seemed fair that this would be the one to send him to Hell:** Opens a sexy historical romance in the middle of the precipitating event; namely, the hero, naked and on the run, takes refuge in the heroine's bedchamber only to be confronted by her with a gun.
- **He liked it when they begged:** Opens a dark romantic suspense in the middle of the precipitating event; namely, a serial killer claiming his next victim.
- **"Two specials for Table Six and, Marilee, there's some cute guy claiming to be your husband up at the counter":** Opens a long contemporary romance in the middle of the precipitating event; namely, the hero's arrival back in the heroine's life after he left her pregnant and heartbroken six years earlier.
- **Dating was hard in the twenty-first century, especially for the single vampire:** Opens a humorous paranormal romance by setting up the intriguing premise; namely, when the heroine—a single vampire in the big city—decides to join a dating service to find her Mr. Right . . . or at least her Mr. Right Now.

An opening line should capture both your style and tone, as well as introduce the reader to your fictional world, so choose wisely. After all, if your opening line isn't the right fit for your book—or doesn't spark curiosity—you're likely to lose a reader's interest. Then again, if you choose the right opening line, you'll have the reader moving eagerly ahead to the next sentence, asking questions, such as, Why? or How? And, most important of all, What will happen next?

Avoid the Info Dump

One of the biggest mistakes that new writers make in their opening pages concerns the use of exposition, or backstory. Known in the industry as the dreaded Info Dump, this phenomenon occurs when a writer places a large chunk of background information—such as the heroine's romantic history or the events that led the hero to his fateful meeting with the heroine—into the middle of an opening action sequence. While interesting and perhaps even integral to the overall understanding of the characters' motivation, the information isn't necessary for the success of the current scene.

Of course, the compulsion to explain the story's setup to the reader is a reasonable one—after all, how can the reader understand what is going on if she doesn't have all the facts? But exposition stops the action cold, which you can't afford to do in an opening scene, especially when the reader hasn't yet decided whether she should buy your book . . . or return it to the bookshelf and try something else.

Give the reader only what is necessary to set the stage in the opening pages. After all, you will have plenty of time to explain things once the story is underway. Try to keep your reader firmly planted in the here and now, especially in the opening chapter. The best way to accomplish this is by avoiding the use of exposition altogether. However, if you must include backstory, try to weave it in slowly as the story progresses. Consider the use of a skillfully placed phrase or line of dialogue, instead of a lengthy paragraph that explains things.

Balancing Dialogue and Narrative

Equally important to a novel's success is finding the right balance between dialogue and narrative, especially in the opening pages. While slow-to-start openings were fashionable at one time, modern romance readers generally prefer a faster-paced book—and faster pacing means more dialogue than narrative.

A quick tip for judging if your novel needs more dialogue is to take the White Space test. Print out the first chapter of your novel and evaluate how much white space—the space on the page generated by short spurts of dialogue—you have. If you see long paragraphs with little white space, add more dialogue.

If dialogue is impractical for a scene, consider using a line of internal thought. You can also break up a long paragraph of exposition or narrative into several smaller paragraphs. Both techniques will increase pacing and keep the chapter balanced between narrative and dialogue. (For more information on mastering the art of pacing, refer to Chapter 16.)

The All-Important First Five Pages

Once you've found an opening line that launches your plot and intrigues the reader, you're ready to write the first five pages, which will usually be the first scene of your novel. Even if your opening scene is considerably longer, it's important to pay close attention to those first five pages. Often, they are all a prospective reader will read before deciding whether to buy your book or move on to the next candidate.

Those prospective readers include editors and agents, too. Of course, for them, the first five pages of your romance novel are especially critical, since the sampling is a gauge of both your writing style and their interest in your project.

QUESTION?

Do editors really reject a manuscript after only reading five pages?
Yes. Some editors will continue to read past the first five pages, but many claim to know whether they are likely to reject the manuscript after reading the opening. After all, editors and agents—much like romance readers—know what works for them and what doesn't, both of which are evident in the first five pages of a manuscript.

Since your goal in writing an opening is to convince the reader—whether an editor, agent, or a potential fan—that she needs to read your romance novel, you'll want to make sure your first five pages are rejection-proof. Using this checklist should help:

Do Your First Five Pages . . .

- ❐ Have a great opening line that launches your plot?
- ❐ Introduce the hero, heroine, or villain?
- ❐ Introduce your main plot or major subplot?
- ❐ Hint at your main characters' internal conflicts?
- ❐ Have a sense of time and place?
- ❐ Have little or no introspection?
- ❐ Have more dialogue than narrative?
- ❐ Leave the reader wondering what will happen next?

If you answered yes to all of these questions, congratulations! Chances are excellent that you've written a great opening to your romance novel. Now you're ready to continue to the next step: writing an equally compelling first chapter.

Writing a Great First Chapter

Writers and jugglers have a lot in common. Both toss balls—or as writers call them, plots, subplot, conflicts, and complications—into the air and try to keep them in motion. Keeping the momentum going without dropping a ball takes skill and practice but the professional juggler makes it look effortless. So, too, must the professional writer when creating her first chapter.

The elements that make for a good first chapter are the same ones that make for a good first five pages—set the events in motion and make the reader want to find out what happens next.

Don't try to cram everything into your first chapter. Concentrate on setting up your main characters and plotline and then move on to the next chapter. After all, shorter chapters give the impression of faster pacing, which is one way to keep the reader turning those pages.

Remember Your Hook

You worked hard to hook your reader in the first five pages of your romance novel. Don't let them slip away in the pages that follow. The best way to ensure that doesn't happen is to make sure the "What will happen next?" feeling is present throughout your first chapter. In other words, keep the action moving.

Review Your Checklist

Take another look at the checklist for your first five pages and see how your first chapter measures up since the same criteria apply to both. Is the conflict understood or at least foreshadowed? Does the reader have a sense of time and place? Have your hero and heroine met, or at least have they been introduced? Do you have fast pacing? If the answer is no, you'll need to bolster your chapter's framework.

Remember, pacing depends in large part on the format of your romance novel. Category romances have fewer pages in which to tell your story, so the development of the romance must happen sooner than in a single title.

Ending on a New Hook

Just as your chapter's opening needed a hook to grab the reader's interest, your chapter ending needs a hook to keep them turning the page. Chapter-ending hooks don't have to be dramatic revelations—they can as simple as a character asking, "What did I just get myself into?" following a well-executed precipitating event. The key is to make the reader want to continue reading.

How to Keep the Reader Reading

So, how do you keep the reader reading your romance novel from first page to last? By writing a book that she can't put down, of course. As for how to accomplish that, the best way is to follow the same "formula" you used in your first scene and first chapter, with a few modifications, of course.

Make sure the scenes and chapters that follow . . .

- Further the plot
- Have conflict
- Develop your main characters
- Engage the reader's emotions
- Contain a minimum of introspection
- Make the reader wonder what will happen next

Following these guidelines will ensure that your romance novel is the best that it can be. (For more information on how to keep the reader's interest from waning, refer to Chapter 16.)

Five Newbie Mistakes and How to Avoid Them

Before you click "Save" on your computer and move on to the second chapter of your romance novel, take a moment and review your work. If you followed the guidelines, you probably have a dynamite opening. That doesn't mean you can't improve upon it, however. The following section explains the five most common mistakes made by new authors in their openings. Best of all, it gives you pointers on how to avoid making them.

Leading with Story Setup

Many new writers open with scenes that are little more than just a setup for the precipitating event or the unique premise. For example, take a lighthearted contemporary romance about a runaway bride who hitches a ride with the Good Samaritan hero and embroils him in a series of misadventures. Instead of opening with the Cute Meet—the heroine jumping into the hero's car when he's stopped at a traffic light outside the wedding chapel—the book might start with a scene in the heroine's POV thirty minutes earlier. Several pages—perhaps even several scenes—are then spent showing her having cute but pointless conversations with her bridesmaids and explaining to the reader why she's going to leave the groom at the altar. The scenes are pointless because the story doesn't start until the heroine jumps into the hero's car.

Setup, regardless of how well written, is boring. Your romance should open when the action does—namely, when your plot is unveiled, your conflict established, or your hero and heroine introduced.

Before starting Chapter 1, ask yourself exactly where the action begins. Refrain from the need to explain things. If you've already started the opening and feel it might it be a setup, try cutting those scenes and move straight to the precipitating event or unique premise. If the deleted scenes contain necessary information that the reader needs to know, find a way to weave it back into the new first pages.

Just as problematic as opening a scene too early is ending a scene too late. While there is no need to show unnecessary details, excessive intro-spection, or mundane activities at any time, it is especially critical not to do so at the end of a scene or chapter. Timing is critical in a romance novel.

Telling Too Much

Another common newbie mistake is telling the reader about facts and events after they've occurred, rather than showing them as they unfold. This often happens with the addition of backstory or by the overuse of passive voice—the "to be" verb (*am, is, was, were, has,* etc.)—in your writing style.

Backstory and passive voice distance the reader from the action, which is never a good idea. After all, if a reader's sense of immediacy is lost—meaning she can't visualize the events as they occur—she may begin to lose interest in your plot.

Limit exposition, or backstory, and substitute an active voice for passive voice whenever possible. Consider, for example, the immediate difference between sentences such as *Jane was listening at the door* (passive voice) and *Jane listened at the door* (active voice.) Using an action verb such as *listened*—instead of a passive verb form such as *was listening*—immediately puts the reader into the middle of the action. (For more information on pas-sive versus active voice, refer to Chapter 7.)

Scenes That Lack Conflict

Often, a new writer will concentrate more on polishing a scene's words than on honing a scene's content. But the best-written scene still can't com-pensate for a sagging plot caused by insufficient conflict. Novels, especially romance novels, are all about the conflict, the struggle of a main character to reach a goal. In order for a scene to succeed, it needs conflict caused by the main character's quest to achieve a goal. This is especially true for open-ing scenes.

People just aren't interested when everything goes right. After all, you wouldn't want to hear about your coworker's perfectly normal everyday drive into work, but have a gas station explode, an eighteen-wheeler catch fire, a man try to carjack her, and you'll be all ears. Without some type of conflict, the reader will quickly lose interest.

Reread your scene and ask yourself what the POV character wants at that particular moment. Is the heroine hoping to land a new job? Is the hero hoping to solve a murder? Whatever your POV character's goal may be, make sure that there are obstacles to overcome. For example, have the heroine spill coffee on the hero in the elevator on the way to her job interview—only to find out the hero is the one who'll be interviewing her for the job. Or, have the hero discover that his best chance for a lead in his murder investigation has just been murdered. Find the conflict in your scene and use it—or delete the scene.

FACT

Conflict doesn't mean that your characters are continually arguing. Conflict just means your characters are continually struggling—whether with themselves, with other people, with nature, etc. A romance novel needs characters with clearly identifiable goals, motivations, and conflicts—otherwise, it's little more than a well-written essay.

Writing Unsympathetic Characters

Sometimes a new writer forgets to explain the hero's or heroine's motivation, especially when the character is behaving badly. As a result, the reader begins to find the character unsympathetic and will no longer root for the character's success.

Romance novels, more so than any other type of commercial fiction, need sympathetic characters. After all, readers want to connect emotionally with the heroine and hero—they want to root for them, laugh with them, cry with them. A reader isn't likely to form that emotional bond if she can't understand a character's reason for behaving in a certain way.

Clearly establish the character's motivation for behaving in any manner that might make him or her appear unsympathetic. For example, if the hero is unexpectedly cold and distant to the heroine after they've made love for the first time, the reader may be turned off by his behavior. However, if he acts that way because he's afraid he's falling in love with her and will get hurt, the reader will understand. Make his motivations clear by inserting lines foreshadowing it in previous scenes.

ALERT!

Sympathetic doesn't have to mean likable. Often, readers will love the heroes and heroines of romance novels but hate the villain. Still, readers find the villains "sympathetic"—meaning they can understand the villain's motivations for committing murder and mayhem.

Giving the Reader a Reason to Stop Reading

The final newbie mistake is perhaps the most important one on the list. Namely, giving the reader a reason to stop reading your book. Most often, this happens because a chapter or scene ends on an anticlimactic moment.

If the action has slowed, or the tension lessened, the reader may get distracted and put aside the book. When that happens, you run the risk that the reader won't pick it up again.

Always end your scenes/chapters with a hook. Keep the reader wondering Why? How? and the all-important What Will Happen Next?

CHAPTER 10

The Nuts and Bolts of Characterization

Ask any romance reader what they loved about a certain book and nine times out of ten, they'll start talking about the characters. Characters are the heart of every story. Plot only becomes important when it involves people. But if the people you create don't feel real, if they don't appear worthy to hold the title of hero or heroine, your story will fall short. Creating lovable characters, with the right backgrounds, goals, and flaws, is the key to writing a great romance.

Defining Character

Defining your characters will require you to ask and answer a lot of questions: Who are your characters? What do they look like? What makes them tick? What do they want? What are they afraid of? And probably the most important question—why? Why do they want what they want and why are they afraid?

In the beginning, you may find that you are the one who does the asking—and answering—of questions. But before long, if you are doing your job correctly by breathing life into these story people, it will appear as if the characters themselves are answering your questions. What feels like an amazing little phenomenon is actually a needed step to becoming an accomplished writer. Before you can write characters that seem real to your readers, they must feel real to you.

In essence, creating characters that your readers will love and remember long after they put your book down isn't always easy. It requires lots of work and a lot of thought. So roll up your sleeves and get ready to play creator. You are about to craft some amazing human beings.

Most writers say that at some point in a book's process, it feels as though the characters take over and begin to tell them, the author, what they will and will not do. An author may write a line of dialogue, only to have the character say, "Hey, I wouldn't say that. What I would is say is . . ."

Physical Appearances

Blond hair, blue eyes. Dark and sensuous. You are the artist; you apply the brush strokes to create your characters' physical appearances. It's important to remember that while this is a romance, and your characters should be attractive, attractive doesn't mean the characters are perfect. As a matter of fact, readers seldom want to read about perfect people—especially people who think of themselves as perfect.

Most people have something they hate about their bodies. Does your heroine want to lose ten pounds? Does your hero wish he was a bit taller? Is his hair receding? If your characters could, what would they change about themselves?

To get an idea of how to use your character's physical appearance, answer the following questions:

- Has your character's appearance affected the outcome of her life?
- Does your character feel her life would be substantially different if she looked differently? How so?
- If your character had to describe herself physically, what would she say?
- Who does your character look like? Her mother? Her father? Is she proud of that?

After you have decided how your characters look, stop and think about how those physical traits have helped mold them into the people they are. For a few minutes, wear the skin you have created for them. How does it feel?

FACT

Most minor physical flaws can make your characters more lovable, not only to the reader, but to their love interest in the book. A hero can find the freckles on the heroine's face adorable. A heroine can think the hero's scar on his chin makes him appear dangerously sexy. And readers will identify with someone who wishes they could change their appearance.

What's in a Name?

Much like a parent will do when expecting a child, a lot of writers spend hours coming up with their characters' names. And yes, names can be important. But . . . names are generally given to a person before they are born and even before the parents have a clue about their offspring's personality or appearance.

You, the writer, have more power than a parent. You can choose a name based upon a character's personality and physical traits. Or better yet, you can choose a name that helps mold a person's personality. What would having the name Rene do to a boy? Or how would the name Beatrice affect a girl's personality in the modern age? Names can tell the reader something about the character's ethnic background and age. But clever writers find methods to use names in other ways. Here are some ideas of how you might make a name matter more:

- Names have meanings. Discover the name's meaning and match it to your character's personality.
- Offer nicknames to your characters that hint at their internal makeup, e.g., Sunshine, Flash, Casper.
- Choose a name that contradicts your character's traits and show how trying to live down the image has molded him, e.g., Angel, Damien.
- Give a character the same name as a well-known public figure and use this as a plot device, e.g., Lisa M. Presley, William "Bill" Clinton.

If you are having a hard time finding names for your characters, you might try looking at BabyNames.com (*www.babynames.com*). The site offers millions of names, their ethnic origins, and what they mean.

The Real Question

Remember, you are the creator. So the question isn't, Who are your characters? It is, Who do you need your characters to be? Do you need them to be workaholics or beach bums? Does your plot require them to be quiet and shy or outgoing and charismatic? Or, are you looking to create a serial killer?

You can make your characters be anything you want, as long as you make the reader believe. So if it's a serial killer you are creating, you need to research the factors that turn a person into a serial killer. For a workaholic, you need to know what drives someone to put career over everything else. This isn't to say that you need to create stereotypical people. To the contrary, your characters should and need to be unique, but even their eccentricities have to be believable.

ALERT!

A great book for learning more about creating characters is *Creating Romantic Characters* by Leigh Michaels. Michaels offers insight into creating characters, from goals to conflicts, and targets her information especially for romance novelists.

Character Sketches

A character sketch is the internal and external makeup of a character. While your main characters' sketches will obviously be more in-depth than those of secondary characters, it is wise to have character sketches for all your characters. That way, if you forget what color your heroine's mother's eyes are, you can simply pull up the character sketch, rather than skim through all the back chapters.

Most character sketches include an extensive list of questions for you to answer before you begin to breathe life into your characters. Below are some of the more common things you'll find covered in character sketches:

- Place of birth/Where they grew up
- Parents/Other close family members
- Childhood traumas
- Education/Profession
- Hobbies/Passions
- Bad habits/Attributes
- Fears
- Religion/Moral compass

- Mental/Physical characteristics
- Past relationships
- Current lifestyle
- Goals/Desires/Dreams
- Things they would like to change about themselves and their lifestyle
- Biggest regret/Biggest embarrassment/Biggest secret

The more you can understand about your characters before you write Chapter 1, the better off you'll be. However, a lot of writers are still discovering their characters' secrets several chapters into a book. When a character is truly defined in the author's head, it may require some changes in the prior chapters to make sure the character's internal makeup is clear to the reader. New writers need to understand that this type of backtracking is okay. Very few authors write their books from beginning to end without doing some rewriting.

Don't try to tell the reader everything about your characters at their first introduction. Present your characters to the reader the way you would want to get to know someone in real life. How would you like it if someone you just met started blasting you with every detail of his life? Let the facts about your story people come across the page slowly through action, dialogue, internal thought, and narrative.

Character Types

Is your character an introvert or an extrovert? Is she a type A personality or a type B? Your fictional characters need personality types just like real people. And to create them, you'll need to understand the different types and how their minds work.

A lot of authors start by filling out character personality assessment charts—such as the Myers-Briggs test. Numerous books on the subject exist and can provide you with these tests. However, you can also find them online. (For one such Web site, refer to Appendix C.) Filling out these charts for your characters can help you flesh them out from stick people to real people whom you feel as though you know and understand.

Choosing Your Character's Career

An important part of creating story people is deciding upon a character's profession. Careers not only enhance characterization, they offer clues about personality types and add setting possibilities. In addition, careers can be the catalyst for the plot and can hint at the overall tone of the novel.

Do you remember the point in your life when you began to wonder what you wanted to be when you grew up—trying to decipher what your gifts and talents were, and what job would best suit your personality? Well, now it's time to do the same thing for your characters. What profession suits them? Will you give them a profession they love? Or will you give them one from which they are longing to escape?

FACT

A great resource for choosing your character's career is Raymond Obstfeld and Franz Neumann's book, *Careers for Your Characters: A Writer's Guide to 101 Professions from Architect to Zookeeper.* The book offers everything from the responsibilities that come with the careers to the educational needs and approximate monies earned.

Research proves that certain personality types do better in certain jobs. So, it makes sense that there is a reason your characters have chosen certain professions. This doesn't mean that they haven't chosen the wrong ones, of course. Being caught in the wrong profession can also be a catalyst for a plot. What's important is that you know your character's personality and match them to the right—or wrong—career on purpose.

Character Goals

What do your characters want? Do they long for a big promotion? Do they want to move to Cancun, Mexico, and retire on the beach? Do they long to find a child they gave up for adoption years ago? Do they want to find the person responsible for killing their brother? Do they long to wipe out the vampire race from the face of the earth? In short, what is their reason for climbing out of bed in the morning?

QUESTION?

Can my character's goals change during the course of a story?
Yes. This technique is often used to show character growth. Characters can start the story wanting one thing—perhaps the big promotion with the corner office—and through the course of the story and their journey, they can learn that a promotion isn't really the key to their personal happiness.

Make sure your character's goals are worthy. For a goal to be worthy, the reader must be able to relate to the goal and see it as essential to the character's emotional or physical well-being. If all a character wants is a new outfit, the reader may see the goal as insignificant and not care if she accomplishes her dream. When a reader stops caring, she generally stops reading.

In real life, many of us go through the motions without knowing exactly what we want. In fiction, however, most of our characters must have concrete goals. Why? Because if a character doesn't know what she wants, then the reader is also clueless. Without knowing what a protagonist wants to accomplish and why, readers are less likely to get emotionally involved. For example, if you saw a neighbor get up daily to run five miles, you might be impressed, but when you found out he was training to enter the World

Olympics, your admiration for him would probably deepen. Understanding exactly what a person, or character, wants allows others to care.

Every Romance Novel's Main Goal

While all of your characters will have personal goals, the ultimate story goal when writing a romance novel is for your characters to find love and overcome their romantic conflicts. For a character, attaining these personal goals can, and should, be a part of the hurdles she has to jump over before she can accept love. Therefore, make sure your character's main goal is somehow connected to the love story. For example, if a character's goal is to discover her birth parents, then the hero could be the detective helping her find them . . . or the lawyer trying to prevent her from getting to the truth.

Opposing Goals

When brainstorming your characters' goals, consider the possibility of creating opposing goals for the hero and heroine. Think of it as a one-bone, two-dog kind of story. For one character to attain his goal, the other must fail.

A good example of opposing goals is from the movie *You've Got Mail,* starring Meg Ryan and Tom Hanks. The hero wanted to open a big chain bookstore; the heroine wanted to keep her independent "family-based" bookstore in business. In the movie, the story goal was for these two people to overcome their differences and realize they were perfect for one another. Nevertheless, it was the characters' personal goals that moved the plot forward.

Character Motivations

Earlier, you learned that the most important question to ask your characters is "Why?" Why do they do what they do? Why do they want what they want? Why do they fear what they fear? Generally, the answer to the "why?" questions will lead you to your character's motivation. In real life, sometimes we don't always understand why we do things. Sometimes in books, the "why?" may not be clear to the characters, either, but it definitely needs to be clear to the reader. The reason for this is simple. It is human nature to want to understand what motivates people. If readers can't understand the reason your characters are reacting and acting in certain ways, they have a tendency not to believe in them.

Motivation Leads to Caring

When an action is good, understanding the "why" behind the action increases the reader's anticipation of seeing the character achieve his goal. Remember the neighbor who gets up and runs five miles every day—the one you now know wants to compete in the Olympics? What if you learned that his father's dream had been to make the Olympics, but he was killed while training when the boy was ten years old? Understanding why your neighbor longs to compete adds new dimensions to his goal. In addition to caring more, you are beginning to know the depth of his "character." Hence, the reason that making story goals specific and giving characters believable motivation is so important when creating characters.

Motivation Leads to Understanding

When a character's actions or emotions are somewhat misguided, hard to grasp, or lean toward the unethical (lying, breaking a law, drinking too much, being a workaholic, fear of biscuits), motivation becomes even more important.

Just about any action, no matter how bizarre, can be made believable if given the proper motivation. Use the right building blocks to construct a character and your story people will always ring true. Even a character's actions—those that bend the moral rules—can be forgiven if properly motivated.

Assume that your hero is a single father who puts his career before his own children. This trait does not make the reader like this character. But what if you knew the character had gone hungry as a child, that his lowlife father had never held down a job, and that he'd seen his mother take up prostitution to feed the family. Suddenly, this character's actions, though still not right, become understandable. A reader who understands the character is likely to continue reading, hoping the workaholic father will overcome his past and learn the error of his ways.

Now, what about that fear of biscuits. Could a writer ever pull this off? How could a reader believe in a character who is afraid of a piece of home-baked bread? What if, as a six-year-old child, your heroine watched her grandfather choke to death while eating biscuits? And since that day, when she attempts to eat a biscuit, she feels her own throat closing up.

Villains' Motivation

When a gunman walks into the mall, or a school, and takes lives, the media spend weeks trying to understand what could have motivated the shooter's actions. As stated previously, it is human nature to want to understand why people act in the way they do. Perhaps, by understanding, the impossible appears a little more possible; perhaps by understanding the motives, you think you can prevent it from happening again. Needless to say, when bad people do bad things in your books, the reader demands to understand the "why?" Therefore, it is wise to remember that your villains need motivation, too.

Where to Find the Motivation

If you are having a hard time finding your character's motivation, try to remember that most motivation will be found in your character's past. If your character is afraid to love, ask what childhood drama or relationship mishap could have instilled such behavior. If your character can't say no, what happened in her life to make her afraid to disappoint others? If a character is afraid of water, did she almost drown as a child, or did she have a sister who drowned? Generally, all the answers to the "why?" questions will be found in your character's backgrounds.

Don't make the mistake of thinking the motivation needs to be written in complete flashback scenes. Flashbacks, even for the sake of motivation, are not recommended for today's fast-paced romance fiction. A character's past and motivations can be brought into the present by use of dialogue or internal thought. For example, *Lacy stood on the river's edge, her heart thundered in her chest. Only the flowing sound of the water surrounded her, but in her mind, she could still hear her sister's cries for help as the water pulled her under.*

A great book for insight into showing motivations from a character's past is *Stein on Writing*. The author, Sol Stein, refers to the internal thoughts that brings past motivation into the present as "flashback thoughts" and offers suggestions on accomplishing this technique.

Making Characters Lovable

What makes readers fall in love with your characters? Basically, it is the same thing that makes you care about and love real people. A character has to be sympathetic and worthy of your reader's emotional commitment. Story people have to hold universal traits that draw you to them. Below are some common traits and situations that are considered hero/heroine worthy.

- A character who is an underdog, who has a handicap but refuses to give up
- A character who is willing to admit he made a mistake and sets out to make amends
- A character who is hurting, but remains strong for others
- A character who is kind to the underdog, small children, elderly people, or animals
- A character who is self-sacrificing
- A character who is able to laugh at her own mistakes
- A character who is levelheaded
- A character who is making a mistake, but for all the right reasons
- A strong, silent type who means well but is unable to express it
- A character who takes risks but is willing to pay the price
- A character who has depth, layers, and secrets
- A character who is able to forgive

When reading your favorite romance authors, notice how the writers make you love their characters. What is it that makes you care if these characters attain their goals? Why do you keep reading to find out if they are rewarded with finding love?

Even villains have sympathetic traits. Consider all the news segments where a neighbor or work associate of a well-known criminal was interviewed. Doesn't someone always say, "He was always so quiet, never caused any trouble"? No one is 100 percent evil. By showing a villain's good side, you will make him real and even more interesting to the reader.

Making Your Characters Flawed

Perfect people rarely exist in the real world, and they shouldn't exist in your books. Stop and think about your own flaws. What are they? Where did you pick up these personality defects? What are the flaws of the people closest to you—people you love in spite of their imperfections? Now, which of these flaws can you borrow for your own characters?

When brainstorming characters' flaws, consider this: A lot of people, real or imagined, attain their imperfections in one of two ways:

1. **By making the same mistakes as their parents.** For example, the father had a temper; therefore, the son has a temper. The mother smoked; therefore, the daughter smokes. The mother used food to feed her stress; therefore, her children overeat when things are going bad. A parent is a hypochondriac; children grow up to become regulars at their doctors' offices.
2. **By going to the extreme to not be like their parents.** A girl refuses to eat at all when upset because she saw her mother abuse food. A father never disciplines his own children because he's afraid of being abusive like his father. A character refuses to go to the doctor because he sees that as a weakness.

Once you understand the root cause of a character's personality weakness, you can create a flawed character that romance readers will love.

Proactive Characters

Instead of constantly having things happen to your characters, look for ways to have your characters make things happen. Editors will tell you that one of the more common characterization problems seen in new writers' manuscripts is having characters do only the reacting, versus having them participate in the forward thrust of the plot.

Most novels start out with something happening to the characters:

- A heroine's husband announces he wants a divorce at her fortieth birthday celebration in front of her friends, family, and work associates.
- A nanny's charge is kidnapped while she buys the toddler an ice-cream treat from the street vender.
- A hero steps into his shower first thing in the morning and finds a dead woman.

Yes . . . things *do* happen to your storybook characters. But once a dilemma has been tossed at your character's feet, he shouldn't go take a nap and wait and see what happens next. He should become proactive and set out to fix what appears to be an unfixable situation.

ESSENTIAL

To make your characters proactive, show them, mentally or physically, coming to forks in the road during their story journeys. Have them consider their options, and show them making choices. Some of those choices will be the right ones. To make it interesting, though, some should be the wrong ones that lead to yet another place where they have to make more decisions.

The key to creating proactive characters is to have them become involved in solving their own problems, rather than depend on others to solve them.

Characterizing Secondary and Minor Characters

Now that you realize what goes into fleshing out your protagonists—goals, flaws, careers, hobbies, and secrets—you might be wondering if you really need to give your secondary characters the same attention.

The answer is yes.

Every character appearing in your novel needs to come across as real to the reader, no matter how small a part he or she plays. The more vivid your writing, the more a reader loses herself in your story.

Just because the character isn't your main protagonist doesn't mean they should be a cardboard character. Secondary characters who play a role in the novel need depth, goals, and layers of interest. But how many of those layers you pull back and expose for the reader will depend on the character's importance and how those layers of interest will play to the novel's main theme and plot. If you go into that character's point of view in the novel, then the reader will automatically expect to see more of the character's internal makeup.

ALERT!

Every character introduced into your romance novel should serve as a mirror to reflect your main protagonists. By using the technique of compare and contrast, a good author knows secondary and minor characters are great tools to enhance the characterization of the main characters.

If the character is only on stage a short time, you may not need to paint the entire life story of this person. But this doesn't mean you can't give insight into a character using very few words. Sometimes, quick brushstrokes can not only tell you what a character looks like, but give the reader insight to background, moral compass, and immediate goals. Never add description solely for description's sake, though. Use other characters and their characterization to allow the reader to get a better view of your protagonist. For example:

Sarah pulled off her wedding ring, and tucked it into her jeans' pocket. Trying not to think too hard, she pulled the employment application closer and then looked around the truck stop that smelled like bacon, burgers, and loneliness. Who knew loneliness had a smell?

The older waitress set the coffee pot down with an end-of-a-shift clatter. Sarah noticed the woman's lipstick—freshly applied—looked a little too red, her blush a little too purple, and the wrinkles creasing her mouth and spanning out from her tired eyes told stories of too many cigarettes and bad husbands. She looked like a woman who could wear the "been there, done that" T-shirt and didn't mind sharing her stories. And if the way she glanced over to the old truck driver sitting alone at the counter and popped open an extra button on her grease-stained uniform was any indication, she'd have a new story to tell real soon.

Looking back at the application, Sarah couldn't help but wonder if that would be her in twenty years.

While the waitress may not appear again in the novel, the author uses the character of the waitress to show insight into the heroine's situation and emotions. How much you choose to expose of your minor characters depends on their importance to the plot and if it will help you create emotion in a scene.

CHAPTER 11

The All-Important Conflict

People crave a problem-and-stress-free existence. They live for the days that are filled with nothing but smooth sailing. Ah, but this isn't what people want to read or hear about. Stop and think about the books you've enjoyed, the movies you've seen, even the fairytales your mother read to you as a child. The common denominator in all forms of entertainment is conflict. Conflict is what keeps your characters on their toes, what propels your story forward, and more important, what keeps your reader turning pages.

No Conflict = No Story

It may sound harsh, but the truth is that without conflict, your story is probably destined to be rejected. Why? Because while it's the Happily Ever After ending that makes your reader sigh; it's initially the struggle that captures her interest. Without the struggle, the reader wouldn't hang around long enough, or care enough, to experience the sigh.

FACT

The importance of conflict in storytelling is apparent in nonfiction, as well as fiction. Consider the "triumph over tragedy" and the "underdog prevails" stories seen in today's magazines. Every entertainment medium loves to cover true-life heroes. And the reference to the hero signifies that these people have triumphed over some obstacle, hence conflict, to arrive at a place of honor.

Conflict isn't something that just shows up in the black moment of the book. Conflict should be present in every scene and practically on every page. Most novels have one major conflict driving the story, but then each character will generally have one or more personal conflicts. In a romance novel, you will also find the romantic conflict. And all of these problems go hand-in-hand to create even bigger problems. So, if conflict is so important to the story, where does an author find it? Better yet, how do you go about creating it?

Where to Find—and Not Find—Conflict

In real life, conflict is everywhere. It can stem from the weather, from traffic, from other people, from bad potato salad, or even a neighbor's gerbil. However, in your books, it is crucial that the conflict be a natural extension of either your plot or your characters. Before you can define what your characters' conflict will be, you need to have a clear definition of both your story goal and the personal goals of your characters. The conflict in your novel is whatever stands in the way of your characters' achieving their goals. Conflict is not something a writer just magically pulls out of thin air.

Yes, unexpected and unusual circumstances do happen to your characters. They can have a flat tire on the way to an important meeting. They can get caught in traffic. However, have more than one or two of these coincidental incidents occur that are not directly related to your story or character, and the plot becomes contrived. In other words, one flat tire might be acceptable, but the second and third flat might only be suitable if the heroine learns someone is flattening her tires on purpose. Therefore, the conflict is no longer just a coincidence, but an actual part of the story's plot.

Sizing Up Your Conflict

If the conflict is big—meaning, it makes a huge emotional impact, as in a natural disaster or a kidnapping—it had better be a part of the plot and not just an occurrence. For example, if the conflict keeping a heroine from arriving home to visit her mother on Mother's Day is an earthquake, then the story needs to be about these characters surviving the earthquake. In other words, don't make the conflict that is stopping your character from achieving a small goal be more dramatic or more interesting than the main story conflict.

Too many contrivances, or what some authors call convenient problems, and readers will stop caring about your story. The best conflict grows naturally from your characters or plot. A problem that is merely a fluke is seldom considered a strong conflict.

Internal Conflict

Internal conflict means that the problem arises from within your character. An internal issue can be a fear, a lack of trust, a misguided belief, an obsession, or an inability to get emotionally close to someone. Most internal conflicts are seen as character flaws, something that your characters will either overcome or come to terms with by the end of the story. Most internal conflicts are connected to the romantic conflict. Though some characters might be dealing with more than one internal issue, generally there is one main internal conflict that carries the story.

Internal conflicts are generally due to an emotional setback or trauma in your character's past. For example, a hero who as a child was placed in the foster care system may not allow himself to get emotionally attached. Or a heroine who lost her entire family in an automobile accident may be obsessed with building her own family to replace the one she lost.

A character may or may not be aware of his internal conflict in the beginning of the book. A novel can open with a character believing his actions and motivations are completely justified. Then, through the course of the story journey, the hero and heroine learn to accept their internal flaws and to change their behaviors or belief systems.

Of course, your characters' issues could stem from something as common as being the middle child who never felt special, or being the only girl in a family of six brothers. Perhaps their internal flaws are a result of their financial status—being raised poor or being raised with a silver spoon in their mouths.

The incidents leading to your character's internal conflicts need not be tragic. No one has to die, be abandoned, or be abused, but the incidents must be emotionally significant enough to cause the hiccup in your character's internal makeup.

The more an author understands and cares about the reason her characters act the way they do, the clearer they are able to communicate this in the book, which leads to the reader caring and understanding.

Internal Conflicts Must Be Believable

Being a writer is like being a psychologist, you must delve beneath the surface to explain why your characters are who they are and what makes them tick. This, in essence, makes them real to the reader. This isn't to say that all internal conflicts are logical. Many phobias and obsessive fears are illogical by nature. However, even the most illogical conflict must be believable. If a character has a bizarre internal issue, connect it to a bizarre incident that makes her actions and reactions credible.

External Conflict

External conflict is generally plot-driven and can be anything that prevents your characters from accomplishing their goals. An external conflict can be a person: a coworker who stands in the way of your hero getting a promotion or the villain out to kill your heroine. External conflict can be a place: a town that hasn't forgotten the sins of your heroine's past or a jungle with danger lurking at every turn. External conflict can be a thing: the legal system that refuses to hand over the name of your heroine's child's adoptive parents or a missing lottery ticket with the winning numbers.

ALERT!

Make sure your conflict is worthy of being called a conflict. Whatever stands in the way of your characters must be substantial enough to make the character feel the burn of the struggle. Making it too easy for your characters will make it too easy for the reader to put the book down.

To come up with ideas for external conflict, make a list of your characters' goals and then make a list of five things that could *logically* come between them and reaching their goals. Logical means keeping the apparent miracles or acts of God down to a minimum. Another essential key to making conflict believable is to allow much of the conflict to derive from some wrong choices your characters made, either during the course of the story or in their past. In real life, people bring much of their conflict upon themselves, and so should it be in novels.

Giving Your Conflict the Right Amount of Muscle

When brainstorming conflict, make sure what is at stake, the consequence of not achieving the goal, is substantial enough to make your character really want to fight. Only when your character is willing to fight and cares deeply will the reader care about the outcome. Make sure your conflict is strong enough to present itself as a worthy opponent. That said, a writer should also be careful that the conflict is not so overwhelming that the reader loses hope. The reader should fear the character may not win the battle or meet the challenge set before them, but they should never completely lose hope.

Romantic Conflict

What stands in the way of your hero and heroine falling in love at the end of Chapter 1? To make the romance satisfying for the reader, you must not only make the conflict believable, but make it substantial enough to carry the book.

The romantic conflict is probably the most important conflict in a romance novel. In most novels, the major conflict keeping the hero and heroine apart will be introduced in the first chapter. This issue will follow the characters through the course of the story—sometimes appearing resolvable, sometimes not—and will reappear even stronger in the Dark Moment of the book. While the main romantic conflict will drive most of the story, it is common that a book will have more than just one romantic conflict. In most novels, the hero and heroine will have their personal reasons for not wanting to fall in love, or for not wanting to fall in love with each other. It's important to know which conflict carries the book, and make sure secondary conflicts are set up and resolved in a way that it doesn't lessen the story flow.

FACT

In most romance novels, both the hero and heroine will have their own romantic conflicts. However, one is generally the driving conflict of the story. The smaller conflicts are generally resolved earlier in the book and the character with the lesser conflict will accept the relationship and emotionally commit before the other.

If you read a lot of romance novels, you probably have discovered that most romantic conflicts are internally motivated, meaning they stem from some emotional baggage from either a character's childhood or from a past romantic relationship. It is also common for the internal conflict of your characters to be directly related to the romantic conflict.

The Path to Discovering Your Characters' Romantic Conflicts

The best way to discover your hero's and heroine's romantic conflicts is to ask the characters two questions:

1. Why haven't you already fallen in love and married the person of your dreams?
2. What was the reason your other relationships failed?

The pat answer of, "I just haven't met the person of my dreams" isn't going to work. Why? Because if that's the only reason this person hasn't fallen in love, then you have no problems/conflict to introduce into the new relationship. And remember, no conflict equals no story. Often, this type of answer masks the real truth—be your characters' psychologist and probe deeper. Why does your character only date "safe" romantic partners, the kind who aren't likely to engage his emotions? Is he afraid of being hurt?

If the answer is, "I've just been too busy in my career to date," then consider why your character has put his career before his own personal life and happiness. Does he suffer from low self-esteem and believe that without a solid career, he has no worth? In other words, dig deeper until you find ways, emotional ways, to create his romantic conflict from his internal motivations.

Revisit the Character Sketches

Once you define your characters' romantic conflicts, look back at the character sketches and see if you have given your hero and heroine the proper motivation to develop these types of romantic conflicts. It's okay if you need to go back to the drawing board and add or change some facts so your characters develop naturally into who you need them to be. Remember, it is the motivation that will make the conflict believable.

The External Connection to the Romantic Conflict

Just because most romantic conflicts are internally motivated doesn't mean the external issues don't come into play. External conflicts can and do play a part in keeping the hero and heroine together or apart, depending on what the plot requires. They can also keep them from confessing their love for each other sooner. For example, if your hero and heroine are being chased by a drug lord who is trying to kill them, they may be forced to stay together for protection, and it's also obvious that these two people will have little time to work through their personal differences.

Nevertheless, in a romance, it's important that what prevents your characters from making that leap into love is more than just external forces. It's wise to remember that love is a matter of the heart, and not about the events, even dramatic events. So make sure the final resolution of the romantic conflict comes from inside your characters and not from the events.

A book should not feel compartmentalized. While scenes may focus on events and cover certain internal elements more than others, all scenes and chapters should involve the story's main theme of romance. As the story unfolds, the scene conflicts should be a blend of the external and the internal complications.

How to Link the External to the Internal

The key to making a romantic conflict carry through the book is linking the plot to the romantic conflict. In other words, whatever is happening externally in the plot should somehow reinforce what's going on internally in your characters' hearts and minds. Think of the plot as a journey where your characters face obstacles that help them confront their inner demons and conflicts.

What if your heroine's romantic conflict is fear of loving because she has lost everyone she has loved? Just as she is about to conquer her demons and admit her love for the hero, something happens that threatens the hero's life, which reinforces the heroine's fear.

The Goal-Conflict Connection

It simply can't be said enough: Conflict is directly connected to your character's goals. If you are having a hard time defining the conflict in your novel, refer back to the character sketch and reconnect to what it is your character wants, desires, and needs. Then, as you define your plot and the conflict, think of the chapters and scenes as the stepping stones that your character must cross to arrive at his or her main goal.

Opposing Goals

One of the easiest ways to establish conflict is to give your hero and heroine opposing goals. When it appears that only one can win, and someone must lose, the conflict is forever present. The one difficulty with writing opposing goals is that you must still find a way to have that important Happily Ever After ending. Generally, an author will have one of the characters realize that his or her goal has changed, maybe discovering a better goal along the way, or the author may redefine the situation and prove that the hero and heroine can both win after all.

Every Romance's Underlying Goal

Remember, no matter what your characters' goals are, in a romance novel there is always the implied goal of finding love with that perfect person. And the best way to keep the romance and story flowing together is to make sure that the romance and external plot are dependent on the other and somehow linked. For example, your hero needs something from the heroine to achieve his main quest or your heroine must rely upon the hero to complete her lifelong goal.

Main Story Goal/Main Story Conflict

Most novels, even romance novels where the romance is essentially the principal theme, have what writers refer to as a main goal. This is generally the innermost quest of the character. Once you have the main goal clear in your head, it helps to be able to define the main conflict. So, in a nutshell, what is the thing standing in the way of your character achieving his goal? Some examples of main goals and conflict follow:

- The hero, a cop, wants to catch the man who killed his father, but the villain is not only a master at evading the police, but a master sharpshooter who never lets anyone get too close.
- A heroine sets out to find the mother she hasn't seen since she was a child, but the mother is running from an abusive husband.
- A heroine who is really an alien wants to find a man to impregnate her so she can become a mother, but the one man who interests her wants more than a one-night stand.

QUESTION?

Why do most romances start out with the hero and heroine butting heads?

The answer is simple: conflict. In most romance novels, the characters find each other attractive upon their first meeting, but generally the conflict prevents them from even liking each other. This push and pull between attraction and conflict is a big part of what readers want to experience.

Once you know your main story goal and conflict, you start linking the internal conflicts to the external conflicts. Make sure the things that will happen externally will have an emotional impact on what is going on internally with both the romance and any other internal issues the characters may have. Once you have outlined your conflicts and goals, it's time to start thinking about the needed steps your characters must take to achieve their goals. These steps are your scene goals and with each scene goal comes a scene conflict.

How Scene Conflict Works

Once again, scene conflict goes back to the all-important goals. What is it that your hero wants to achieve in this scene? New writers often find defining scene goals very difficult. They know what will happen next, but they haven't plotted the scene in a way that the hero has a concrete goal.

Many new romance writers question the need for scene goals. They are quick to point out that in real life, people don't always have an "agenda." And perhaps in real life, people don't *always* have a concrete goal. However, they generally have an implied goal. Think of the average Joe who gets up every day and goes to work. He may not have a stated/concrete goal, but his implied goal is probably to have a normal day.

FACT

Conflict, Action & Suspense by William Noble is a good book for any writer wanting to learn more about adding conflict to her novel. Noble gives you clues to making your book a page-turner by upping the conflict, drama, and suspense.

Yes, like in real life, sometimes your characters enter scenes with implied goals, but it's wise to remember that while you want your books to have a sense of realism, you are writing romance fiction. The characters in your books must be more proactive than the average Joe. Readers don't necessarily want to read about people who just have things happen to them; readers want to read about people who *make* things happen.

The closer your scene goals are linked to the character's main goal, the more involved your readers will be in the story. Readers want and need to see the characters on the path to accomplishing their dreams. If the characters detour off the main path, a reader will likely feel less emotionally connected to the story.

Sizing Up Your Scene Conflict

Once you define what your characters want in a scene, you need to decide what conflict they will face in their quest for the goal. The size of your scene conflict will depend upon the importance of the scene. If the scene is a turning point in the book, naturally, the conflict will be more dramatic. However, every scene will not contain a breathtaking event. Conflict should escalate during the course of the book, and the lows are just as important as the highs for maintaining proper pacing.

A scene goal can be as small as a hero asking the heroine out for a date and moving their "just good buddies" relationship to the next level. The conflict can be another coworker who barges in on the conversation, making it difficult for the hero to ask. Remember, your hero should both win and lose some of his struggles as he moves through the story. The loss of a scene goal ups the tension for him to reach his main story goal.

Opposing Goals

A good way to increase the conflict is to give another person in the scene a goal that directly opposes what your character wants. If your heroine's goal is run into the drugstore to buy birth control and be at home before her date arrives, have her run into an old friend who's been trying to reach her. If she wants to get an appointment with her vet right now, have the vet's wife at the office needing to talk to her husband before he takes another client. If your hero needs to find out what happened to his kid, have a lawyer in the room who tells the ex-wife she shouldn't talk to him. Opposing goals up the conflict.

Most Common Conflict Mishaps

Because conflict is so important, you should watch out for the common pitfalls. Here is a rundown of the most frequently made conflict mistakes and their quick fixes:

Too Little Conflict

First, read your work to make sure you have defined and given credence to your character's main goal and introduced scene goals. Second, make your characters fight for what they want.

FACT

A great measure of the strength of a romantic conflict is to ask yourself if the conflict could be resolved simply by having the hero and heroine sit down and discuss the situation. If the conflict arises solely because she assumes something untrue about the hero—or vice versa—this is not a valid conflict. Make your conflict real and believable.

Contrived Conflict

Make sure that most of your conflict stems from either your character or the plot. Reconfirm that internal conflict is properly motivated. Change any conflicts that feel like flukes or acts of God.

Repetitive Conflict

Don't rely too heavily on any one type of conflict. Mix it up. Use the internal conflict, the different types of external conflicts, and the romantic conflict to keep the story moving. For example, if your hero is in a jungle, and all you have him come up against are snakes, the reader will eventually grow tired of seeing him fight the same battle. Think of the other dangers that could lurk in the jungle. Think of internal issues that could be brought to his attention as he attempts to face external issues.

Good Conflict That Doesn't Matter

Review your characters to make sure they are sympathetic and likable. If your reader doesn't care about your characters, chances are they won't care about the conflict they face.

Bickering Disguised as Conflict

In almost every romance you'll find the hero and heroine arguing at some point. However, there is a difference between a valid and usable disagreement and bickering. If the subject they are quarreling over isn't directly related to internal conflicts, then a heated exchange isn't a valid conflict and, therefore, is just bickering. And even if it is related, make sure the issue isn't rehashed or the readers will grow tired of hearing it.

Finding the right conflict and avoiding the common conflict mishaps will quickly move you out of the amateur status and into the rankings of a romance writer on her way to publication.

CHAPTER 12

Mastering and Choosing the Right Point of View

Through whose eyes will the reader experience your story? Whose ears are hearing the dialogue? Which character's mind is collecting the data and recounting the bits of information to the reader? Point of view, or POV, is probably the most mangled and misunderstood aspect of the craft of writing. And yet it is one of the most powerful tools writers use to bring life to their characters. Mastering POV will help you get closer to your dream of publication.

What Is POV?

POV is simply the perspective from which your story is being conveyed to the reader. Loosely translated, it means . . . who is telling your story. Whose head are you in during this particular moment, in this particular scene?

At first glance, it seems like such a simple thing to understand. Yet mastering POV can be harder than herding three-legged cats. The reason for this can partly be blamed on the many variations and subcategories of the different POVs. Add to that fact that the rules are not carved in stone and it's understandable why beginning writers are easily confused.

Most published writers who have mastered point of view have at one time or another chosen to bend the rules to accomplish a certain element in their stories. The trick is to know the rules and to be able to bend them without jarring the reader.

Types of POVs

There are many different types of POVs. An experienced writer may be able to blend varying POVs into her story. But generally, new writers should stick to the guidelines of one type.

- **First-person point of view:** *I saw the pain in Jake's eyes.*
- **Second-person point of view:** *You saw the pain in Jake's eyes.* (While often used in nonfiction, this POV is seldom used in fiction.)
- **Third-person point of view:** *She saw the pain in Jake's eyes.*
- **Omniscient point of view (also commonly referred to as author's POV):** *No one could see it. Jake didn't even know it was there, but pain reflected in his eyes.*

First-Person POV

The "I" character speaks directly to the reader. When done well, this type of POV can bond the reader to the character more closely than other forms of POV. While first person is regularly used in mysteries and "chicklit," it's not the most common POV in the romance genre.

Advantages to Writing in First Person

First-person POV creates an intimate bond between the reader and the character. This bond is definitely seen as an advantage. Most first-person writers also find their ability to get into deep characterization easier than some third-person writers.

When a third-person writer is having trouble getting into her character, a good piece of advice is to attempt to write the scene in first person then go back and change it to the third-person voice. Many times, the "I" voice will allow the writer to get closer to her characters.

Disadvantages to Writing in First Person

In most cases, first-person POV is not the norm for romance publishers. Therefore, first-person authors find a more limited market to submit their work. Category lines rarely use it. Even in the single-title houses, most traditional romances are written in third person. Basically, this is due to readers' expectations of having both the hero's and heroine's POV. With only a few exceptions, first-person romance novels are written in only the main character's POV. This means that your main character will have to be present in every scene. And your only method of communicating with the reader is through what this character experiences.

Third-Person POV

This is the most common POV used in fiction, especially in the romance genre. Third-person POV filters the events of your novel through the eyes of a single character by use of pronouns such as *she* and *he*. The trick to mastering third-person POV is learning to stay in one person's POV until a proper shifting point and learning how to shift POVs without jarring the reader.

Advantages to Writing in Third-Person POV

Because third-person POV is the most common point of view used in romances, you are not limiting yourself with markets. Also, the third-person techniques allow you to move into the heads of other characters, adding depth and layers to your novels through characters.

Disadvantages of Writing in Third-Person POV

The freedom to move around into different characters will often encourage a writer to bend the rules too freely. New writers need to refrain from shifting too quickly from one point of view to the other.

Omniscient or Author's POV

While omniscient or author's POV is not the most common POV in the romance genre, it is embraced in many other genres: mystery, suspense, mainstream fiction, and science fiction to name a few. Some well-known romance authors also use this POV in some of their scenes because the tone or story elements require it.

ALERT!

Omniscient or author's POV blended into a manuscript with third-person POV is generally viewed by experienced and published romance writers as a point of view "slip." If your manuscript is entered into a RWA-sponsored writing contest, you will generally be counted down for using it.

Advantages of Writing in Omniscient POV

Omniscient POV is often used when the identity of a character, perhaps a villain, is being withheld from the reader. By describing a scene without going into the POV of the character, the identity is easier to disguise. Foreshadowing an event is also easier to do in the all-knowing voice, for your characters need not have the information for the writer to give it to the reader.

Disadvantages of Writing in Omniscient POV

Generally speaking, omniscient POV is one of the most difficult to write without confusing the reader. For the most part, it is frowned upon by romance writers and many readers. While this may seem an easy way to get some information across to the reader, ultimately you are pulling your readers away from your characters, possibly allowing them to lose the all-important reader/character connection. So while the omniscient or author's POV can work, new romance writers should be forewarned that adding this type of POV is probably best left up to those with a proven track record of sales.

Multiple POVs

Most of the third-person romance novels contain more than one POV character. Most important, you will be in the head of your heroine and your hero. Depending upon the book's length and genre, you may use additional POVs along with your two main characters. Some books include POVs from more than one secondary character and possibly even a villain's POV. How do you deal with multiple POVs? The simplest way is to limit each scene to only one POV.

Each POV character must be different enough that the reader never confuses him or her with another character. One way of individualizing your POV characters is by giving them different backgrounds, ages, social status, and careers.

Establishing POV

To establish POV, you need to get the reader inside the character's head. In essence, the reader becomes the POV character. The reader knows the character's thoughts, and experiences the world through the character's senses. In the two scenes that follow, notice how the reader is immediately clued into whose head she is in.

Scene One

Sarah walked into the kitchen, the smell of bacon and the familiar sound of the sizzle had her mouth watering, and she hoped her roommate was in a sharing mood. "Hey. . . ." Sarah stopped short at the sight of her ex-husband standing over the frying pan, a piece of bacon dangling from a raised fork.

It had been six months since she'd seen him, and blasted if his hard body didn't look scrumptious in his tight jeans and black T-shirt. Good enough to eat. Her heart hiccupped at the same time her stomach growled. But then she remembered why she left him. "I don't know how you got in, but you obvi-ously know where the door is. Use it." She paused a minute. "You can leave the bacon."

Scene Two (Same scene written in different POV)

Mark heard the footsteps padding down the hall, and felt certain the smell of breakfast would lead Sarah to the kitchen. The old adage about the way to a man's heart was through his stomach wasn't just true for men. Cooking for Sarah had been how he'd won her heart the first time. But could he do it again? Hell, it would be a lot easier if he understood why she left him.

"Hey. . ." Suddenly she was there and still as beautiful as he remembered. Shock widened her eyes, and then her gaze whispered up and down his body. Right then something else flashed in her baby blues. Hunger. And it wasn't just for the bacon. Maybe paying her roommate a hundred bucks to leave was going to be worth every cent.

Sarah blinked, and just like that, all the wanting left her expression. "I don't know how you got in, but you obviously know where the door is. Use it." She paused a minute. "You can leave the bacon."

One trick to establishing POV is to use one of the five senses: sound, touch, smell, sight, or taste. When a character experiences one of the senses, the reader automatically slips into that character's point of reference.

Choosing the Right POV for Your Romance

One of the quickest ways to know if your story would work in first person or third is to ask yourself if you plan to add any other POV characters, other than your heroine, to your story. Do you have a villain whose character you wanted to show in-depth? Do you have your hero fleshed out in your head and hear his voice so clearly that you are excited about telling his story from his perspective? If you really want more than one POV character, it is wise to go with third-person POV.

The other way you can know if you prefer first- or third-person POV is to write in both and see which one feels right for your story. However, do keep in mind that third-person may be the easier sale if you are writing straight romance. It is also comforting to know that just because you write the story in one POV, doesn't mean you can't change it later. Many published writers admit to writing a story in one POV first, rewriting it in another and making a sale.

Another POV rule of thumb to follow as you begin to write is always try to open the first chapter of your book in one of the main character's POV versus that of a secondary character. As an orphaned goose might imprint with the first being it sees after birth, a reader may imprint with the first character introduced and feel disappointed to discover that he or she isn't the main protagonist.

Choosing the Right POV for Your Scenes

Most authors who use third-person POV will tell you they decide on the POV character for a scene by looking for the person who has more to lose in the scene. Whose internal thoughts and viewpoint would bring the most tension to the book in these pages? For example, let's say you are using the villain's POV in a romantic suspense. You also have your heroine's POV. Let's say you want to write a scene in which the villain has captured your heroine and has a knife to her throat. Which POV would offer the most tension? Obviously, the heroine—with her life at risk—has more at stake. Choosing the heroine would probably be the best option.

When a scene isn't flowing or it just doesn't feel right, try writing the scene from a different POV. Often the author will realize that the character they thought had the most to lose isn't really the one with more at stake in the scene. The switch in POV characters will often get the author back on track.

Another reason a writer may choose one POV over the other is that one character knows something only he or she can share with the reader. Let's say your hero is a cop and he's questioning your villain in the presence of his partner. All three characters—hero, villain, and hero's partner—are POV characters. Your villain may seem like the obvious POV character for this scene. His freedom is at risk, therefore he might have more at stake. However, let's say that your hero's partner is hiding something. Something he is reluctant to share. What if he knows that the villain is actually his long-lost father? If you want the reader to know his secret, then choosing his POV allows the reader to discover this key piece of information.

Writing Deep POV

Writing deep POV means you have written the scene so "in character" that the reader feels immersed in that POV. She feels what this character feels, tastes what the character tastes, and sees what this character sees. The reader experiences the story as if she is the character. Every word of dialogue filtered through this character is true to the character's voice. Every reaction to what is said is a response that this character would make due to her life experiences.

FACT

Writing a scene in such a way that the reader doesn't know for sure whose head they are in is called vague POV. Vague POV is the opposite of deep POV and can be fixed by adding internal thoughts, reactions, emotions, or one of the five senses.

So, how does one accomplish deep POV? By making sure that every word on the paper is filtered through the character's thoughts, emotions, and senses. Imagine you are in a ladies' tearoom, surrounded by fine antique china, an abundance of pastel colors, lots of lace and ribbons, and cucumber sandwiches. Now attempt to write a description of this tearoom. But wait . . . can you really write this description without knowing who your POV character is? What if the character is a ninety-year-old woman? What if the character is a 300-pound NFL football player?

Even narrative descriptions must be written in your chosen character's POV. The best way to accomplish deep POV is to look at all the elements in each scene and make sure they all sound as if they could only come from inside your POV character. Here are some of the elements to consider when attempting to write deep POV:

- **Narrative descriptions** (Are they written the way the chosen character would describe them?)
- **Dialogue** (Would this character really say these words?)
- **Internal dialogue** (Do the character's thoughts reflect his speech patterns, his sense of humor, and his outlook on life?)
- **Emotional responses** (Is this how this character would respond to this situation?)

Too many POVs, especially in the first chapters, keep the reader from getting to know your main characters. Only bring in another POV character when that character has something that only he can give the reader, and even then, only when the reader has to have this information.

Most Common Mistakes and Quick Fixes

It's best to think of your POV character as your camera, your recording device, and your only method of gathering story data. If your POV character can't see it, you can't describe it for your readers. If he can't hear it, you can't let your readers hear it. If your POV character doesn't know it, you can't tell it to the reader. If your character wouldn't think that way, then you can't write that way.

Character Can't See It

What if your character can't see the action she is describing? Consider this example: *Annie stared straight ahead, her hands fisted so tight that her nails cut tiny half moons into her palms. Her ex stood directly behind her, his arms crossed over his chest, his blue eyes scowling at her short skirt and his frown deepening every second. She swung around to face him.*

Why It's a Problem

If he's standing behind her and she doesn't have a mirror in front of her, eyes in the back of her head, or a secret spy camera, then she can't see what he's doing. And remember if she can't see it, you can't describe it.

The Quick Fix

Use the other senses. She can smell him, she can hear him, and she can imagine what he's doing. For example: *Annie stared straight ahead. His familiar footstep echoed behind her. His cheap aftershave assaulted her senses and her fists tightened until her nails cut into her palms. She envisioned Brent standing there like a rock, his arms crossed, scowling. Was he looking at her skirt? She'd bet her best bra that he thought the skirt was too short. Hadn't he always accused her of dressing like a cocktail waitress?*

Character Can't Hear It

What if your character can't hear the event she is describing? Consider this: *Annie continued down the dark street. Several blocks away, another set of footsteps echoed into the darkness, but Annie never suspected she was being followed.*

Why It's a Problem

If she can't hear it, she obviously can't describe it. Moreover, if she didn't suspect it, who is telling the reader this information? This is not in her POV.

The Quick Fix

Set the mood that hints at what you want the reader to fear. You can also have your character imagine the worst. For example: *Annie continued down the dark street. Her feet hit the wet pavement.* Slap, tap, slap, tap. *She closed her eyes and concentrated on the sound. Her steps. Just hers. Weren't they? The tapping seemed to come closer together. She shook her head. No, it was just an echo. No one followed her. All the same, she quickened her pace.*

Character Wouldn't Think That

Consider the problems if your character wouldn't think the thoughts ascribed to them. For example: *Annie looked at her hands, beautifully long fingers, graceful digits, like those belonging to a pianist. Brent walked into the room, and she looked up and smiled. Her beautiful lips parted exposing her perfectly straight extra-white teeth. She shifted slightly, positioning the slit in her skirt to offer him a view of her creamy, soft, and sexy inner thigh.*

Why It's a Problem

We all know that if we did have beautifully long fingers, we would probably hate them and want smaller hands. Unless your character is a self-centered person with an ego problem, she probably wouldn't think of herself so highly. Also, notice that the second and third sentences in this example are written as if from the POV of the person who is seeing the scene unfold.

FACT

If someone accuses your character of being egotistical, check to see if you have allowed the character to describe herself in a way that would be best coming from the POV of another character.

The Quick Fix

The best way to describe a character is to do it in another person's POV. The hero could easily think about the heroine's beautiful lips and straight teeth. Or, you could still use similar thoughts in the heroine's POV, but change the wording so it doesn't sound as if she thinks so highly of herself. Also, make sure the descriptions don't read as if she's seeing herself in a nonexistent mirror.

Consider this revised version: *Annie looked at her hands. She'd inherited Aunt Kay's fingers but not her tiny waistline. Growing up, Annie had hated her fingers. She'd wanted to hide them in her pockets. Only recently had she learned that some people actually admired them. So today, she'd painted her nails candy apple red and when she ran her palms across Brent's chest, she hoped . . . she hoped he'd notice her hands and not her waistline.*

She looked up and smiled when she heard his steps fall on the tile floor. He stopped, his gaze lingered on her mouth, and she shifted slightly, placing her leg in the skirt's slit to give him a peek of her inner thigh—the part of a woman's body that always seemed to catch a man's attention.

Character Doesn't Know That

Another type of POV problem involves information that your character couldn't possibly know. For example: *The ghost waited in the next room with his chains held over his head. His white beard hung mid-chest and a trail of blood was smeared on one sleeve. Annie walked in, never knowing what she would find.*

Why It's a Problem

To be true to third-person POV, you can't write what your character doesn't know. To do this, is what the POV "police" may refer to as either omniscient POV or author's POV. Your character can think of all the things that might wait in that room. She can guess, imagine, and surmise, but she can't know what she doesn't know or describe what she doesn't see until she sees it and knows it.

Below are a few other omniscient or author's POV slips that are often used:

- *DeeAnn got out of her car, shut the door, and walked away. She never realized that she'd left her keys in the ignition.*
- *John decided to take the job. He wouldn't find out for several months that it would turn out to be the biggest mistake of his life.*
- *Shala walked right past the window and never noticed that someone had left it open.*

When someone says they are not bonding with your main character, you may be switching POVs too often. Remember, your main characters should have more POV page time than your secondary characters.

Head Hopping

Head hopping is when an author is in one character's POV and suddenly hops into a different character's POV. Nora Roberts, along with numerous other well-established romance authors, have mastered this POV style. But not everyone is Nora or has her quick-switch capabilities. And here's why.

When a writer changes POV, she needs to make sure that the reader follows this shift and doesn't feel jarred. Have you ever been reading and suddenly wondered . . . Who is thinking this? Generally, this means that the author has hopped into someone else's head and you, the reader, didn't follow the shift. When you jar readers, no matter how slightly, they are very likely to put down the book.

There are many authors who are POV purists, who never change POVs within a scene. Some, however, do find that moving once within a scene is acceptable. New authors who may be tempted to head-hop are cautioned to make sure that the switch is done in such a way that the reader is never confused.

Mastering the POV Switch

Every writer has come upon a scene where she feels as if she needs two people's POV to accomplish a certain purpose. For those times, there are some tips to help make that switch without jarring the reader.

The After-Dialogue Switch

After someone speaks, especially after a longer piece of dialogue, a POV change can move more smoothly.

For example: *Luke watched the way Sarah nipped on her bottom lip as if nervous. She had good reason to be. Which was why he decided to help her. "I told Ms. Brown that she could be looking for your resignation."*

"What? You told her what?" Sarah edged closer. "I will not let you do this to me. I'd rather eat road kill than resign." She couldn't believe Luke thought she would walk away. She really would rather eat road kill. Or maybe she'd rather just kill him.

The Sense-This Switch

When someone feels, smells, or tastes something, the reader seems instantly aware that they are in that POV character's head.

For example: *Brent spotted her standing by the counter, wiping a worn Formica countertop that didn't need wiping. His gaze swept over her soft curves and remembered how it had felt to hold her next to him. His heart picked up speed. Oh, yeah, she looked good.*

The hot smell of strong coffee tickled Annie's nose as she gave the counter one more swipe. She knew Bret stood behind her. Would he smell the coffee and know she'd made it just for him? Would he notice she'd worn his favorite perfume and guess she'd worn it for him?

The Pass-It-On Switch

Pass something from one person to the other. As the object moves from one person to the other, the readers seem to pass the POV over as well. It can be a physical object or it can be just an expression.

For example: *Brent watched her move, mesmerized by the soft, swaying of her hips as she came closer. Tomorrow she would be his. He held out the pen for her to sign the contract.*

Annie looked up at Brent's eyes as she took the pen from his hand. The smooth gold pen still held the warmth of his touch and she wondered how his touch would feel against her skin. If she signed the contract, she'd find out soon.

Again, switching POV during a scene is not the recommended formula to follow. But when you must . . . make sure the switch is smooth.

CHAPTER 13

Setting the Stage for Romance

Once you have your characters and a dynamic plot, you'll want to choose a setting that will make your story come alive. But be forewarned: to please a romance reader, you'll need to pay strict attention to the details of your fictional world. That means you'll need to research your setting and write about it convincingly, whether it's small-town America or the Elizabethan court. Most of all, you'll want to make every word used to describe your setting count. Luckily, it won't be as hard to accomplish as you think.

Why Setting Matters

So, does the setting of your romance novel really matter that much? Absolutely. Consider this: Would you enjoy a nail-biting contemporary romantic suspense set in New Orleans just as much if there were no mention of drunken revelers in the French Quarter during Mardi Gras, no reference to jazz, beignets, voodoo, energy-sapping humidity, or any of the other things that set this city apart from the others in the United States?

Or, what about a rollicking Western romantic comedy set in the Wyoming Territory just prior to the territory's induction as the 44th state in the Union? Would you still enjoy the romance if the novel didn't specify the actual timeframe? Or if it didn't have at least have one reference to the things that made the Wyoming Territory unique, such as its towering mountains and vast plains, the cattle and sheep ranchers who were often at odds with one another, or the women of the territory who had full voting rights long before the passage of the 19th Amendment?

FACT

For many romance authors, the setting of their novel is as important to the success of their plotline as the characters themselves. Indeed, setting, much like every other element of your novel, should support the book's theme. Best of all, it should evoke the emotional response from the reader that you're trying to achieve.

If the setting of the novel doesn't "ring true"—or if the setting's unique components aren't fully utilized—you run the risk of alienating the reader. Research can help, of course, but even when you have all the facts, the trick is to use only the details that matter to your story.

Defining Setting

To understand the importance of setting, you'll first need to understand what it is. Setting refers to the specific time, place, and social context in which your novel is set. It's the fictional world or backdrop—the canvas on which you paint your story, if you prefer an artistic metaphor. It sets the overall tone of your novel.

Don't confuse setting with travelogue-type descriptions of your characters' environment since long, beautifully written descriptions without emotional relevance don't advance the plot and should be cut. Instead, guide the reader's visualization of your setting by keeping the descriptions short and scene-specific, and always remembering to filter the images through the POV of your characters.

The way setting is used in a romance can vary. For some authors, their novels need little more than a generic "Current Day, Town in the Midwest" type of time and date stamp since their use of setting focuses upon the social context of the story. For other authors, however—particularly for those who write historical and paranormal romances—the establishment of time and place truly does set their romance stage.

It's More Than a Pretty Backdrop

Setting is more than just the sum of the parts of a location's description. As mentioned previously, it sets the tone of your novel. It can also establish the mood of the scene and foreshadow coming events as well as offer insights into the POV character. For example:

It was past midnight. Micah ducked down an alley and hurried toward her meeting with the informant, Boudreaux. Her high heels made a click-clack-clicking *sound against the cobblestone street. A light rain had begun to fall and it chilled her skin. She walked faster. Here, the streets were deserted but she could still hear the revelers celebrating Mardi Gras along Bourbon Street a couple of blocks over. Raucous laughter, followed by a loud whoop of male approval. She'd heard it enough times when she'd been a beat cop to know what it meant: Some drunken frat boy had just asked an even drunker coed to flash her breasts, and she'd complied. Mardi Gras. It was sanctioned insanity in a city never particularly known for being that sane in the first place. But Micah didn't have time to worry about drunken tourists. She had to talk with Boudreaux before the drug dealer changed his mind.*

Her sister's life depended on it.

This excerpt offers the reader several details about the scene, while raising several more questions. For instance, you know that Micah is on her way to speak to a drug dealer informant named Boudreaux who may be able to help Micah save her sister's life, though exactly how and why her sister's life is in danger is not made clear. The scene sets the time and place as midnight in a dark street in the French Quarter of New Orleans during Mardi Gras.

FACT

It helps to have firsthand knowledge of a location before you decide to set a novel there, which is why experts often suggest that you write about what you know. Even so, having a reliable street map and an up-to-date travel guide for the location you're writing about is a handy resource for every writer.

What makes the scene come alive are the sensory details. The reader can hear the sound of Micah's high heels clicking against the cobblestone street, hear the laughter from the drunken frat boys a few blocks over. The reader can also feel the mist of a light, chilling rain as it falls, which adds to a feeling of unease as Micah hurries down the dark street.

With these few details, the setting ceases to be just a backdrop for the action and becomes a seamless part of the story itself.

Using the Five Senses

As you noticed from the previous example, evoking the power of the five senses can bring a scene to life in the reader's mind. After all, romance readers, more so than the readers of any other genre, want to experience the novel as though it were happening to them. They want to pretend they are the characters you've written about on the pages of the book. They want to live your story.

To make this happen, always ask yourself the following five questions when writing a scene:

1. What can my POV character hear?
2. What can my POV character see?
3. What can my POV character smell?
4. What can my POV character taste?
5. What can my POV character touch?

While it's important to know the answers to these questions when you write your scene, you don't have to include an example from each of the five senses. Just choose the most vivid ones that best describe the scene you're writing.

ESSENTIAL

When you're visiting a location that you're researching for a novel, keep a notebook handy. In addition to making a note of the various sights you see, along with the facts associated with them, make a list of your sensory experiences. What can you hear? What can you smell? Often, the answers to those questions are more important for the success of a scene than a litany of dry facts.

Remember, also, that the setting should reflect the tone of the scene you're writing, so choose descriptions of your characters' sensory experiences that reflect the mood you're trying to create in the scene.

In other words, if your purpose is to instill a sense of fear, for example, you should focus on the five senses that fuel that particular sensation. Your heroine might think she sees a shadow move in a darkened hallway or hear the echoing of footsteps as she walks down an empty hallway. She might smell the acrid scent of a cigar in an empty room and suspect that the killer—a man known for his love of cigars—is nearby.

As your heroine becomes frightened, so should your reader. More than simply mentioning the various sensory observations, however, you must use the descriptions to propel the story forward. After all, word choice can help evoke emotions in a reader, so choose your setting descriptors wisely, just as you would the wording in the rest of your novel. (For more information about making the right word choices, refer to Chapter 7.)

Different Uses for Setting

Sometimes, the use of setting is subtle, such as in most contemporary romances. In other words, setting supports the action, rather than serves as a basis for the action itself. In those instances, the setting provides more of a social context for the story. In other romance subgenres, however, the author may be required to build a fictional world outside the reader's realm of everyday existence. That's when the setting becomes part of the story.

Deciding which method is right for your novel largely depends on the subgenre you're writing in, as well as your particular style of writing.

FACT

Setting can also be used as a form of symbolism in a romance novel. Often, writers use weather in this way—the rapid approach of a storm, for example, with its sudden transformation of a blue sky into a dark, threatening mass of clouds could symbolize an increase in tension in a relationship. When setting embodies symbolism, the descriptions serve dual purposes—the first is factual and the second implied.

Setting as Social Context

When setting isn't defining the specific time and place in which the story takes place, it is usually providing more of a social context for the story as a whole by explaining the cultural issues at work. For example:

- A contemporary romance might be set in a small-town where all of the various idiosyncrasies of small-town life are described for comedic effect.
- A romantic suspense might be set on a fat farm where people are literally "dying" to be thin; the setting focuses on America's obsession with weight.

- A lighthearted Regency romance that follows a young woman's quest for a suitable husband could be set against a backdrop of the intricacies of life and love in Regency England.

When the setting is used as a social context, the setting becomes more than just a description of the weather, time and place, and environment. It becomes a commentary on society at large.

ALERT!

Don't get carried away with using your setting as an opportunity to comment on the society's ills as you see them. Most romance readers are looking to be entertained, not to be lectured. Losing sight of the romance in favor of espousing your views on a particular subject would likely result in your book being tossed aside—assuming, that is, it ever got past an editor in the first place.

Setting as World Building

Settings can also play a significant role in a romance novel in their own right. This occurs when the setting stops being the backdrop and becomes part of the story itself. For example, in historical romances that take place hundreds of years ago, setting becomes more crucial to the story because an actual historical event, such as a war, might become an external conflict. Most paranormal romances will also use setting as a potential for external conflict—whether with a futuristic romance set on a hostile planet or with a story set in present-day Ohio with a band of otherworldly creatures running amok.

Small-Town America Versus Exotic Locales

There are no hard-and-fast rules about what constitutes a "proper" geographical setting for a romance. Some publishers may have specific dislikes for a particular time period or setting, but generally, anything goes as long as you can write about the setting convincingly. After all, an isolated military base in Antarctica can be just as romantic as a tropical paradise in the hands—and imagination—of a skilled romance novelist.

QUESTION?

How do I find out which locales and settings are unacceptable to a publisher?
Generally, this type of information is available in the editorial guidelines provided by the publisher, which can be obtained by visiting the publisher's Web site. Submission information, including editorial likes and dislikes, can also be obtained through various writing organizations, such as Romance Writers of America (*www.rwanational.org*).

Generally, the only limitation facing an author on the issue of setting is the need to make it seem as believable as possible. Write what inspires you. Chances are excellent that your enthusiasm for the subject will inspire the reader.

Getting Your Facts Right

Regardless of the type of romance subgenre you're writing, you will want your novel's details to be accurate. Part of that requires that you keep track of your novel's internal timeframe—if you have your hero meet the heroine on Tuesday and not see her again for three days, you can't say their next meeting occurred on Saturday. (Three days from Tuesday would be Friday.)

It's equally important that you do the necessary research for the setting of your novel. After all, having your hero stop for a traffic signal on the 101 Freeway in Los Angeles when no such traffic signals exist would immediately jar a reader who is familiar with the area.

Details, whether large or small, matter.

Research Tips

Nothing can take the place of actual firsthand knowledge about a location, of course, but that isn't always possible, especially in the case of a futuristic or historical romance. The next best thing to visiting the location is to do your research.

The following resources can help:

- Travel guides for a particular location or how-to books for a particular occupation
- Your local library
- Internet resources, such as universities, city government and professional organizations (Always double-check your facts since Internet resources are only as good as their source.)
- Local historical societies
- Local newspapers

When researching your setting, don't forget the importance of incorporating sensory observations (your five senses) into your work. This may require that you dig a bit deeper for the details, even calling an "expert," such as someone who has actually been to the location or performed the job in question. Generally, people are happy to talk about their occupations or hometowns.

Using a Timeline

Just as important as researching your setting is getting the chronological order of events in your novel correct. One method that might help is to create a written timeline. List the dates (days of the week, especially) that events occur in a spreadsheet or on a piece of poster board and hang it on the wall next to your computer.

Many authors use a similar method to keep track of their characters' details, such as age, height, eye and hair color, especially when writing a continuing series or a larger-format romance novel. Keeping notes, in whatever form works for you, can save you time and aggravation.

Of course, not all writers feel it's necessary to keep a written timeline. But having one handy can certainly help during the final review process.

Five Tips on How to Use Setting to Advance Your Plot

Ideally, every aspect of your romance novel—character descriptions, dialogue, and narrative—should advance your plotline. In a romance, that means bringing your story closer to the hero and heroine's achieving their HEA (Happily Ever After). Setting is no different.

Don't waste words. Describing the hero's living room from the heroine's POV only gives the reader a description of furnishings. However, if you use the description to offer insight into both her personality and his, you'll move your story forward.

The easiest way to use setting to advance your plot is to make sure the setting details are relevant on more than one level. Following are five tips that might help:

1. **Use setting to show the passage of time.** For example, if you are writing a historical romance, you can jump ahead months by using a short description in the heroine's POV of how the weather has changed from summer to winter.

2. **Use setting to introduce an internal conflict.** For example, assume you are writing a contemporary romance where the heroine can't trust men because her father had abandoned her and her mom years earlier. If you add a scene where the hero and heroine visit a casino, the setting could trigger the heroine's memory of her father's compulsive gambling, which was the reason he had ultimately left.

3. **Use setting to turn the plot in a new direction.** For example, you could write a romance in which the heroine and hero are traveling together by necessity. If you foreshadowed in Chapter 2 that the heroine will leave the hero once they arrive in Abilene, Texas, the destination becomes a part of the plot. Once they arrive in Abilene, reader expectation for forward movement of the plot is understood.

4. **Use setting to become the catalyst for a shift in the romantic relationship.** For example, if the heroine and hero find themselves having to seek shelter in an abandoned barn after a sudden downpour, they might end up making love in the hayloft.

5. **Use setting to reveal hidden aspects of a character's personality, which propels the story forward.** For example, assume the heroine has thought of the hero as a tough, by-the-book cop who has no empathy for other people. Then she watches him at a Safety Awareness class in a school-room full of third graders. He's a different person from the gruff cop she's known. He's softer, kinder . . . and much more attractive to her in the new setting.

Setting, if used correctly, can work as any other element of the story. Don't think of setting as simply the backdrop for the action. Make it count by finding a way to use setting to advance your plot.

How to Build Conflict Through Your Setting

While setting can enhance conflict, it can also be the source of the conflict itself. After all, external conflicts are often the hero and heroine struggling against outside forces that threaten to tear them apart, such as a war, surviving the aftermath of an earthquake, or a long trek through a jungle following a plane crash.

Choosing a setting that will create conflict for your characters is another way to add depth to your story. The result means more questions for the reader to answer . . . and more reasons to keep turning the pages of your book.

CHAPTER 14

Dialogue—When People Talk, Readers Listen

Silence may be golden, but it is when your characters talk that your readers listen. Putting words into your characters' mouths isn't always as easy as some new writers imagine. Unlike real conversations, your dialogue has to create curiosity, generate tension, build emotion, or incite laughter. Good dialogue jumps off the pages and heads straight to the heart of the reader like a jolt of adrenaline. Fortunately, writing snappy dialogue is as much of a rush for the author as it is the reader. So get ready to get creative.

Why Dialogue Is So Important

While novels are divided into paragraphs, scenes, and chapters, your words belong to one of two categories: dialogue or narrative. You will probably never hear a reader complain that she would have loved more narrative from an author. While both are needed to build a novel, the narrative is considered the passive component, while the dialogue is the "going places" component.

Conversation is the communication between two or more people. While dialogue is words spoken between your characters, the real communication in dialogue is between the writer and the reader. When you place quotation marks around words, it's as if you are saying to the reader, "Pay attention; this is important."

Readers not only expect dialogue, they demand it. One of the first things a potential reader will do in a bookstore is to open a novel and check for the white space on the beginning pages. A lot of white space generally means a lot of dialogue. Readers are no dummies; they know if written correctly, more dialogue means a faster pace and more conflict. White space is a good thing.

ALERT!

A word of caution for those writing historicals: your dialogue will need to be written to reflect the time period. Readers are very savvy about their favorite time periods, so be aware of the words and speech patterns of the era you have chosen for your novel.

The reader also assumes that if characters are talking, something worth talking about is happening. In real life, you make small talk; you may discuss the weather, and exchange pointless chitchat. Not so in your novels. If readers wanted casual chatter, they would pick up the phone and call their aunt who talks too much about nothing. In fiction, dialogue has a job to do. And if your dialogue can do double duty, that's even better.

Dialogue Shows Character

You've heard the adage, "You are what you eat." When considering dialogue and your characters, you might say, "They are what they speak." The words that come from your characters' mouths will tell the reader who they are. Well-written dialogue can also give the reader information about other characters. Here's an example:

Picking up a five-pound catfish she'd caught from the lake that morning, Thelma Baits slapped it down on the cutting board and grabbed a knife. "People around these parts are known for being friendly, Mr. Nelson, but we don't beat around the bush."

She lopped off the fish's head and tossed it into the sink. "I'm plum grateful that you want to protect us and all, but I ain't impressed that you walk into my home dressed like some big-city doorman and talking with those high-dollar words. My niece has already been hurt by your kind once. You lay a pinky on that girl, and I'll skin your well-dressed ass just like I'm skinning tonight's supper."

Every piece of dialogue spoken by your character is an opportunity for your reader to get to know your character. Dialogue gives the reader information about where your character is from, hints at their education level, and shows what the character cares about.

Dialogue Moves the Plot Forward

Dialogue keeps the story moving. Instead of telling the reader what's going to happen next, let the reader learn it through dialogue. For example:

Ashley stormed up to the desk clerk. "I'm here to see Mr. Logan."

"You must be Ashley." The man reached into the desk, rustled with some papers and then handed her an airline ticket. "Mr. Logan said to tell you that if you wanted to talk to him, you'd be there before morning."

Ashley stared at the ticket, then blinked, her fury brought tears to her eyes. "That egotistical ba—" She bit off her last word. "He seriously thinks I'll fly to freaking Paris to see him?"

The man half-smiled. "Yeah, and what really chaps my ass is that he's generally right."

Dialogue Sets Up the Conflict

Good dialogue can introduce the conflict and get a story rolling with a bang. What can someone say to your character, or your character say to someone else, that can set the conflict in motion? Here's an example:

Detective Brit Hansen hailed the cab, glanced at his watch, and jumped into the backseat. He friggin' couldn't believe he'd overslept. "Airport." He slapped the seat.

The man looked over his shoulder. "You not listen to the news?" He spoke with a heavy accent.

"Forget the news," Brit said. "A woman I already don't deserve is waiting on me and I'm an hour late. Drive."

The man frowned. "Ah, Señor, airport is closed. Men with guns. And police say maybe they have bombs. This country, it get as bad as my own."

Dialogue Helps Create Sexual Tension

Whether it's pillow talk, flirting banter, or whispered promises of seduction, dialogue can up the sensual heat of your romance. For example:

Beth looked up from her menu at her brother's best friend. "Do you see something you want?"

Tom's bedroom eyes crinkled around the corners with his smile. "I do. But what am I going to have to do to talk you into it?"

The heat in his gaze felt like summer sun on her skin. She leaned in so only he could hear her words. "I'm not going to bed with you."

He leaned in closer, his lips a breath away from hers. "So I guess the double-decker banana split is out, too?"

Don't be afraid to have fun with your dialogue. And do let the tone of your book be reflected in your characters' speech. If you're writing a romantic comedy, use the dialogue to make your readers laugh. If you're writing a drama, use the character's words to bring a tear to your reader's eyes.

Dialogue Creates Suspense

Good dialogue always creates questions in your reader's mind. When a reader is wondering what will happen next, it's called suspense. Every book, be it a romantic suspense or a romantic comedy, needs suspense. The reader's urge to turn every page is fueled by suspense—she has to know what will happen next. Dialogue can create suspense in different ways.

- By stating a question that the reader should be wondering. For example: *"If Harry didn't try to kill her, then who did?"*
- By having a character say something so surprising that the reader must read on to see how the others characters will react. For example: *"I did something terrible today." Mary dropped on her sister's sofa. "I . . . I had a big fight with my boss and I left work and broke into his house and then I . . . "*

  "You what?" her sister asked.

  "I kidnapped his goldfish."
- Dialogue can create suspense by showing a character's unwillingness to talk about something. The reader will start to wonder what it is that this character does not want to talk about. For example: *His mom walked into the room. "Melissa called twice today. Do you know what she wanted?"*

  "Yeah." David stood and walked over to the bar.

  "So what was it?" his mom queried.

  He could feel her watching him. "What was what?" David feigned ignorance and opened the bar cabinet.

  "What was it that Melissa wanted?"

  "Did you hear about the accident that happened down the block?"

Avoid the everyday pleasantries in your stories. Routine exchanges as in: "How are you?" "Fine, thank you" are boring. Common greetings, introductions, chitchat, may be needed in life, but not in fiction. Dialogue is supposed to sound real, but not be real.

Why Dialogue Isn't Real Conversation

Dialogue isn't conversation, but you might say that conversation is the rough draft of dialogue. In real speech you hem and haw, use "Uhs" and "You knows" as you gather and reconsider your words. While you may use these words in your dialogue to show nervousness or a reluctance to speak, a little goes a long way.

Dialogue is generally direct, to the point, and punchy. Good dialogue is both confrontational and adversarial. It provokes a response. The best dialogue is like the great lines that come to you an hour after you had a confrontation with someone—they are the perfect comeback or statement that would have been ideal to prove your point if you'd had the presence of mind to say it. Hence, dialogue isn't always what you really might say; it's more like what you wish you'd said.

Conversation Answers Questions

Think about the last conversation you had with a friend. Chances are it was filled with a lot of simple questions and answers about the weather, a television show you saw, or other non-earth-shattering discussions. See the two examples below:

- **Example 1**
  "Hi. How are you?"
  "I've been doing okay. How about you?"
  "Fine, thanks."
- **Example 2**
  "Good morning. Can you believe this heat?"
  "Yeah, it's just too much. Have you heard the temperature, yet?"
  "They say it's supposed to hit the hundred mark today."

It might be hard to admit, but the basic question/answer conversation just isn't interesting, intriguing, or worthy to appear in your novels.

Dialogue Creates Questions

A public speaker is praised for being direct. Much to the contrary, dialogue is best when indirect. As Sol Stein states in his book, *How to Grow a Novel,* "the most important key to understanding this new language is that dialogue involves oblique responses as often as possible."

Below are two examples of how oblique responses can add tension to everyday passages that would otherwise be too boring to include in a novel:

- **Example 1**

    "Hi. How are you?"

    "For God's sake. Don't pretend that you don't know."

    "Know what?"

    "The whole world knows and I'm tired of pretending that they don't!"

- **Example 2**

    "Good morning."

    "So you haven't read the paper yet."

    "What's in the paper?"

    "The truth. For once, someone told the truth and it's not pretty."

A good place to start developing an ear for dialogue is to listen to the soap operas on daytime television. In addition to some over-the-top drama, the writers have tapped into the art of snappy, surprising, plot-forwarding dialogue that creates both suspense and questions with its oblique answers.

Eavesdropping 101

To write good dialogue, you'll need to understand the art of conversation. To sharpen your skills, you'll probably want to hone your eavesdropping ability. The best eavesdropping is usually in a restaurant or coffee shop. Take some paper and a pen or a laptop and be prepared to take notes.

The number-one rule for effective eavesdropping is to be inconspicuous. Actually, you may not want to sneak a peek at the person until after you've listened for a while. Can you guess, just from their voices, how these people dress and their average age?

A good exercise to play while eavesdropping is to try and characterize the person speaking. Can you guess where they are from? Do their speech, tone, and word choice hint at their education and profession? Can you guess the relationship of the two people by their conversation?

Eavesdropping can provide inspiration for your characters' dialogue. Below is a list of things to pay attention to while listening:

- Different speech patterns
- Word repetitions
- Voice reflections
- Word choices that hint at characterization of the person speaking
- Differences in male conversation and female conversation
- Words that reflect the mood of the person speaking
- The lack of sentence structure and proper grammar, such as incomplete sentences and dangling participles

ALERT!

Make sure your men sound like men and your women sound like women. While both sexes speak the same language, they use it differently. Men are generally less verbal and get to the point more quickly; women use more words to say the same thing and give more analogies.

Don't worry if the conversation you've tuned in to is boring. That's part of your lesson. Conversation can be very boring. Something your dialogue should never be. While you may get lucky and actually get a great line or two, you aren't there to steal lines or be entertained, you're there to listen and learn.

Dialogue Tags

Dialogue tags are the lines that tell the reader who's talking. Generally, they are the "she said" and the "he said." While the rules of dialogue tags are simple, it is one of the most common mistakes new writers make. And it's also one of the easiest ways to lose a reader, because, for your story to make sense, the reader needs to know who's saying what. For example: *"If Jack wants to see me, he's just going to have to come to me," Mary said.*

The easiest way to prevent confusion is to make sure you give all your characters a unique voice. This is accomplished by speech patterns, word choices, and by allowing your character's personality and background to come across in the way she talks.

Many new writers forget to give their characters their own voice and therefore all the characters speak the same and use the same vocabulary. Be careful that your storybook people don't all sound like you.

However, even when an author gives characters different speech patterns, dialogue tags are sometimes needed to help a reader keep things straight. When it's just two people talking, you will need fewer tags. Their use becomes more important when more than two people are involved in a conversation.

Where Tags Belong

Dialogue tags can come after, in between, or before a line of dialogue. For example:

- *"I'll take the cookies home. My son will devour them," she said.*
- *"I'll take the cookies home," she said. "My son will devour them."*
- *She said, "I'll take the cookies home. My son will devour them."*

While there are no hard rules about where to place a tag, other than what sounds more natural, writers have their preferences and many authors feel the "before" tag is more intrusive and use it less often. However, alternating your tag-line placements can help make them less noticeable.

Proper Punctuation of Tags

Quotation marks go after the punctuation within the dialogue. For example: *"Do you love me?" Kathy asked.*

Another mistake commonly made with dialogue is tag lines that include things that are not forms of speaking. For example: *"I'll make sure it happens," she grinned.* Grinning is not a method of speech, therefore the proper punctuation should be *"I'll make sure it happens." She grinned.*

Be careful of the number of exclamation marks you use in dialogue. Exclamation marks should only be used to show shouting, or very firm orders. Editors say that a page littered with exclamation marks is the sign of an amateur writer.

Said Is Not a Dirty Word

While word repetition is frowned upon in most cases in novel writing, the word *said* is truly the exception. *Said,* when used as a dialogue tag, is practically invisible to the reader and is generally better than an author trying to get too clever and use such words as *articulated* or *proclaimed.*

Action and Narrative Tags

While using "he said" is clearly acceptable, most writers vary the "said" tag with action and narrative tags. Action and narrative tags are simply attributives that describe action or give a bit of narrative that tells the reader who is speaking. See the following two examples:

1. *Mark crossed his arms over his chest and inhaled. "I'm going to miss you."*
2. *Sarah stormed into the room. "I'm not staying here."*

When using action tags, make sure the action is important to the story and fits the mood of the scene. If not, these little actions can start reading like filler and fluff. A balance of regular dialogue tags and action tags can make your dialogue appear crisper and cleaner.

Be careful not to add someone else's action in another person's dialogue paragraph. The reader may assume that the dialogue belongs to the person performing the action and not the actual speaker. Sometimes, even a mention of another character's name immediately following a line of dialogue can confuse the reader.

Internal Dialogue

Internal dialogue is where you have your character's thoughts written out. Internal thoughts that are italicized in a novel will usually be underlined in manuscript format. And while all dialogue is character driven, internal dialogue takes that to an even a higher level. Why? Because internal dialogue is what you would think, but would probably never really say. In other words, internal dialogue is never censored. Internal dialogue can be very useful, especially when your character is saying one thing but really thinks another. See the following two dialogue excerpts:

- **Example 1**

  "Isn't he a sight for sore eyes?" Candy moved the blanket from the infant's face.

  "You can say that again," Becky answered. *That proved it. Love really was blind.*

- **Example 2**

  "You are going to come visit me, aren't you?" Tom asked.

  Sandy smiled. *"You better believe I will."* *Right after they lower my casket into the ground.*

Internal dialogue is only used when you are in that person's point of view. To use it otherwise would mean you are jumping POV and that can confuse the reader.

Most internal dialogue is written in first person—even when the book is written in third—because the character is talking to herself. However, some authors stay in third person when using internal dialogue. The best rule of thumb is to use what sounds natural.

While the use of internal dialogue is a great key to characterization, and enhances deep POV, too much of it can distract from the story. For some authors, writing internal dialogue comes naturally and works very well with their writing voice. For others, it feels and reads forced. The best way to learn to write internal dialogue is to study other authors who use it regularly.

The Blend of Dialogue and Narrative

While it's been emphasized that the more dialogue the better, it bears stating that without narrative, dialogue would never work. A reader wants to envision these people much as they would watch a movie. Dialogue adds the auditory element, but the narrative provides the brush strokes that paint the picture. Don't cheat your readers out of being able to see your characters and their surroundings.

When mixing your dialogue and narrative, be careful that you don't interrupt the flow of dialogue. If a character asks a question, or if a statement is made that requires a response, don't place too much narrative before the response or answer, or your reader may have to backtrack to remember the context.

Narrative's Communication: Body Talk

While dialogue is the verbal communication in your book, it doesn't mean your narrative can't do some talking. Basically, characters communicate with their bodies. Be it a shrug, a raised eyebrow, eye contact, or a tug on the socks. These slight gestures mean something. And when writing romance, this nonverbal communication can lay a foundation for your dialogue and your romance.

Describing the nonverbal communication, using them as action tags or simply as description to help flesh out the scene, is a great way to set a mood and make your words on the page feel real to the reader. You can increase your knowledge of body talk by buying a book on the subject, but don't forget the more personal approach of people-watching. Going to a single's bar and watching the men and women can really be a quick and wonderful way to study body language.

Dialogue Don'ts

Mastering fast-paced, plot-forwarding dialogue is a must for writers of romance fiction. However, learning what not to do is a big part of mastering this element. Following is a list of dialogue don'ts:

- Don't use a lot of dialect. This can be very hard to read. Instead, choose one or two words to give the tone and flavor of the dialect.
- Don't repeat in dialogue what you've just said in internal thought. Repeated information is boring.
- Don't let your characters tell something to someone, or explain what they already know. Delete any line of dialogue that starts with *"I know you already know this but . . . "*
- Don't allow your characters to tell the entire story again to another character when the reader already knows it. Opt instead to fade out of the conversation. For example: *"I went to work and . . . ." Sarah told Brent the entire story.*
- Don't use high-dollar words or avoid the use of contractions in dialogue unless it is a character trait.
- Don't repeat names in dialogue. For example: *"I want to go home, Cindy. Please, Cindy. Listen to me. Cindy, I'm serious."*
- Don't allow your characters to give a speech in dialogue. If someone has something lengthy to say, break it up with internal thought, other people's dialogue, or action.
- Don't allow everyone to sound the same. Use speech patterns and word choices to make each character's dialogue unique.

Probably the biggest "don't" when writing dialogue is . . . Don't be boring. Your readers expect your dialogue to be exciting, invigorating, and provoking. Don't disappoint.

CHAPTER 15

Sex Scenes and Sexual Tension

Sex. That little three-letter-word can stop many writers cold, whether it's their first novel or their hundredth. The idea of writing love scenes is difficult for a lot of romance authors. However, with the exception of some Inspiration Romances, most romance novels will include sexual tension, with the larger percentage including explicit, yet emotional, love scenes. Learning to write about sexual desire, allowing your reader to experience the titillation of your character's relationship, while writing it at a level that is comfortable to you, is a challenge but it is a crucial ingredient in a romance novel.

What's Hot/What's Not—Varying Degrees of Sexual Explicitness

Romance is hot, but to pinpoint which degree of sexual explicitness is the hottest on the market is almost impossible. Why? Because the level of sexual explicitness will depend on the subgenre you are targeting, the publisher, and the current market trends.

FACT

To get a good idea of the level of sensuality that certain lines or subgenres are targeting, check out the latest releases in that particular line. Note the number of sex scenes, the length of the scenes, as well as the choice of language used in the scenes. Also, don't forget to see if the publisher has editorial guidelines.

Studying books for the degree of sexual content is the best way to get an idea of what the publisher expects. While some authors may push the envelope and raise the level of heat, others may just barely meet the established standards. A study of five or more books should give you a basic idea of the publisher's expectations.

New Trends in One Market Affect Other Markets

In recent years, the erotic novel has gained some respectability—no longer just sold in adult bookstores, erotica is now marketed in some of the major bookstore chains.

With the popularity of this genre, a new subgenre of erotic romance (sometimes called romantica) was born.

As the erotic romance grew in popularity, the level of sexual explicitness began to show up in the romance genre as a whole. In part at the encouragement of the publishers, the focus on the sexual relationship in single-title romances, and even in some series lines, began to increase.

ESSENTIAL

The erotic romance is a hybrid of a traditional romance and an erotic novel. The erotic romance contains more sex scenes and more focus on the sexual experience. It is also written with more explicit language than the typical romance, but generally the genre holds to the Happily Ever After ending.

Different Flavors for Different Folks

At the same time, and almost as an answer to this, inspirational romance became the new romance subgenre editors were desperately seeking. New lines were opened, and many authors have found their place writing inspiration romance fiction.

This isn't to say that the traditional sweet romances aren't still on the market today. Publishers are smart. They understand that romance novels are like ice-cream and they should come in varying flavors to meet the variety of consumers' tastes. This said, when the trend heads toward hotter reads, the sweeter romances are harder sales. When the pendulum swings toward less explicitness, the hotter books become the harder sale.

Going Hot or Not

Understanding the market trends, including the degree of sexual content, is important for a new author. However, ultimately, the decision of how much sexual explicitness should be included in your book should be based on your own comfort zone.

Attempting to write outside your comfort level is never a good idea. Not only will you lack a sense of pride for the work if it gets published, you will find that writing outside your comfort level will generally show in your ability to write the scenes.

However, you shouldn't use your initial foreboding about writing sex scenes to judge your comfort zone. Most new authors experience difficulty with love scenes. Allow yourself some time to adjust to writing these more private scenes.

A lot of times, the negative emotions tied to writing love scenes are due to an author feeling as if the experience is practically autobiographical. Yet, as a writer masters the art of getting deeper into their characters' points of view, the scenes magically become about the people they have created and not about themselves.

Discovering Your Real Comfort Zone

What level of sensuality are you comfortable writing? Often, the answer can be found in another question. What level of sensuality are you comfortable reading? Many writers find their comfort zone for writing falls within the same comfort zone of their reading pleasure.

If you love hot, steamy romances, then attempting to write a sweet romance may not be the type of book of you'll enjoy writing. However, if you cringe and often skip over the sex scenes in the books you read, then you might question if you have what it takes to write a book with lots of sensual sizzle.

FACT

Even erotica writers have comfort zones when writing sex scenes. What one writer considers taboo, another has no problem exploring on paper. The trick is to discover your creative limits and stay within your own boundaries.

You may be thinking that while you are comfortable with reading and writing the sex scenes, you worry what your family and friends may think. Frankly, this is a common issue most romance authors face. While the majority of published authors admit to having a friend or relative who is surprised and sometimes offended by their stories, most writers have found that people who truly love them accept their chosen career. Others will employ the use of a pseudonym so the issue never arises. Determining your own comfort zone needs to be considered when you decide on the type of books you intend to write and the level of sensuality you plan to include.

Sex Versus Sexual Tension

Some writers can write novels in which the hero and heroine never consummate the relationship, or they have far fewer sex scenes than other books in the same genre, yet the author is dubbed as a very "hot" writer. Basically, the author has keyed into an essential part of writing romance for women. They have mastered the art of sexual tension.

For female readers, sexual tension is to a romance novel what foreplay is to sex. It is the teasing, the seducing of the senses, that leads one to feel desire and to feel desirable. Sexual tension is achieved when a reader becomes absorbed in the sexual awareness and emotions of the hero and the heroine.

So, how important is sexual tension in a romance novel? Very. Even in romances where the hero and heroine may never consummate the relationship, sexual tension is essential to the reader's pleasure.

Building Sexual Tension

Just as in real life, sexual tension in a romance novel doesn't usually come on fast. It's slow, seductive, and builds as the hero and heroine get closer. The tension should feel natural. It should grow naturally from the plot and characters and not feel forced.

Be aware of the differences between a man's reactions to a sexually charged situation compared to a woman's. A man's approach will be more sexually blatant, where a woman may react to it with a more emotional viewpoint.

While a writer's goal is to make sure your men sound like men and your women sound like women, don't forget who your audience really is. Because women make up the majority of the romance readership, the sexual tension should be written to appeal more to the feminine viewpoint.

Dialogue Builds Sexual Tension

Dialogue is one of the best tools a writer has to build and show sexual tension. What can your hero or heroine say that ups the sexual tension?

From pillow talk, to words they wish they could take back, dialogue can be sexy. See the following example:

"What do you want from me?" Sarah asked as he headed out the door.

Nick swung around, stormed back across the room, and didn't stop until he stood inches from her. "I want you. All of you. Naked and willing. Is that too damn much to ask?"

Romantic/Sexy Gestures Can Melt a Reader's Heart

What does a man do to impress his date, to seduce her into his arms and his bed? From the opening of a car door to a gift of roses, romantic gestures and gifts will tug on a woman's, and a reader's, heartstrings. See the following example:

Jenny spotted the gift box and one red rose lying on top of her desk. Her chest tightened. It couldn't be from him. He didn't know where she worked— didn't even know her real name. She glanced around to see if any of her colleagues were watching. They weren't. Then she slipped the red ribbon off one corner of the lid and opened the box. Her breath caught when she read the note. "Once wasn't enough." Below the note, lay a sheer negligee.

He knew.

Oh, Goodness. Don't Look at Me Like That!

Have you ever watched two people across a room who are attracted to each other? The heat in the looks they give each other is palpable. The old cliché, "They couldn't keep their eyes off each other," says it all. For example:

His hungry gaze swept around the parlor, taking in all the females, searching, as if he knew exactly what he wanted. Then his soft blue gaze met hers. She could swear his irises darkened with something primitive, something she didn't quite understand. She told herself to look away, to silently send him the message that she wasn't willing to play his game. Sweet heavens, she didn't even know the game, but her gaze seemed locked, frozen with something akin to hope.

The Power of a Simple Touch

The power of touch is amazing. Goosebumps rise, nerves tingle, and the heart races. But sometimes what's sexier than a blatant touch to one of the more erogenous zones is a simple touch meant to seduce. See example below:

It was a just a dance, something men and women did in social situations every day. So why did the light pressure of his hand against her hip feel way too intimate? Why did his whiskey-scented breath against her temple send shivers down her body? He moved closer, her breasts brushed over his chest and the sweetness of it started tremors deep in her abdomen.

A Penny for Your Thoughts

If only you could hear what he's thinking. Those internal thoughts can be very sexy, slightly naughty, and extremely seductive. Your characters may be able to control what they say, what they do, but seldom can they control what they think. Use internal thoughts to add sexual tension to your novels. See the following example:

He watched her move, the way her body swayed with her steps, and how the red silk dress slipped and slid across all her more interesting body parts. What he wouldn't give to be able to remove that dress, along with his brother's engagement ring from her finger, and claim her as his own.

What Makes It Work

Sexual tension isn't always as easy to write as you might assume. You can't just toss in a kiss, or have the hero notice the heroine's body and imagine her naked. Of course, that isn't to say kisses and naughty thoughts couldn't create sexual tension. They can. But, generally, sexual tension is accomplished in the following ways:

- The mood in the scene
- The right words
- The way the words were said
- The characters' disposition

The art of delivering sexual tension that works is about as problematic as delivering a perfect come-on line. For a come-on line to be successful, it has to be delivered at the right time, in the right tone, and by the right person.

While boldness sometimes works when introducing sexual tension, crudeness seldom does. Unfortunately, for many new authors, it can be a fine line between being bold and being crude. If your sexual tension is coming off as being too raw, turn it down a notch and look at countering the bold statements with something softer, something that shows emotion.

The "Scene": Is It Love or Is It Sex?

Are you calling it the sex scene or the love scene? We all know that having sex and making love are not the same. And to write "the scene" successfully, you need to be aware of the difference.

Not too long ago, romance novels only featured love scenes. Meaning, the hero and heroine only consummated the relationship after one or the other had fallen in love. But times change.

Today, it's not unheard of to have the hero or heroine having sex with someone other than each other, especially in the erotic romance subgenre. While that's not the norm in single-title romances, what is normal is the hero and heroine falling into bed—or on the sofa, the backseat of a convertible, or the kitchen table—before either are committed to a serious relationship.

In other words, in most of today's romance novels, sex is taken a lot more lightly. It can be more playful, more graphic, the language more direct and daring than it was several years ago.

ALERT!

While sex between the hero and heroine early on in the book can be viewed by the characters as casual, the scene is generally written in a way that the reader knows there is an emotional connection. The romance should always be present during sex scenes between the hero and heroine.

While sex may not be viewed as a major commitment in today's romance novels, you should never forget the one word that describes the genre in which you are writing: romance. And for a sex scene to be romantic, there has to be some emotional connection between the hero and heroine. The characters may not even be aware of the connection, but the reader must always feel the budding of a relationship.

The Heart Grows Fonder

With each love scene, the characters' awareness of the connection between them becomes harder to deny. Generally, there is always one love scene when the hero and heroine both realize that the sex has stopped being casual and turned into something much more meaningful.

Find ways in each love scene to show these people coming closer. Show the trust between the characters getting stronger. Show how the pleasure of sex becomes less important and how pleasuring each other becomes the main goal.

A great example of how a sex scene can gradually change into a love scene appears in the movie *Pretty Woman*. Julia Roberts (Vivian Ward) plays a good-hearted prostitute who's hired by Richard Gere (Edward Lewis), a wealthy businessman, to spend a week with him. From the first time they sleep together, the reader is aware of the chemistry between them, both the emotional and physical chemistry. Vivian's rule of never kissing a john on the lips is constantly tested by Edward. When she finally does kiss him, it becomes clear that things have changed between them. Their relationship is no longer strictly business.

What Makes a Sex Scene Sizzle?

We've all read them—oh, those scenes that make us breathless. How does a writer do that? While there are many techniques that can help achieve the writing of a really hot love scene, generally what makes these scenes work is the same thing that makes every other scene work in a romance novel. Namely, characterization.

> Make sure that your characters remain true to their personalities while making love. Passion will and should expose your characters' deepest secrets, and hidden personality traits, but it should always be believable. Find ways to make the scenes about the characters and not just about the sex.

A good writer manages to pull you into the story by making you care about the characters. You feel what the characters' feel, you want what they want, and you care about what they care about. So when these characters are in the tantalizing experience of passion, you are there with them.

When writing your love scenes, never allow the scene to be clinical. Readers know what happens during sex, they want to know what happens when these two individuals come together. Make sure the love scenes are as unique as your characters.

The Senses

Incorporating the sense of smell, taste, touch, sight, and hearing is what brings any scene alive for the readers. From the feel of the heroine's hair sweeping across the hero's chest, to the sound of the hero's heart beating, the senses are what make the scene real for the readers.

Anticipation

The success of a love scene will also rely on the anticipation of the characters and the readers. Have you added enough sexual tension so that when this moment arrives, the characters and your readers are totally hooked and ready?

When in doubt, take the slow approach. Don't be in a hurry to get to the sex scene. Part of the fun of these scenes is the anticipation. Tease and seduce the reader just as your characters do to each other during the song and dance that leads to the mating ritual.

Many authors include what they call the "almost scene" before writing the actual sex scenes. This is when the hero and heroine almost make love but stop because of external forces or just plain cold feet. If your sex scenes aren't as hot as you'd like, try writing an almost scene earlier, teasing the characters and readers a little more before things really heat up.

Tension

The need for conflict in each scene holds true even in love scenes. Refer back to your favorite books and check out their love scenes to see what types of conflict can exist during sex. Below are some common things that may cause tension during a love scene:

- One, or both characters, have doubts about the wisdom of allowing the relationship to progress to the new level
- Fear that one will not perform up to the expectations of the lover
- Insecurities about one's appearance
- Fear of being caught
- Fear of where the sex might lead emotionally
- Fear of losing control to passion
- Fear of intimacy

While external conflict can be used in sex scenes—for example, someone/something interrupts the couple or the setting isn't conducive for lovemaking—the best conflict will be internally motivated. Look deep into the character's internal issues to discover what problem might naturally arise during these intense and private moments.

While new writers often find it difficult to get into deep point of view during a sex scene, these scenes are where point of view needs to be the strongest. For a reader to fully experience the romance, they must understand how the ultimate intimacy has bonded these two people.

Emotion

Of all our body parts, the most important erogenous zone is the head, which is closely followed by the heart. What a character is feeling and experiencing is much more important than what is actually happening. The hottest scenes are those written with an abundance of emotion.

To pull in emotion, work on language, not only on your prose, but the words spoken between these two people. Also, make sure you focus not only on the physical pleasure but the emotional sensation of giving yourself to another person. Make sure you include how it feels to be touched and held, but don't exclude what it feels like to touch or to hold.

Explicit Versus Implied

How explicitly you write your sex scenes will first depend on the type of romance you are writing. The series lines generally have the requirements spelled out in their guidelines. Most erotic romance lines will expect the explicitness in both the language and the descriptions.

However, if you are writing single-title romance, to some degree, the level of explicitness may depend on your own comfort zone. Some writers choose to use strong language and straightforward descriptions of the love scenes. Others rely on symbolism or euphemisms to describe certain body parts and to depict the actual sex act. When done well, both can be effective.

Be careful that the euphemisms you use are fitting to the story and characters, and are not clichéd. Nothing can ruin the mood of a love scene quicker than a wrong word that pulls a reader out of the story.

Most single-title romance editors will not care about the degree of explicitness you use. What they do care about is that your scenes work, that the imagery and words elicit the emotions of the readers—that the readers feel as if they have journeyed into the world of romance.

CHAPTER 16

Writing a Book They Can't Put Down

Do you remember the first time you got so swept up in a novel that you stayed up half the night reading it? As a reader, you hope you'll find that with every book you read. As a writer, you hope yours is the book that readers can't put down. There are many reasons a reader finds a book a compelling read—great writing, wonderful characters, unique plot. But pacing, or the speed with which an author tells the story, is why they keep turning the pages.

Understanding Pacing

Pacing plays an important role in creating a salable romance novel, but it's probably one of the least understood elements of the craft of writing. Basically, pacing is the author's way of controlling how fast—or slow—a reader reads the book. The author does this by controlling the length of the sentences and paragraphs, the ratio of dialogue to narrative, and the amount of descriptive details offered in a particular scene.

Think of a scene as a song. Just as each song has its own rhythm and tempo, some fast, some slow, so will your scenes. Your choice of words, how short or long you make the sentences and paragraphs, the ratio of dialogue to narrative in your scene—all of these combine to form the pacing or tempo.

For a romance novel to succeed, it will need scenes that take away the reader's breath (fast pacing) and scenes that make the reader sigh with pleasure (slower pacing). Like most aspects of writing, finding the right balance is critical.

Generally, when you want to speed up pacing, you will use the following techniques:

- Shorter sentences
- More dialogue
- Crisper, sharper nouns and verbs

Conversely, the following techniques result in a slowing pacing:

- Longer sentences
- More narrative
- More descriptive passages

So, how do you strike the right balance? The answer largely depends upon the type of subgenre you're writing. After all, a lushly sensuous historical romance will usually have a much slower pace than a tightly plotted contemporary romantic suspense. Still, even within the same subgenres, certain scenes and situations call for a specific type of pacing.

E
ALERT!

When you're looking for ways to quicken your writing's pace, focus on making your scenes all take place in the here-and-now, rather than using flashbacks or dreams. Both techniques, as a whole, have been overdone. Even when they're used properly, they slow down the action and the story's pacing.

Another way to balance your pacing is to vary the sentence structure you use. Instead of writing sentence after sentence that follows the same "subject-verb-object" format, mix it up by trying "predicate-subject" or other variation. This, combined with varying the length of your sentences and types of scenes, should ensure your pacing is well balanced.

When to Quicken the Pace

Most romance novels published today are faster paced than romance novels published thirty years ago. That said, there are still certain scenes that require faster pacing than others. Action sequences, for example, generally require faster pacing. So would a scene designed to build suspense.

When writing such a scene, focus on the mood, keep the description and introspection to a minimum, and as said before, strive to use short sentences. Notice the differences in the original and revised paragraphs below:

Original: *Susan crept down the dark stairs to her Aunt Margaret's living room, trying to get a fix on the noise that had awakened her but she couldn't. Of course, she wasn't even sure what had awakened her, only that she'd heard something. It was dark but she could still make out a few details in the large, shadow-filled room, thanks to the moonlight pouring in through the partially open floorlength beige-colored drapes that covered the bank of tall windows against the east wall. She glanced from the overstuffed, Queen Anne–style, camel-colored easy chair in the corner to the two mocha-colored leather sofas and glass-and-chrome coffee table that sat in the center of the room. Then one of the shadows seemed to loom larger than the rest and started moving* *toward her. She gripped the baseball bat harder and raised it above her head, and demanded, "Who's there?"*

Revised: *Susan tightened her grip on the baseball bat and crept down the dark stairs to her Aunt Margaret's living room. She wasn't sure what had awakened her but something had. She looked around the room. It was shrouded in shadows, each more ominous than the last. Then one of the shadows started moving toward her.*

She raised the bat above her head. "Who's there?"

Both examples describe the same event, but the second one is more effective at building suspense. Not only is it shorter, it uses a minimum of visual details about the living room. While those descriptions may paint a visual picture in the reader's mind of the room, they are unnecessary for the success of this scene.

Notice, also, that the reference to the baseball bat was moved to the first sentence. By leading with the image of Susan creeping down the stairs in the dark with a baseball bat in her hand, you immediately set the stage for suspense in the reader's mind.

When to Slow the Pace

Just as there are times in a romance novel that naturally call for faster pacing, there are also scenes that require things to slow down. One example might be a scene of heightened emotions, such as when the hero and heroine make love. When slower pacing is needed, use longer sentences with more visual details. Again, notice the differences in the original and revised paragraphs below:

Original: *Meredith studied Luke, trying to memorize every detail. "Guess I'll see you around," she said, surprised her voice didn't crack.*

Revised: *Meredith studied Luke for a long moment, trying to memorize every detail . . . not that she really needed to. Lucas McFall's image had been branded into her soul the first time they'd met. Even now, there wasn't a part* *of him that she couldn't close her eyes and imagine if she tried. The scent of his bare skin, his oh-so-kissable mouth—even the tiny scar above his left eyebrow that he'd gotten in a motorcycle accident when he was a kid. "Guess I'll see you around," she said, surprised her voice didn't crack.*

The second example delivers much more of an emotional wallop than the first. The added details, both about Meredith's memories of Luke and her feelings for him, strengthen the tug on the reader's emotions. Since the pacing for this scene should be slower, these added descriptive details slow down the tempo of the scene.

Keep the Story Moving

Writing a romance novel is a lot like toppling a carefully arranged line of dominoes. The first falling domino starts a chain reaction—each subsequent falling domino knocks over another piece and continues until all of the dominoes have been toppled. Timing is critical, of course. If a domino falls too soon, the chain will be broken. In writing, you have scenes instead of dominoes. Each scene leads to the next, which, in turn, leads to the one after that.

Consider creating a timeline for the important—and not so important—events of your novel. Not only will a timeline help you keep track of the events, it can help maintain pacing. Often sluggish pacing is due to a lack of action in your plotline.

While plotting sets the dominoes, or plot points, in place, pacing ensures that they all topple at the correct time.

Crafting Great Chapter Hooks

As discussed in previous chapters, a great hook at the end of a chapter, or scene, ensures the reader will continue reading your romance novel.

It's human nature to want to solve mysteries. Smart writers use this to their advantage by ending a chapter with a question. Will the heroine kiss the hero? Will the villain claim a new victim? If the reader is involved in the story, she'll turn the page to the new chapter, eager to find out what happens next.

Remember the old adage, "Less is more?" This is especially true when it comes to chapter endings. Never answer all of a reader's questions about what is happening before ending a chapter. Make the reader feel she must turn the page and see what happens next.

But "tricking" the reader into turning the page by promising an exciting development and then not delivering on that promise will quickly wear thin. Having the heroine react to a perceived danger at the end of a chapter, only to discover that the "danger" was nothing more than the hero's cat and her own overactive imagination will probably generate a laugh the first time. Overuse the technique, however, and you'll likely alienate the reader.

Bolstering a Sagging Middle

Generally, new writers can do a great job of starting a romance novel with either a unique precipitating event or an intriguing premise. They also can craft the perfect ending for their romance, whether it's a comedy, a dark paranormal, or a novel of nail-biting romantic suspense. The problems arise somewhere in the novel's midsection. That's where the action begins to slow and the reader's attention wavers.

ESSENTIAL

A good technique for analyzing the pacing of your romance novel is to read a scene aloud. Do you find yourself losing track and having to start over? Does it seem like a paragraph goes on for too long? If so, there's a good chance your pacing is off. Try tightening the scene and increasing the pacing, then see if you get better results.

Luckily, faster pacing can help to eliminate the problem of the sagging middle. If you feel your midsection isn't as exciting as your opening or ending, try turning the action in a new direction or add a new complication to an existing conflict.

Upping the Stakes

By the middle of the book, the goals of your hero and heroine should be clear. So should their fears and the obstacles standing between them and certain victory. "Upping the stakes" means you increase the tensions that are already in play. For example, if a killer is stalking the heroine, have the killer claim the life of someone close to her. This doubles the heroine's determination to unmask the killer and increases the odds that she and the hero are facing.

Upping the stakes isn't restricted to romantic suspense novels. For example, if the hero and heroine are ad executives at the same company competing for a big client's account in a sexy contemporary, you could up the stakes by having the rules of their "game" suddenly change. Perhaps, their boss has decided the loser will lose more than just the account. The executive who bags the client gets a big raise while the executive who doesn't is fired.

This raising of the stakes increases the tension, which by default quickens the pacing of the story.

ALERT!

Always remember that when you raise the stakes in a romance novel, the outcome of the HEA (Happily Ever After) must be threatened in some way. Raising the stakes in a subplot is fine, as long as it will affect the main characters. If there is no danger to the hero and heroine's HEA, however, the status quo hasn't been altered—and the stakes haven't been raised.

Increase the Suspense

Nothing quickens the pace of a story like a ticking clock counting down the seconds while the hero works frantically to defuse a bomb. Give the hero and heroine a short timeframe in which to reach their goal—whether they are striving to find their romantic bliss or stop a madman from annihilating a planet. By increasing the number of complications that stand in their way, you automatically increase the suspense.

For example, if at the beginning of the story, the hero and heroine had eight weeks in which to resolve their romantic conflict, a complication could arise that cuts that timeframe by more than half. With less time in which to reach their goal, the hero and heroine must intensify their efforts, thereby increasing the suspense . . . and increasing the pacing as well.

Tweaking Your Story Arcs

Sometimes the problem with your romance novel's pacing has more to do with the timing of the events in the story, rather than the tempo of your individual scenes. This usually happens when all of the elements that are needed to make a great romance exist in your plot—though not in the proper order. Tweaking your story arcs can help.

QUESTION?

How do I know if my novel's pacing is off?
Sometimes it's hard to be a fair judge of your own writing. Generally, though, if you find your attention wandering while reading a scene aloud, it's a safe bet your readers' attention would wander also. Radical shifts between long, contemplative chapters and short, action-filled chapters are another indication that something may be amiss.

Ideally, your subplots should support your main plot. Not only by adding texture and layers to the main plot, but by supporting it as well, either through added insights into your characters or by introducing new obstacles for them to overcome. The timing of this support, however, is important. If you're having a pacing problem, take a look at the timing of your subplots. Do the highs of your subplots exist during the lows of your main plot?

If not, move the subplot to a new timeframe within your novel.

Tips for Faster Pacing

Not all romance novels require fast pacing, of course. Some books—such as a sweeping historical saga, for example—seem to demand a slower tempo. But for the majority of the novels being sold today, faster pacing is a necessity. Luckily, you can increase your odds of making a sale by mastering a few tried-and-true techniques for speeding up the pace of your romance novel.

Shorter Scenes and Chapters

Romance readers, like most readers of fiction, generally prefer to stop reading at the end of a chapter or scene. Often, they will flip ahead to see how many pages are left until the next break. If you write short scenes and short chapters, they'll likely keep telling themselves "just a few more pages" until the next stopping point. Your goal when they reach that new stopping point is to hook them so they'll continue reading "just a few more pages," and then repeat the process until they ultimately finish the book.

On the other hand, if your chapters are longer, readers may decide to put your book down in the middle of a scene . . . and never pick it up again. A novel with shorter chapters and scenes, even when the book has the same number of pages as a novel with longer chapters and scenes, will often take a reader less time to read.

Varying both the length and structure of your sentences can also make for faster pacing in your novel. Experiment with single-word paragraphs, or single-word sentences. Not only can their occasional use add impact to your writing, they can keep the reader turning those pages.

Keep Them Moving

Another way to keep the pace moving at a fast clip in your romance is to focus on action, rather than narrative. Descriptions, of any kind, slow down pacing while action sequences speed them up.

Nothing slows down your novel's pacing like lengthy paragraphs of character introspection. While it's probably impractical to eliminate all introspection from your romance, try to intersperse it with dialogue and action, to keep the story moving. Read through your scenes and cut any unneeded descriptions and wordiness.

Keep Them Talking

Dialogue—especially the short, snappy variety—is another excellent way to increase the pacing of your romance novel. For scenes between your hero and heroine, experiment with using dialogue exchanges that don't include tag lines (*he said, she said*).

For this technique to work, make sure that you:

- Use distinctive voices for each character
- Have short dialogue exchanges of no more than one line in length

Naturally, the dialogue should advance the plot or clarify some aspect of characterization. (For more information on writing great dialogue, refer to Chapter 14.)

Subplots That Advance the Main Plot

Another way to ensure fast pacing is to use subplots that support the main plot. For example, if you are writing a romantic suspense, the suspense subplot would advance the main romance plot because, ultimately, the two are connected. (If the mystery is not solved, the killer not caught, the hero and heroine cannot have their HEA.)

The key to a fast-moving novel is to maintain the focus on the main plot. For a romance novel, that would be the romantic relationship between the hero and heroine. Anything that propels that forward ensures faster pacing.

CHAPTER 17

Writing the First Draft

With the plot, the characters, and the setting of your book already laid out, the only thing left for you to do is start writing the first draft. Of course, if you're like most new writers, that thought probably fills you with dread. If so, relax. First drafts don't need to be perfect—they just need to be written. Are you ready to begin writing yours?

Why a Rough Draft Is Important

Every romance novelist writes a rough draft of her novel. Some drafts may be "cleaner" than others, meaning they have fewer grammatical errors and mangled sentences. Other drafts may be unpolished and focus on getting the story committed to paper, rather than on making the words sparkle. Of course, new writers must ultimately choose the method that works for them creatively. Either way, completing the book is a necessity.

For some successful romance authors, a first draft is really a detailed outline that lists in narrative form precisely who the book is about and what happens to them. These outlines can be quite lengthy—in fact, writing a detailed outline of 60 to 100 pages is not unusual. For authors who use this method, completing a detailed outline first helps them write a more polished draft later.

Being able to take a novel from story idea to first draft strengthens a new writer's confidence level. After all, completing a first draft is tangible proof that your goal is within your reach. And with that rough draft in hand, you're ready to take the next steps along the path to publication.

FACT

In rare cases, editors and agents have signed a new writer who hasn't completed the romance novel in question. This usually happens because the novel's hook is both unique and topical, meaning the project is very marketable, and the editor or agent feels the book's potential is worth the risk of signing an unproven author.

It Proves You Can Write a Book

Have you ever wondered what goes through the minds of editors and agents when they read a dynamic first three chapters of a romance novel by an unpublished author? If you think they're imagining themselves offering the author a contract, you'd be mistaken. Chances are excellent, however, they are wondering if the author can finish the book, since many new writers never get beyond writing those great opening chapters.

The reasons new authors fail to complete a manuscript vary. Some lose interest in the story idea and move on to something new. Others hit a snag in the writing process—a plotting mishap, for example—and decide to give up on writing altogether. A few encounter problems of a different kind. They succeed in completing the manuscript, but only their first three chapters are ready to be submitted for publication.

The latter scenario seems to happen most frequently to "contest junkies," or those who enter—and become finalists—in dozens of writing contests. For them, the goal becomes more about winning a contest than selling a manuscript. As a result, they polish their contest entry until it shines . . . while ignoring the rest of their manuscript.

ALERT!

Don't become a contest addict! Writing contests, especially the ones offered by RWA's various chapters, provide a great opportunity for an unpublished author. They can get your work critiqued, as well as get it placed in front of acquiring editors and agents. But you can't make a sale if you don't have a completed manuscript. Finish the book!

Having a great first three chapters is important, but having a completed manuscript is the only proven way to make a sale. After all, editors and agents want a great book, not just a great first three chapters and synopsis.

You Can Revise Anything but a Blank Page

Don't worry if your first draft isn't very good. First drafts rarely are, nor are they supposed to be. It isn't even necessary for the first draft to meet the word count of your projected romance novel. Ultimately, all that matters is getting the story down on paper. Once you have a completed first draft, you can rewrite, polish, tweak, and expand until the finished novel shines as brightly as your first page.

Getting Past the Blank First Page

As discussed in previous chapters, staring at a blank first page is probably the most frightening aspect of writing a romance novel. Probably for good reasons, too, when you consider that finding the opening line—the right opening line—is a challenge for even a seasoned pro. What most new writers fail to recognize, though, is that more often than not, the much-sought-after "perfect opening" doesn't reveal itself until the author is already involved in the writing of the book.

Accept That Writing Is Rewriting

Bestselling author Michael Crichton probably put it best when he said that books aren't written, so much as they are rewritten. Experienced authors of all genres recognize the wisdom in his words but many new authors often find it difficult to embrace the concept that writing is rewriting. However, it's true. Most writers, regardless of genre, spend more time polishing and tweaking their revisions than they do on writing new copy.

Romance writers are no exception.

QUESTION?

How many drafts do most romance writers write of a novel?
The answer varies from author to author. Some writers may do numerous rewrites, while others only do one or two. Of those who do multiple rewrites, some revisions could be minor tweaking. Other writers may do more extensive revisions or focus on one particular aspect of the novel, such as intensifying conflict or adding sexual tension.

Accepting the inevitability of revisions can free your creative muses. Once you've given yourself permission to create imperfect work, you are more likely to focus on the creative aspects of writing. That's when elements such as adding unique twists to your plot or incorporating a fresh take on familiar characters take priority over producing "perfect" copy. It's a good tradeoff. After all, the technical aspects of writing, such as proper sentence structure, tweaking the language to make a suspense scene more suspenseful, etc., can be easily accomplished during a rewrite.

Writing Your First Page

So, are you ready to write the first page of your romance novel? By this point, you probably have the opening scene visualized. This includes knowing whose POV you want to use, the tone or mood of the opening scene and whether it reflects your intriguing premise or precipitating event. However, knowing what you want to write about doesn't always lead to an easily created first page.

Or, to a first line, for that matter.

FACT

Many authors confess to rewriting their first chapter multiple times, and for good reason, too. First chapters—first lines and first pages, especially—are critical to a novel's success. However, when you start a novel, you don't know your characters and their story as well as you will by the time you write the ending. Hence, the need to revise and rewrite.

Fear is usually the culprit. One of the first "rules" that new authors grasp about writing a publishable romance novel is the importance of having a well-written and compelling opening. But those attention-grabbing first lines are usually the result of multiple revisions, rather than a first try in a first draft.

In other words, you shouldn't worry overly much about the quality of your first draft. Focus, instead, on getting your story down on paper. Chances are excellent that you will have many opportunities to find the perfect opening as you write your romance novel.

If You Still Can't Write That Page . . .

If you're still worrying about writing that first page, try using a declarative sentence that summarizes the conflict in your opening scene. Then, follow it with another few sentences that build upon that opening until you've completed your first page. Think of these first lines as temporary placeholders that you'll replace once you feel the rhythm of your novel take hold.

A good temporary placeholder doesn't always have to be a declarative sentence. Think about having your POV character ask a question that alludes to the opening scene's conflict. Make it actual dialogue or a line of internal thought—what matters most is that it sets the story in motion.

For example, if your opening scene for a romantic comedy has the slightly shady bad-boy hero telling the skeptical-about-trusting-men heroine to trust him while he handles a potentially disastrous business deal, you could open with a declarative statement that summarizes the situation and establishes the tone of the book. The placeholder might read as follows:

"Trust me," Jimmy Ray Darlington said with a slow grin.

Jessie Simmons tried not to punch him in his nose. Trust him? She'd learned to stop trusting men at the ripe old age of five when her daddy promised he'd be right back after leaving her in the Jitney Junior parking lot while he "ran a quick errand" with his friends. That errand had been a bank job and she hadn't seen her father again until she was twelve.

She had a hunch things with Jimmy Ray wouldn't turn out much better.

It's doubtful the opening lines will survive a final edit but they serve their purpose as temporary placeholders: They allow you to start your novel. What's more, they also establish the book's tone and hint at the romantic conflict ahead for the hero and heroine, as well as put you into the middle of a scene. Who could ask for more?

Silencing Your Inner Critic

One of the biggest challenges facing a new writer is learning to silence the inner critic. That's the nagging voice inside your head that reminds you when your writing isn't as sparkling as it can—or should—be. While having that self-awareness about your work is important, especially during the editing process, problems can arise when your inner critic threatens to extinguish the creative spark. That's when you need to silence your inner critic . . . or at least ignore it for a little while.

Three techniques that might help include:

1. **Turn off your word processor's automatic spelling and grammar checker while you're writing.** Seeing the alerts and notifications of a misspelled word or grammatical error can distract you, especially when you're trying to create.
2. **Don't read through your work as you write.** Writers have a tendency to write a sentence, then immediately read over it. While this can be useful for the editing stage, it can sound the death knell for creativity.

3. **Don't share your unedited rough draft with anyone.** Constructive criticism can help you grow as a writer but receiving feedback on an unedited rough draft will only activate your own inner critic. Save the critiques for the editing stage.

Learning to block out the voice of your inner critic while you write isn't easy—your inner critic wants to help make your work better, after all. But mastering the technique of when to ignore the unsolicited advice is probably the best gift you can give yourself as a writer.

Setting Goals

To succeed at any profession, you must establish goals—both for the long-term and the short-term. Writing is no different. Since authors only improve their craft and hone their skills by writing on a consistent basis, you will need to make a writing commitment.

Setting Aside Writing Time

Some authors find that they are most prolific in the morning. Others become creative late at night. The best way to find out which time of day works best for you and your creative muse is to experiment. Take a week and try writing first thing in the morning, then try writing later in the evening for another week. Naturally, you may have to factor in the obligations and responsibilities of family and work. As a result, you could find yourself having to write at a time of day when you're not at your best creatively. Fortunately, it's not the time of day that matters as much as the commitment to set aside a block of uninterrupted writing time on a regular basis, and stick to it.

ALERT!

Set realistic writing goals. Just as a new runner can't compete with an Olympic-caliber athlete in a track meet, a new writer can't produce the same number of quality pages each day, every day, as an experienced author can. Start with an achievable goal, such as writing one hour a day, and build upon it.

Setting Your Daily Goal

New writers often have no idea what a reasonable daily output for them will be. In fact, it's rare that an author, even a seasoned professional, will write the same number of pages each day. That's because writing is a cumulative process. The work you do today may not be measured in actual pages completed today. You could just be laying the foundation for the pages you will complete tomorrow.

FACT

Some writers perform better when their daily writing goal is measured in time, rather than in actual pages produced. If your commitment to your romance novel is to write for one hour each day, and you achieve that goal each day, you have succeeded—regardless of the number of pages actually completed.

Rather than setting a goal based upon daily totals, set a goal for a weekly total. For example, if your goal is to write one page a day, change the goal to writing seven pages a week. This produces the same number of pages each week, but allows your creative muse to operate under its own time schedule.

Dealing with Writers' Block

Don't be surprised if you occasionally find yourself facing your computer screen in the middle of a scene or chapter and having no idea what to type next. Sooner or later, every writer will experience a creativity slowdown. When that happens to you, don't despair. Writers' block is a real phenomenon but it can be overcome, with practice and perseverance. The following tips might help:

- **Try to discover the cause of your blockage.** Is it your plot or is it your inner critic? If it's the latter, ignore the voice and keep writing.
- **Recharge your creative battery.** Take a walk in the park and appreciate the beauty of Mother Nature, visit an art museum, or simply spend time with family and friends. Return to your computer feeling refreshed.

- **Look at the scene that has you blocked.** Would a change in POV change things? Would a rewrite? Or is the scene in question even necessary?
- **Put the book away and focus on doing something physical, such as exercise or working in the yard.** Physical activity, especially tasks that you can perform with your brain on autopilot, are an excellent way to work through writers' block.
- **Call up a writer friend and talk through the problem.** Your critique partner may be able to see the solution to your problem when you can't.

Often a few hours away from your computer will be all that is needed to break through a creative blockage. If you find that you suffer frequent bouts with writers' block, however, you may need to re-evaluate your creative process. After all, writing should be fun. If you're finding that the joy of creating is missing from your writing life, take a short break and work at restoring the balance.

Pros and Cons of Reading While Writing

Writers need to replenish their reserves of creativity frequently while writing the first draft of their romance novel, and one of the best ways to do that is by reading the work of other writers. Not only will reading other romances keep you current with the changing marketplace, it can fire your imagination in unexpected ways. Unfortunately, the flip side is that reading romances, particularly those in the same subgenre you're writing in, can have a detrimental effect on your work. For example:

Advantages
- **Reading can keep you motivated.** Whether the book you read is good or bad, it can inspire you to write.
- **Reading new titles can keep you aware of market trends.** This can be especially critical when writing a category romance or in a hot subgenre.
- **Reading debut authors can keep you aware of publisher expectations.** Knowing what grabbed an editor's interest at the publisher you're planning to target can be especially helpful while you write.

- **Reading refills your creative reservoir.** Authors are artists who need to have their creativity batteries frequently recharged; reading is an excellent way of firing up your imagination.

Disadvantages
- **Reading can subconsciously alter your own writing style.** This is especially problematic if it happens during the middle of a book.
- **Reading too much cuts into your writing time.** Writing will probably be a part-time job; spending too much time reading can eat up valuable writing time.
- **Reading in the same subgenre while you're writing could lead to unintended plagiarism.** New writers often find themselves emulating the work of their idols. Reading a new novel by your favorite author could backfire, though, if you find yourself lifting phrases and plot devices and incorporating them into your own.
- **Reading in the same subgenre while you're writing could stifle your creativity.** If you're writing a scene with a talking house pet, for example, and read a similar scene by another author that didn't work, you might be tempted to change, or eliminate, your own scene unnecessarily.

Some authors have no difficulty reading similar works while writing their first drafts; others restrict their reading material to novels outside their particular subgenre. As with all things related to the writing craft, you should choose the method that works best for you.

Learning from Your Mistakes

Writers become better at the craft of writing through practice and repetition. Simply put, this means that to become a better writer, you must write consistently. But more than that, you must learn from the mistakes you make along the way. Reading a completed first draft for your first romance novel will likely fill you with pride . . . and a certain amount of dread. After all, writers are usually their own worst critics. But by completing a first draft, by reading through it and correcting the mistakes, then revising and starting the process over, you will not only grow as a writer, you will find yourself moving steadily closer to your ultimate goal of publication.

CHAPTER 18

Stepping Stones to Publication

You're on your way. Almost ready to send your baby—your manuscript—out into the big world of publishing. Is it ready? Are you ready? It's not a secret that breaking into the publishing business can be hard and scary. But don't worry, this chapter offers you easy-to-follow tips and methods for increasing your self-confidence, strengthening your writing muscles, and helping you prepare to take those final steps toward becoming a published romance writer.

18

A Fresh Pair of Eyes

If you haven't joined a critique group already, now would be the perfect time to find one. Having someone read and proof your work before you send it out to an editor is a must. Not only will you learn from reading and critiquing another person's work, your work will receive a cold read from a peer.

FACT

Just because you don't live close to another writer, don't think that you can't be critique partners. E-mail allows you to partner up with anyone . . . anywhere. With most major word processing software's ability to track changes, online critiquing has become as popular, if not more popular, than meeting at the local coffee shop.

After all, few writers are immune to at least some typos and grammatical mishaps. Having a fresh pair of eyes read your work can catch things you may have missed. (For more information on critique groups, see Chapter 6.)

Help with the Little Things

A critique group can help identify the typos in your romance novel before you ship it off to an agent or editor. Good thing, too, since a manuscript with too many typos and grammar errors will earn a quick rejection. Editors seldom expect perfect copy, but a manuscript filled with too many errors is a sign of sloppy work. If a writer can't get the basics of writing down, an editor is likely to assume the writer's storytelling talent is just as weak and stop reading.

Help with the Bigger Things

Typos and grammatical mistakes aren't the only things a critique partner can shed light on. Typically, writers fall in love with their characters. And just like in real love, when you first find that perfect person who makes your heart beat faster, you don't see your new love's less-than-appealing characteristics. So, as you create your characters, you may be blind to their flaws.

And these negative features can prevent your characters from standing up to hero status.

Yes, it's a must that your characters have flaws, but the reader must fall in love with the character before his negative traits are too apparent. A critique partner can tell you if they are or aren't falling in love with your hero and heroine as fast you would like.

Another blinded-by-love piece of advice: Don't expect someone who thinks you are perfect or someone who would never tell you if you weren't to offer a valid critique. Honesty may hurt at times, but it will hurt more coming from an editor than someone trying to help you improve your manuscript.

Are You Up for Some Competition?

Is your work ready to go to market? How will it stand up against the manuscripts of other romance writers? While most writers don't like to think about their new career as a competition, the truth is that competition is the nature of the publishing business. An editor can receive ten or more manuscripts a day. You need to make sure your work has that something special.

So, how can you know if you've got what it takes? Belonging to a critique group will help tremendously, but sometimes even your critique partners become so close to your books that they can't be objective. When that happens, the answer is simple: Contests.

Writing contests have been popular for decades in the romance publishing industry, but just in the last five years, the number of contests has grown to enormous proportions. Most contests are sponsored by the local, or special interest, chapters of RWA.

QUESTION?

Where can I find information about contests for romance novels?
If you belong to RWA, you will get a monthly magazine that contains a list of upcoming contests. Or, there is the contest Divas Web site (*http://contestdivas.blogspot.com*) where new contests are posted monthly, as well as the results of the contests.

Most contests offer a selection of categories. It's up to you to place your book in the best-suited subgenre (single title, paranormal, historical, romantic suspense, among others.) An entry fee, usually in the $25 range, will normally get you two or more critiques from other writers and an opportunity to get your work in front of an editor if you place in the finals. In most cases, the top three to five scoring entries in every category are sent to an editor or agent to judge.

Each contest has its own rules and guidelines covering everything from the number of pages entered to whether or not a synopsis of the book is required. Not all romance-writing contests are sponsored by RWA chapters but the majority are. Of those that are, many require the entrant to be a member of the national organization. A review of a contest's rules and guidelines will help you decide if the contest is right for you.

The Pros of Entering Contests

Many authors have found contests offer unbiased feedback that has helped them improve their craft. Even better are the stories of authors who sold as a direct result of a contest. This occurs when an editor is impressed with an entry in a contest and requests to see more of the manuscript.

Putting your work out there for someone else to read and comment on can be daunting, especially for the new writer. However, contests offer many benefits, such as:

- The cold reads and critiques of your work can help you get your manuscript ready to submit to publishers.
- Contest finals are a great way to spice up your query letters to editors or agents.
- Contests keep you motivated to write.
- Contests can provide the validation that you are on the right track.
- Contests can get you an agent. (If the final judge is an agent and likes your entry, he or she will ask to see the full manuscript.)
- Contests can get you sold! (One of the authors of this book, Christie Craig, sold four of her manuscripts as a result of a contest.)

Entering contests is a tool that may help you achieve your goal of publication, but it isn't the right tool for everyone, or the only way to get your work where it needs to be. A smart writer will evaluate the best route for her, and make choices depending on her personal situation.

The Contest Lessons

In so many ways, entering a contest mimics the publishing industry's mode of operation. Therefore, entering contests prepares a new writer for what she might expect once she gets closer to the publishing business. For example:

- **The Deadline:** Contests force a writer to have a certain amount of pages polished and mailed by certain dates.
- **The Rejection:** Like it or not, the odds are that you will have to deal with rejection sooner or later. When you don't place in a contest, the rejection is real, just not quite as devastating as a rejection from a publisher.
- **The Patience:** Contests, much like the publishing industry as a whole, consist of a lot of waiting. Some contests take up to six months to announce their winners. Some editors take almost a year to respond to a submission.
- **The Subjectivity:** It is likely that you will get some judges who love your work, and in the same batch of judges, you'll get someone who equally dislikes your work. Editors are just like judges.

ALERT!

Be careful that you don't become addicted to the contest game. While it's questionable if Gamblers Anonymous lists writing contests as one of the things to be aware of, needless to say, it's easy to lose your objectivity when competition is involved with someone's passion. And for most writers, writing is a passion.

The Cons of Entering Contests

Nothing is perfect, and no one who has entered more than a few contests can honestly tell you that there aren't some flaws in the contest circuit. Some of the more common contest woes include:

- **Contests can be addictive.** The validation one receives in contests can become like a drug to desperate authors seeking approval.
- **Contests can be costly.** Some contest addicts have invested thousands of dollars in them over a year's time. Naturally, the amount you spend on contests should depend on your business budget.
- **Contests can lead to an author's loss of focus on her main goal.** Entering contests should be a tool to help achieve publication, but it should never distract from the goal of finishing a manuscript.
- **Contest judges can offer bad advice.** A writer needs to be secure enough in her craft to distinguish bad advice from good.

Make sure you enter your manuscript in the right category of a writing contest. Generally, contest score sheets will have a place where the judge can count the entry down if the work entered is not within the boundaries of the category in which it is placed.

Contests as a Tool

Entering contests is a tool that can help authors, but it isn't the only tool. Writers should not neglect the other avenues available to them, such as querying editors and agents and making face-to-face contact with them at conferences.

As with any type of tool, a writing contest needs to be used correctly to get the best result. Used improperly, contests can be a waste of a writer's time and money. A wise writer will educate herself on how to make contests work best for her.

Only Your Best Work Leaves the House

Reconsider entering a contest in a rush. Take the time to polish and repolish your manuscript before submitting it to a contest, just as you would when submitting to an editor. Because if you become a finalist, that manuscript will be going to an editor or agent. In addition, many writers have missed the finals due to a point or two being taken off because of typos. You are paying for this opportunity, so don't shortchange yourself by not giving it your best shot.

While becoming a finalist in a contest can mean you are on the right track, missing the finals doesn't necessarily mean you aren't. Many published authors have entered contests and never won with the same manuscript that went on to be a bestseller.

Work Hard at Hooking Your Reader

One of the best ways to increase your odds of doing well in a contest is the same method you'd use to increase your odds of getting a "yes" from an agent or editor. Open with a good hook that pulls the contest judge into the manuscript, and then close with an even better hook at the end of the entry that leaves them screaming for more.

Color Inside the Lines

Contest judges tend to be sticklers about the rules of the craft. Bending the rules when it comes to point of view and passive voice will generally get you counted down heavily in contests. While it's okay to bend the rules on purpose, contests are not the best place to enter rule-bending manuscripts.

Judging Those Judges

If you are entering contests mostly for the feedback, perhaps the final judges might not be so important. However, if you are entering for the opportunity to get in front of an editor, then it is wise to make sure the editor judge reading your category is from a publishing house that buys the type of manuscript you're writing.

Probably the most prestigious contest for unpublished romance writers is RWA's Golden Heart Award. While the contest offers little feedback, editors and agents are impressed by the finalist's status. And for good reasons, too. Many finalists go on to sell their manuscripts.

Know How You'll Be Judged

Most RWA chapters post their score sheets for authors wanting to see how their manuscript will be scored. A quick review of the score sheets might help you do some revisions and give you a better chance of making the finals. Some critique groups use the score sheets to score each other's work before entering the contest.

Volunteering to Judge Contests Is a Win/Win

As soon as you feel your knowledge is at a level that you're capable of judging other writers' work, do it. You'll not only be doing this for the good of the chapter or organization that you're volunteering your time to, but the learning gained by judging a contest is a benefit.

Offering even more learning potential than working with a critique group, judging contests is an eye-opening experience. Reading a stranger's work with direct questions on how to score on craft allows an author a clearer view of her own craft mistakes. Things like confusing POV, or too much backstory, are easy to pick up on in someone else's work and can lead to a judge's self-awareness of her own mistakes.

Some contests require their judges to be trained and some even offer online classes to their judges. Others take it upon good faith that if you have offered to judge, then you have enough knowledge in the field of writing to complete the task.

How Do You Know If You're Capable of Judging?

Judges don't have to be published. Generally, contests offer contestants one or more published author judges and others they call experienced writers. But what is considered experienced? You should only judge after you've acquired a certain amount of know-how in critiquing and writing. Remember, you need to understand the basics and what is and isn't acceptable in the genre you are judging. You probably should not judge a contest until you've entered a few and understand how they work from the inside out.

It's Never Too Late to Learn . . .
Or to Learn More

When a marathon runner wins his first race, he doesn't stop his daily practice runs. If he wants to continue to compete, he must continue to work his body and to challenge himself to get better. Just because you understand the basics of writing a novel doesn't mean you can't improve. The more you learn about writing, the more you realize how much there is to know.

FACT

Writing is a form of entertainment and the entertainment industry is constantly in a flux of change. Learning and updating your knowledge of the craft of writing is not only beneficial to getting you published, it will help keep you published. Learning is job security. To paraphrase Deepak Chopra, you don't grow old, you get old when you stop growing. Keep your writing fresh and young by feasting on knowledge.

Go Back to School

Taking writing classes is one way to keep your writing muscles strong. Colleges and continuing education classes generally offer some writing courses. Just because they might not be specific to the romance genre doesn't mean they won't help you with writing. Also, most writing organizations hold conferences where writers at all stages of development can learn from the knowledge of others.

Online Education

The Internet is truly the information superhighway and the online writing courses offered today are endless. Online classes are generally affordable and offered by published writers or experienced teachers. You can usually find one to address your specific problem areas. If you belong to writing organizations or RWA, you will probably find the posting of available classes on your group's loop. Here are three Web sites where you might also find the perfect class to help you improve your craft:

- *www.worldwidelearn.com*
- *www.writingclasses.com*
- *www.writewithus.net*

Create and Give Your Own Course

Perhaps once a month, decide to work on a weak area of your writing. Buy or get from the library a how-to book that covers one specific area of the craft. For example, if you think your characterization is weak, read a book specifically about creating characters. Be your own teacher and assign yourself homework that involves creating characters and character traits.

Joining a Writer's Group

If you haven't yet joined a writer's organization, don't think about it anymore . . . just do it. For most writers who are serious about writing a romance, that means joining RWA (*www.rwanational.org*). Your local chapter will be where you'll meet other writers, find support and possible critique partners, learn more about your craft and the business in general, and be able to share your woes about rejection. The benefits are endless and even more so when you become a part of the group by volunteering. Don't stop looking just because you found RWA, though. Many different multigenre organizations also exist. Most writers find themselves joining a couple of writing groups, including some online guilds. Different clubs may offer different benefits and good writing advice is good writing advice, no matter what genre is being discussed.

Balancing Writing Group Involvement with Writing

While getting together with other writers, volunteering, e-mailing writing buddies, and chatting on the phone is a needed resource for authors, a writer should never lose focus of her goal of writing and completing her novels. Make sure you balance the volunteering and talking about writing with the actual process of writing. Becoming too involved with too many organizations can be harmful to your career. Remember, you joined the organization to become a better writer, not to become a better volunteer.

A good place to find writing organizations is in your own neighborhood—try your libraries, colleges, and bookstores. You may also try doing a Web search for key words like "writing organizations" and the name of your hometown. Don't forget, if you live in a rural area, online chapters of RWA, or other online writing organizations, are always as close as your computer.

Writing in Different Genres

Two mindsets exist on the issue of writing in more than one genre. Some say that to be successful, you need to focus on only one area. In other words, don't go to school to be a brain surgeon and a lawyer at the same time. Or, to put it in writing terms, don't try to become the best suspense writer and the best romantic comedy writer at the same time. The reasoning is that by dividing your time, you are dividing your growth potential and chances of making it. These experts also argue that if the two projects have different tones, a writer can find it difficult to keep them from crossing over and being evident in each manuscript.

Others disagree and say that what you learn from one genre can help you be more successful in the other. With practice, a writer can learn to keep the right tone in the right book. Experts also point out that many writers who hit stumbling blocks and spend days not writing could actually be working on another project. And by working, a writer can reconnect with her creative juices, and return to her other manuscript.

ALERT!

If you are constantly jumping from one project to another without finishing them, you might ask why. Is it that your plots are not holding up? Is it that your characters are not defined enough? Find your problem, and fix it by taking a class or by reading a how-to book instead of automatically jumping into another book where you'll probably face the same issues.

Perhaps each romance author must discover what works best for her. But if you are stuck on one project, consider the idea of working on something different. Try something that will challenge you—something that may recharge your writing batteries.

Reading to Learn

You've already heard that becoming a romance writer is going to change the way you read. But as your skills advance, the opportunity to use reading as a tool grows even stronger. Every book you read is an opportunity to study the writing craft, to study story structure and pacing for particular lines. Reading is even an opportunity to get inside the head of an editor or agent. Don't pass up the advantage of learning from the books you read.

Craft Lessons from Reading

When you read to study craft, be aware of how the writer uses words to create her novel. How does the writer shift point of view without leaving you confused? Look for dialogue tags and study how they work. Notice how much dialogue is on the page compared to narrative. Analyze how the character's backstory is brought in.

Story Structure and Pacing Lessons from Reading

To study story structure, find a book similar to yours in plot—for example, a romantic suspense, or a romantic comedy that is similar to your own style. Then look at the scenes and what is happening in them. Do the hero and heroine meet on page one? Or is this a romantic suspense and the suspense plot is introduced first? Where does the romance start carrying the story?

FACT

Different writers for the same line might approach their plots differently, but there will still be some continuity in the lines. Discover the continuity and your odds of selling to this house will increase.

Compare your pacing of the romance, the level of sexual tension, and the introduction of other plot elements to those published by that particular line. How does your story measure up? Is your book written to fit these lines? Do you need to tweak your novel, or maybe look toward another publisher?

From the Written Page to the Editor's and Agent's Head

Readers have favorite types and tones of books. Some love humor; some would prefer the darker stories. Now, think about agents and editors. They chose their careers because of their love of the written word. But just because they added a title to their nameplate doesn't mean their favorite types of books cease to exist.

When reading a book, try to find out the name of the agent who represented it and the editor who bought it. If you read a book similar in tone to your own book, then it's pretty clear the agent liked the book enough to represent it, and the editor loved it enough to buy it.

When talking to editors or agents at conferences, ask them what type of books they love and what type they are looking to represent or buy. Then, read the books to see if your writing style matches the editor's or agent's taste.

To find out who edited and agented a book, look at the author's acknowledgments page. Some writers mention their editors and agents by name. You might try checking out Publishers Marketplace (*www.publishers marketplace.com*) for a list of the latest romance novel sales, which includes the name of the acquiring editor as well as the author's agent. Another great resource for discovering the name of a writer's agent is Agent Query (*www.agentquery.com*).

CHAPTER 19

The Last Polish

Often, the biggest difference between a published writer and an aspiring writer is their willingness to polish a manuscript before they submit. Many published writers admit that only by completing a book, and setting the story aside for a while, will they know where they went wrong—or where they went right—with their novel. This chapter will help you revisit your manuscript and characters to make sure they are ready to go out into the big publishing world.

Reaching the Finish Line

You've finished your manuscript. Typing "The End" is a big deal because while a lot of people can start a book, not everyone can, or will, finish one. So, congratulations! Celebrate your accomplishment.

But before you say farewell to your cast of characters or place your book in an agent's or editor's hands, take the time to give your book its last polish. Is your prose tight enough, your plot paced fast enough? Are your characters lovable from page one to the end?

It's common for writers to resist rewriting. Some want to believe their words are perfect, and need no revision. Others are tired of the story and want to move on to a new idea. However, the truth is that most authors get the words right, not by writing, but by rewriting. The difference between a rejection and acceptance may depend on your last polish.

The unwillingness to revisit your book, to nip, tuck, and improve what's on the paper is a sign of an amateur. Don't be in a hurry.

Time to Refresh

It's okay to take some time before diving back in to polish. Actually, it's probably best. You will need some distance from your work before you can look at your book and see where it might need tweaking.

QUESTION?

How much time should I be away from my book before doing the last polish?
For some writers, a week away from their work allows them to read with fresh eyes. Others need a month. However long it takes, remember the time is probably worth it. Your ultimate goal is to build a career, not simply to get the manuscript to the agent.

Many writers use the time between books to either plot out a new book or to write a shorter piece in hopes of publishing them so they can beef up their resume. Others take the time to read a how-to book, take an online class, or do some market research about where their work best fits. You don't have to waste the "distancing" time; use it wisely to improve your craft.

Sampling Your Book a Bite at a Time

If someone placed a savory meal in front of you and then asked how it was, you might say, "It was great." But if they asked, "Did you taste the garlic in the potatoes, and were the green beans a bit salty?" You might be tempted to grab the fork and taste the potatoes and then the green beans again.

Polishing your manuscript is like a taste test for an entire meal. You need to focus on one item at a time to really be subjective.

Polishing your book will probably require several reads as you focus on different aspects. If you attempt to do one read-through and look for all possible problematic issues, you may miss something.

By focusing on one or perhaps two aspects at a time as you read and polish your book, you are much more likely to get a real taste of what's right and what might need to be seasoned a little differently.

Cutting Clichés

Clichés are clichés for a reason; they are so commonplace that they create an immediate image for the reader. Clichés are stereotypes or trite phrases or expressions. And writers never want their work to be stereotypical or trite. So, either cutting or putting a new twist on an old cliché is a good idea.

Personalizing a Cliché

A good way to find a replacement for a cliché is to look within your character and personalize the phrase to some aspect of the character's life, career, interest, or experience. See examples following:

Cliché Example One
- **Cliché:** *She looked sweeter than honey.*

- **Personalized Cliché (from the hero's personal experience):** *She looked sweeter and more tempting than the chocolate mousse they'd shared last night.*

Cliché Example Two

- **Cliché:** *Her temper was hotter than fire.*
- **Personalized Cliché (from the hero's career as a firefighter):** *Her temper had the making of a three-alarm fire, and not one that he or any firefighter could survive.*

Putting a New Twist on an Old Cliché

Find a way to tweak an old cliché by either taking it to the next level, or by mixing it up a bit so it reads fresh. See the following examples:

Cliché Example One

- **Cliché:** *Her expression was colder than ice.*
- **Twisted Cliché:** *Her expression should have come stamped with a frostbite warning.*

Cliché Example Two

- **Cliché:** *Ever since she'd walked into his life, he couldn't think straight.*
- **Cliché Taken to the Next Level:** *Ever since she'd walked into his life, he couldn't think, walk, or even pee straight.*

By changing a few words, you can take an old cliché and make it feel fresh, make it something of your very own.

Cookie-Cutter Characters

Characters and character traits can also be clichéd. Think of dumb blondes, doctors who can't write legibly, and engineers who carry around a pocket calculator. It is okay to use some of the common traits—people are sometimes characteristic of their chosen careers, their backgrounds, and ethnic makeup—but make sure your characters are fresh and unique, not carbon copies of what people might expect them to be.

A good book is one in which the characters stay in the minds and hearts of the reader long after the book is finished. Making your characters memorable, perhaps a bit eccentric, will help get you on the bookshelves, and make a place for your book on your reader's keeper shelves.

Make sure each of your characters has something that makes them memorable. Look at habits, obsessions, weaknesses, passions, or hobbies, anything that will make them stand out in a crowd.

Add the Element of Surprise

If the reader can tell you what is going to happen in your story by reading the first few pages of your book, then why should he read on? If everything that happens in your book is predictable, a reader, be it an editor or agent, will grow bored. Shake things up by adding the unexpected.

If, when doing your reads, you discover your book is predictable, look at all your plot points and make a list of ten different things that could happen. The first three may be as predictable as the one you've already written, the last three may be too farfetched, but study those in between. You may find a new twist to give your plot just the excitement it needs.

Did He Really Say That?

Look for those mundane conversations that lack sparkle. How can you add some bling? Can you make a suspenseful scene more suspenseful through dialogue, a humorous scene funnier, or a sexy scene sexier? See the following example:

Without Bling: *As soon as the meeting was over, Jody walked through the restaurant to the booth where Tom waited for her. "Sorry it took so long. Can I buy you a beer to make up for it?"*

Tom glanced up and scooted over at the same time. "It's okay. But a beer would be nice."

With Bling: *As soon as the meeting was over, Jody sashayed through the restaurant to the booth where Tom waited for her. "Hi, sugah," she said, her voice oozing Georgia charm. "Sorry it took so long. How's about I buy you a drink to make up for it?"*

Tom's blue gaze slid over her. "It depends. Are you the type of woman who thinks one drink means I'll be going home with you tonight?"

She blinked. "Do I look like that type?" Then she noticed the corner of his lips turning up in a sexy, crooked smile. That one smile of his had butterflies playing Hide n' Go Seek in her stomach.

He patted the small space on the booth's seat beside him. "A guy could hope."

Use dialogue to make your characters jump off the page and come to life for your readers.

Did She Really Do That?

Your characters react to everything that happens to them in the course of the book. While to some degree, they should respond to the situation "in character," it's wise to remember that in tense situations (which should happen frequently in your book), it is human nature for people to occasionally react and make choices that might seem shocking to others and sometimes even to themselves.

ALERT!

Creating characters means you motivate your characters to react in certain ways in different situations. However, as it is with real life, your characters should sometimes do the unexpected. Having your characters make surprising choices that still fall into the realm of their characterization while raising a reader's eyebrows is one way to keep your reader reading and enjoying your book.

When doing your last polish of your book, look for character responses to stressful situations. Have you taken full advantage of your character's reactions? Do their responses sometimes give the reader an unexpected surprise or insight into their characters?

Amputating Dead Scenes

Nothing will slow your story down more, or lead to a rejection faster, than pages that don't move your plot forward. Read your book and look for scenes that weigh your story down. Sometimes these scenes can be disguised with lots of beautiful words, humorous dialogue, and cute anecdotes, but the fact is they offer no new information to the reader. Below is a list of other indicators of scenes that may need to be cut:

- A scene containing mostly repeated information
- A scene lacking conflict
- A scene whose sole purpose is to set something up
- A scene lacking a goal
- A scene that doesn't encourage the reader to turn the page

A good book to help you decipher lagging scenes and help you pace your fiction is *Scene & Structure* by Jack M. Bickham. Bickham gives excellent advice on crafting compelling scenes that keeps your readers reading from the beginning to the end.

Another way to help master the art of scene amputation is to rent/buy movies where you have the added bonus of being able to watch the scenes that were cut from the movie. One great example is the movie *Love, Actually*. Over an hour of scenes were cut from the movie's original version. By watching those scenes, you will see that while some of the scenes were cute and funny, they were not needed for the movie to work. After all, it takes more than being cute and funny to move the story forward.

Step Up the Pace

In addition to scenes that require amputation, you may find some scenes that just need a little more get up and go. Scenes can lag due to some extra weight or the wrong focus. Look at your sluggish scenes to see what shouldn't be there and check if the focus of the scene is on target. Following is a list of reasons your scenes may not be moving along at the right pace:

- Too much casual chitchat
- Too much description and narrative and not enough action
- Not enough emphasis on the scene goal
- Not enough conflict to create interest
- A scene written in the wrong point of view

By removing the extra weight from the scene and adding significance to what matters most, you will have your scene moving at the pace your readers crave.

Get Rid of Passive Voice

Sometimes what slows your scenes down isn't so much the amount of description or narrative, but the manner in which those words are written. Passive voice can be the culprit in bad pacing. Look for an overabundance of the verb *was*, or the "to be" verbs.

Another sign of passive voice is telling instead of showing. For a quick review on what passive voice is and how to pinpoint telling versus showing, refer to Chapter 7.

Remove the Fluff

There's also a chance it's not what's on the page, but how many words you took to get the idea across. Tight writing makes for a faster read. Below is a list of words that could be weighing down your sentences, and examples of how they are used and could be removed.

Example	Weightier	Tighter
That	He told her that he wanted to go.	He told her he wanted to go.
Up, down, over	His gaze slipped down from her eyes and over to her lips.	His gaze slipped from her eyes to her lips.
Very	He knew she was very happy to see him.	He knew she was thrilled to see him.
Suddenly/almost	She suddenly blinked and her expression changed.	She blinked and her expression changed.

To say these words shouldn't appear in your manuscript is wrong. All words serve a purpose. It's when your manuscript is peppered with them that they add unnecessary weight to your story.

Remove the Purple from Your Prose

There's nothing wrong with beautifully written, descriptive passages. But sometimes a little goes a long way. Are you overdescribing something? Are the visuals you're creating important to the story? Does the description enhance the mood or add something to the story other than just being beautiful? If the answer is no, then cut back on the adjectives and focus on what is important. You may also find adverbs that can be removed and replaced with stronger verbs. This isn't to say all adverbs should be sent packing, but when used in excess, they could be hindering your pacing.

Tie Up Loose Ends

A writer's job is to pose questions so the reader reads on to discover the answers. Sometimes writers pose so many questions that when they get to the end of the book they accidentally forget to answer all of them.

FACT

Books that are written as series will often pose some questions to be answered in an upcoming book. However, even in a series, each book has a set of plot problems and issues that must be tied up within the course of that novel.

Look at all the internal and external problems you gave your main and secondary characters. Have you solved all their issues? Were there two people who had a misunderstanding during the course of the story? Did you resolve that issue? This doesn't mean everything needs to be tied up with a perfect bow, but the characters need to come to some sort of a conclusion.

Have you had a character ponder a question or even search for a lost item? Amazingly, when readers close your book, they will expect your character's curiosity to have been sated, and either that lost item to have been found, or the character to have accepted it as lost forever.

Reassess Your Characters

Have you created characters your readers will fall in love with? Are their flaws forgivable and the motivations behind those flaws clearly stated on the written page? Because writers' characters are sometimes like their children, it's easy for writers to love their story people in spite of their downfalls.

If you find your heroes or your heroines behaving inappropriately, make sure you have balanced their good qualities with their flaws and that you have written the motivation behind their less-than-favorable qualities.

In many cases, it isn't so much the author's blind love that is the problem, but a writer's inability to get the character's internal makeup on the page. In other words, an author knows why his characters behave the way they do, but he hasn't spelled that out for the reader. So, in that final polish, make sure your reader has insight into what is really making your characters tick.

Add Emotion

When polishing your final draft, look for at least one way in each scene to add more emotion. If the scene is tense . . . make it more tense. If the scene is funny . . . make it funnier. Find the main emotional focus in each scene and up the ante in some way.

Readers read romance looking for the emotional connection and to relive the wonder of falling in love. Help make your manuscript rejection-proof by making sure each chapter, each scene, and each page of your book is rich with emotion.

In tense scenes, turn the conflict up a notch, give the antagonist the most power, or figure out another way to push the heroine to work harder to accomplish her goal. Find a way to remind the reader what it is the hero has to lose if he fails at his scene goal. Pay close attention to the sentence structure in tense scenes to help build the tension.

If your scene is sad, dig deeper and pull tighter on the heartstrings of your reader. The more you allow your reader to see and feel the pain of the characters, the more emotionally involved they become in your book.

In humorous scenes, toy with your word choices to see if you can tap the funny bone a little harder. Look for a play on words that could induce a chuckle. Ask yourself what your hero or heroine could say that would be so unanticipated that it would cause the reader to laugh. Remember the secret to humor is surprise—the reader expects to read one thing and instead you give her something completely different.

The scenes in which the emotion should really be the strongest are in the love scenes. Love, and being able to experience all the emotions connected with falling in love, are the reasons your reader picked up a romance novel. Readers want to feel the desire, the tenderness, and the longing induced by meeting that right person.

POV really is the key to writing a good novel of any kind, romance included. To maximize the emotional quotient of your scenes, make sure they're written from the POV of the right character.

While not all romances will have the same level of sexuality, most will have sexual tension. Make sure you build the level of sensuality in your novels to meet the standards of the subgenre you are targeting.

Most important, remember that you are writing a romance. Allow the reader to experience the journey, the excitement, the wonder, the temptations, and the fears that come with falling in love.

CHAPTER 20

Submitting Your Work

Congratulations! You've completed your romance novel and you're now ready to submit your work. To get started, you'll also need to write a synopsis, or a short description of your book that will give an editor or agent a clear, concise outline of your story. Plus, you'll need a marketing plan—who to contact, in what order, and what to start working on while you wait. Are you ready to begin?

20

Formatting Your Manuscript

One of the most commonly asked questions of publishing professionals at writer conferences concerns proper manuscript formatting. Debates have waged for years—both online and offline—about the "proper" font to use and how to calculate word count for a manuscript. While it's true that some publishers have house guidelines that specify the font to be used, most publishers don't care as long as the copy is legible and easy to read. What counts most is good writing.

That said, the following guidelines should ensure that your manuscript looks professional:

- One-inch margins for top, bottom, right, and left of the manuscript page
- Header on the first page of your manuscript with your name, address, phone, e-mail address, manuscript title, word count, and genre/subgenre information
- Header on all subsequent pages with the name of the manuscript in caps on the left, your last name and the page number on the right
- Easy-to-read 12-point font, such as Courier, New Courier, or Times New Roman
- Each chapter begins one-third of the way down a new page

If you are printing out a hard copy of your manuscript, use a good quality, 20-pound, white, 8" × 11" type of paper. (Office supply stores generally refer to it as standard copy paper.)

Many writers use Microsoft Word as their word processing program of choice, although any fully functional program will suit your needs. Many agents and editors now accept manuscripts via e-mail attachment. If so, they will advise the specific format that your manuscript should be in, such as Rich Text Format (RTF).

Researching Markets and Agents

Remember when you researched the market before you started work on your romance novel? Well, it's time to research it again. This time, you'll want to make sure that your targeted publishers are still acquiring your particular subgenre of romance and how to submit to them. (After all, a lot can happen in the publishing industry in the months it's taken you to finish your novel.) You'll also need to compile a list of literary agents if your intended publisher only accepts agented submissions.

Deciding whether to target agents or publishers is a tough call, even for a seasoned pro. However, if you're planning to use a literary agent, it's best to target an agent first before submitting to the publisher. Then, if your agent hunt is unsuccessful, and you feel your work is appropriate for a particular publisher who is open to unagented submissions, contact the publishers yourself.

When verifying the status of a previously researched publisher, pay close attention to the following two details:

1. **Editorial staff changes:** When editors change houses, it can often signify changes in editorial policies.
2. **Submission policy changes:** Always double-check the specifics of how to submit your work to a publisher.

The best way to research a publisher's submission policies is to check with their Web site. Using the Market Update section of the Members section of the Romance Writers of America Web site (*www.rwanational.org*) will also provide you with the current status of an RWA-eligible romance publisher.

ALERT!

Beware of agents who charge a reading fee or an upfront charge for anticipated mailing costs, manuscript preparation fees, etc. Reputable agents never charge fees for reading your manuscript. While many agencies do charge an annual fee for office expenses, such as photocopying and mailing, those fees are rarely charged up front.

You can research agents in much the same way, although the type of information you will want to acquire for a literary agent is often different. True, you will want to make certain that the agent handles work similar to yours and is open to new submissions, as well as the proper way to contact the agent, i.e., sending an e-mail query, sending a partial along with a cover letter, etc. You'll also need to make sure they have an established track record in your particular genre and adhere to the guidelines of the Association of Author Representatives (*www.aar-online.org*).

How to Start Your Agent Hunt

Generally, the best place to start your agent hunt is on the Internet. Great resources such as Agent Query (*www.agentquery.com*) and Publishers' Marketplace (*www.publishersmarketplace.com*) contain an active database of literary agents—their names, their contact information, the type of work they represent, the number of years they've been in business, and how to submit to them. An advantage of using the online database searches is that you can search by an author's name and find the name of the literary agent who brokered the author's last book contract.

Generally, you will want to find an agent who has experience—either as an intern to an established literary agency or as an editor for a publishing house, for example. For an agent to be successful at her job, she will need professional contacts at several major publishing houses. Most of all, however, she will need to have a genuine passion for your work.

Ten Questions to Ask a Prospective Agent

Often, new writers will jump with joy when a literary agent—any literary agent—offers representation. While it's true that having an agent is often a career necessity, especially in the single-title romance market, you should handle the selection of an agent with the same care and consideration you would when considering a prospective mate. After all, having a bad agent is far worse than having no agent at all.

Many agents will request an exclusive when reading the work of a prospective client, which means that the author agrees not to submit her work to another agent until the first agent has had a chance to respond. Generally, exclusives benefit the agent, rather than the author. However, if the agent requesting the exclusive is your first choice, it might be beneficial to agree, especially if the agreed-upon time is fairly short (say, two to three weeks).

When looking for an agent, consider signing with a new agent at a large established agency. New agents usually don't have large lists of authors to represent and can give a new author more attention, while being part of an established agency affords the agent, and author, access to resources not usually found with a smaller agency.

To help you make the best choice of literary representation, ask a prospective agent the following questions:

1. **Does the agent require a signed agent-author agreement?** Some agents have signed contracts that spell out the exact role that each will play in the partnership; others have a verbal agreement. If the agent has an agency contract, ask for a copy ahead of time and review it carefully. Also ask to see a copy of the agency clause they will place in the publishing contract.
2. **How does the agent prefer to keep authors informed of submissions?** Some agents forward e-mails and hard copies of correspondence; others don't. Find out what your prospective agent's policy is and make sure that you will be comfortable with it.
3. **What happens in the event of the agent's death or incapacitation?** If the agent has an agency contract, this will usually be covered. If there is no signed contract, verify that the agent has provisions for protecting the rights of her authors in the event of the unthinkable.
4. **How many authors does the agent and agency represent?** If the agency is a one-person operation, the agent won't be able to handle as many clients as another agent in a large multiagent office. Some authors feel they need more handholding, while others do not.
5. **Does the agent offer editorial feedback?** Some authors enjoy having an agent critique their manuscript before submission; others do not. Knowing how your prospective agent works ahead of time can save you both unnecessary headaches.

6. **Does the agent offer career planning?** Some agents become actively involved in planning an author's long-term career goals while others focus more on a book-to-book sale. Make sure the agent you choose is right for you.

7. **Does the agent handle sub-rights, ancillary rights, and/or movie rights?** Each of these rights is usually negotiated separately in a publishing contract. While smaller agencies rarely handle the sale of these rights themselves, they will usually have other agency contacts who can handle them, rather than rely upon the publisher to exploit them.

8. **What novels has the agent or agency sold in the past year?** Before you sign with an agent, make sure she or her agency has a track record of legitimate sales.

9. **What is the agent's normal turnaround time for responding to e-mails and phone calls?** Busy agents usually handle routine correspondence in twenty-four to forty-eight hours, although some may have longer turnaround times.

10. **How can the agent-author contract be severed?** Agents and authors part company for a variety of reasons. Knowing what the procedure is for severing a relationship ahead of time can save you both a lot of anxiety and frustration later.

With the exception of question number 8, there is no right or wrong answer to these questions. The purpose in asking them is to give you the information you need to make an informed decision. After all, knowing how a prospective agent works, knowing her expectations for your working relationship in advance of agreeing to work together, is the best way to avoid a nasty breakup later.

QUESTION?

Who is the perfect agent and how do I find one?
The perfect agent varies from author to author. In fact, the agent that one author considers to be perfect for her may very well be the same agent another author fires for incompatibility. To find your perfect match, look for an agent who believes in your work, who loves your voice, and whose vision for your future matches your own.

With your list of prospective agents, and publishers in hand, you're ready to begin the submission process. First up: Writing the query letter.

The Query Letter

A query letter is a short, single-spaced, one-page letter that pitches your romance novel to a prospective agent or editor. Basically, it's a sales letter. Rather than a life insurance policy or a new computer system, the product you're trying to sell is your novel . . . and you, the author.

The Basic Elements of a Good Query

Some authors write queries in the same tone or style as their novel. In other words, if their book is funny, their query letter will be funny. Other authors are more comfortable with writing a business-letter type of query. Generally, the best approach for you is the one that feels most comfortable for you.

That said, a good query letter should have the following elements:

- The correct name and title of the addressee
- A strong hook for your novel
- A brief description of the book's main characters and conflict
- The book's title, word count, and subgenre
- Your publishing credentials, if any
- Your name and contact info (usually in your letterhead or signature block)
- SASE (Self-Addressed Stamped Envelope for their reply)

Agents and editors see thousands of query letters each year. What they want to see—actually, *all* they want to see—in a query letter is a well-written sales pitch that tells them what your book is about so they can judge its marketability.

If you're a new writer, you probably won't have writing credits to include in the paragraph about your publishing credentials. Instead, mention your membership in writing organizations, such as Romance Writers of America, any writing workshops or classes you may have taken or awards you may have won from unpublished writing contests. All of these prove your commitment to the craft of writing.

For more information about what to include—and how to obtain—publishing credentials for your query letter, refer to Chapter 22.

A Sample Query Letter

Assume that you've written a single-title romantic comedy that you want to pitch to an agent. The text of your query letter might read as follows:

Career-focused Melissa Wesson has the perfect job, the perfect boyfriend, and the perfect life in It's Vegas, Baby, *my 100,000-word romantic comedy. Or, at least that's what Melissa thinks until a routine three-day business trip to Las Vegas ends in murder, mayhem, and marriage to another man. Melissa's world is turned upside down, and she can't decide if she's more upset about her boyfriend dumping her via Text Message, the dead body of a casino pit boss turning up in her bathroom, or her quickie wedding to Derek Kincaid, the single, most infuriating man on the planet. And then there are those police detectives who want to question her about the dead body, along with the trio of wiseguys and an angry casino owner who are all on the lookout for a missing fortune in casino chips.*

For laidback Derek, a commitment-phobic bachelor, the quickie marriage—a necessary move on their part to get them out of a tight spot with the wiseguys—is potentially more problematic than the murder rap, the wiseguys, and the angry casino owner combined. After all, marriage is the last thing on his mind, especially with someone who micromanages every minute of her life the way Melissa does. So why can't he keep his hands off her oh-so-sexy body? And more important, why does the idea of an equally quick annulment keep getting harder and harder for him to accept?

I am an active member of my local RWA chapter and my work has finaled in several RWA-sponsored contests, including the Golden Heart. I would be happy to send you the first three chapters and synopsis of It's Vegas, Baby *for your review. An SASE is enclosed for your convenience.*

Some writers prefer to open their query letters with a more straightforward pitch, followed by the plot description, such as:

I am interested in securing representation for my 100,000-word romantic comedy It's Vegas, Baby. *Your Web site states that you represent novels of this type, and since I am a fan of your client, Betty Bestseller, I am contacting you.*

The specific approach you use isn't as important as making certain that your query letter contains all of the things the agent or editor will need to know about your romance novel before she can make a decision about requesting to read your manuscript.

Writing a Synopsis

As previously stated, most agents and editors will request that an author submit a proposal, which is the first three consecutive chapters of their manuscript along with a synopsis. A synopsis is a summary of your novel. It is written in present tense using the same style and tone as your novel, and it explains the main characters, their conflict, the plot, and its resolution. In essence, a synopsis describes your book from first hook to HEA (Happily Ever After).

A great resource for writing a synopsis is *Give 'Em What They Want: The Right Way to Pitch Your Novel to Editors and Agents, a Novelist's Complete Guide to: Query Letters, Synopses, Outlines* by Blythe Camenson and Marshal J. Cook. Novelists Camenson and Cook offer practical advice on writing query letters and synopses and provide lots of examples of each in their book.

There are two basic types of a synopsis: the short synopsis, and the detailed synopsis. A short synopsis is usually one to two pages in length, while a detailed synopsis can be five to ten pages long. (A good rule of thumb for writing a detailed synopsis is to include one page for every 10,000 words of your novel.) Often, an editor or agent will specify the length of the synopsis you should submit; always follow the instructions of the agent or editor when submitting your manuscript.

Sometimes an agent or editor will use the term "outline" when referring to a synopsis. In nonfiction, an "outline" refers to a detailed synopsis that breaks the book down chapter by chapter. However, when most agents or editors ask for an "outline" of a romance novel, they are usually referring to a detailed synopsis, unless they specify "outline by chapter."

Some authors write their synopses single-spaced while others prefer a double-spaced synopsis. Also, some synopses will start with brief character sketches and then move into the narrative of the story, while other writers prefer to keep their synopsis in narrative form throughout. Either method can work. Just as with the length of your synopsis, the method you should use is the one requested by the particular editor or agent. If none is specified, go with double-spaced and all narrative. The formatting should be the same as for your manuscript; that is one-inch margins on all sides with a header on each page that contains your name, the title of your book, and the page number. Use a standard, good-quality white copy paper if printing a hard copy.

Regardless of synopsis length or format, a good synopsis should focus on the following information:

- The hook
- The hero and heroine and their emotional response to each other
- Their conflicts—internal, external, and romantic
- The novel's main plot points
- The resolution of the conflicts and the HEA

Depending upon the length of your synopsis and the complexity of your novel, a brief one- or two-line description of the following elements is also recommended:

- Secondary characters and their purpose in the story
- Subplots and their purpose in the story

Keep extraneous information to a minimum. Ideally, a synopsis should focus on the main plot points, the main characters, their feelings, and the development and resolution of their internal, external, and romantic conflicts.

ALERT!

To avoid a fast rejection, make sure your synopsis doesn't skimp when it comes to the romance between your main characters. Remember that the more emphasis you place on secondary characters and subplots, the more attention the agent or editor will assume you've paid to those elements in the novel itself. Keep the focus firmly placed on the romance.

Last but certainly not least, make sure your complete contact information is printed on your synopsis. Generally, the first page should contain your name, address, phone number, and e-mail address, along with the title of your book, its projected word count, and subgenre.

To read examples of a short synopsis and a detailed synopsis, visit the coauthors' Web site, Write with Us (*www.writewithus.net*).

Tips for Preparing a Great Partial

What makes for a great partial? Generally, it's a well-written synopsis and a dynamite first three chapters (or approximately the first fifty pages of your novel) that leave the reader—in this case, the editor or agent—wanting to read more of your romance. More specifically, however, a great partial should include the items specifically requested by the editor or agent and showcase your work in its best light. The following checklist can help:

Checklist for a Great Partial

❒ Did you follow the agent's or editor's instructions about what to send?

❒ Did you address your envelope correctly and reference that your material was requested in the cover letter? (Assuming it was requested, of course.)

❒ Are your synopsis, chapters, and cover letter free of grammatical and spelling errors?

❒ Does your first chapter open with a hook?

❒ Does your last chapter end with an even bigger hook?

❒ Did you include an SASE?

❒ Is your contact information printed on the first page of your synopsis and sample chapters?

As you read in previous chapters, it's important to end each scene and chapter with a hook, or a compelling reason for the reader to keep turning the pages. This advice is especially true when submitting a partial to an editor or agent.

Developing Your Marketing Plan

Achieving success at finding an agent or publisher requires a good marketing plan. For many people, the words "marketing plan" bring to mind images of accountants, stacks of paperwork, and hours of research. Luckily, a marketing plan for achieving representation and/or publication doesn't have to be that detailed or intimidating. It just has to help you keep track of where you're submitting, in what order, and the status of each.

Many new authors hesitate to submit their manuscripts to more than one editor at a time, especially when the submission instructions for a publisher clearly state "no simultaneous submissions." But those rules don't apply when searching for a literary agent. In fact, most agents generally assume that they are not the only agent considering a submission. Therefore, feel free to query away!

Generally, when you are submitting queries, you should start with your "dream list"—the agents or editors you most feel your work fits best. Then, keep track of your submissions in a spreadsheet, noting the date submitted and the items submitted. (Using delivery confirmation from the post office will confirm delivery of your submission at the publisher or literary agent.) Always know where your manuscript is—whether full or partial—and have your queries ready to submit to the next group, should a rejection arrive.

The Waiting Game

Once you've sent off your manuscript to an editor or agent, you will likely have a long wait ahead of you. How long is "long"? Well, that depends on the agent and the publisher. Some editors and agents respond to queries quickly, especially if they are sent via e-mail. Others may take several weeks to answer their mail. The turnaround time for an actual submission, however, is usually much longer.

If an editor has had your manuscript for several months, don't assume you're heading for a rejection. Some editors have a tremendous backlog of material and take longer to read their submissions than others. In fact, it's not uncommon for an author to sell a manuscript that has been sitting on an editor's desk for a year or longer!

While waiting to hear back from the editor or agent, make good use of your time. Fine-tune your marketing plan for your novel. Have any new markets opened since you began your submission process? Are there any new agents looking for new authors in your subgenre? If so, add them to your list for a future submission.

Better yet, start work on a new romance novel. Nothing can help you pass the time while you wait for a response from an editor or agent than diving into a new book.

CHAPTER 21

Rejecting Rejection

Rejection really isn't a dirty word. No, it doesn't roll off the tongue with a lot of pleasure, and no author likes hearing it, but don't fool yourself: Sooner or later, every writer deals with some form of rejection. A successful writer not only accepts rejection, she uses it to further her career, and ultimately she overcomes it. In this chapter, you'll find tips on how to accept, grow from, and ultimately reject rejection.

The Truth about Rejection

To be a successful romance novelist, you'll need to bank on certain skills and talents. However, for a writer, more important than the art of storytelling, more important than the knack of plotting, is the needed skill of perseverance. To persevere in this business, you'll have to learn to face rejection. It is, unfortunately, a part of the writing profession.

In fact, rejection is such a part of the business, that to arrive at PRO status (a level above general membership designed for writers who are seeking publication) within the organization of Romance Writers of America, you must be unpublished and have submitted one completed manuscript, which was most likely rejected.

FACT

Successful western novelist Louis L'Amour sold countless books over the years. Many of his works have even been made into movies, like *The Quick and the Dead.* However, his stories earned him more than 300 rejections before he ever sold a book.

Yes, you've all heard the success stories of writers sending out their very first book and receiving an acceptance letter with a huge advance check attached by return mail. It happens.

Really.

Okay, the advance check will probably not be attached, but some writers have actually sold their first book without ever tasting the bitterness of rejection. However, for every writer who got to walk the red carpet without first having the door slammed in her face, there are thousands of others who have confronted, been knocked around, beaten up, and abused by, and then ultimately triumphed over rejection.

The number-one truth about rejection is that it happens. The number-two truth about rejection is that it doesn't kill you. And you know what they say, "What doesn't kill you makes you stronger." The third all-important truth about rejection is that a rejection doesn't always speak of the quality or the publishability of the work.

Just because a manuscript is rejected by one or more editors doesn't mean the work will not go on to sell. Consider the ever-popular John Grisham. Did you know that the first manuscript he wrote, *A Time to Kill,* was rejected forty-five times before it was accepted?

Receiving a rejection may feel like the end of your world and especially like the end of your career. But honestly, it is only the end if you decide to make it the end. When most writers give up writing, it's not because they lack talent. It's because they lack the ability to deal with the rejection. Hold on to your perseverance.

No Pain, No Gain

It's an ugly little saying, but where writing and rejection are concerned, there is a lot of truth to it. If you get a rejection and it simply doesn't hurt, then there's a good chance your heart and soul weren't in the manuscript you sent out. And without heart and soul, a manuscript is doomed to fail.

Don't ever mail an editor an ugly response to a rejection. No matter how personal that rejection might feel, understand that the editor didn't mean it personally. Writing is a business. The editor was simply doing her job by making a business decision based upon her subjective opinion.

Your stories become a part of you. They are your creations. In essence, they are your children. And a rejection is the same as if someone calls your baby ugly. It hurts. So if pain is part of the process, how do writers prevent the pain from stifling their creative process?

Surviving the Sting

The first step to surviving rejection is to understand you are among good company. Stephen King, Dr. Seuss, and Mary Higgins Clark all have confronted the ugly beast and won. Unfortunately, there isn't a sure-bet cure for rejection pain. Every writer must find her own way of dealing with the "they-didn't-buy-my-book" blues. Here are several ways to survive the sting:

- Do admit it hurts. Denial isn't going to work.
- Do allow yourself time to rejuvenate. Take an hour, even a day off, but never more than a week. You don't want to fall out of the habit of writing.
- Do nurture your artist. Read a good book, take a walk, or eat some chocolate. TLC is a good thing, but don't wallow in self-pity.
- Do share your news and heartache with close friends, especially other writers whom you know will understand and offer you motivation.
- Do, if you must, sit down and write the editor a rebuttal letter and then tear that letter to shreds and flush it down the toilet. The only reply to a rejection from you should be a thank-you to the editor for giving you her time.
- Do remember that just because the work wasn't right for that editor or that house at that moment doesn't mean it won't be right for another. Also, just because it isn't ready for publication now doesn't mean you can't make it publishable.
- Do get busy on another project. Nothing can soothe the pain of rejection more than excitement over a new project.

A writer not being able to deal with rejection is almost like a doctor not being able to deal with death. But with some armor and understanding, you can, like thousands of others before you, find ways to survive the sting.

Deciphering Rejection

Rejections come in many variations. Personal rejections, form rejections, and then there's the mix between the personal and the form. Every editor may send different types of rejections, and those types will vary depending on her workload, and her feelings about that work. Let's not forget, editors are prone to headaches, bad-hair days, and PMS, just like everyone else. Therefore, it's very possible that the type of rejection you receive could be due to her mood.

Because rejections come in so many variations, and because just receiving a rejection can be an emotional experience, writers often have a hard time deciphering exactly why their manuscript was turned down.

Editors are human and their reaction to your work could be based strictly on a personal preference. If an editor doesn't care for alpha heroes and your hero is alpha, then it's very likely she might reject your work based on her personal taste and not the merits of your work.

Personal Rejection

While no one wants to be rejected personally, in the writing business, the personal rejection is always the best. Personal rejections mean the editor is responding directly to you concerning your writing and novel.

Yes, comments directed specifically at your writing may sting more than the nonspecific comments of a form rejection, but it is only by understanding why your work was turned down that you can attempt to correct the problem. Below is an example of a personal rejection:

Dear Mrs. Smith:

Thank you for allowing me to read TEMPTED. There was a lot to love about this project: great, snappy dialogue, and good humor, and I especially liked the sexual tension seen in scenes such as the first kiss. However, ultimately, I found the hero unsympathetic, the plot a bit contrived, and the story just didn't work for us. Sorry to disappoint.

Sincerely,
Ms. Editor

A personal rejection may hurt more, but editors seldom take the time to write critiques unless they feel their constructive comments could actually help a writer who has creative talent. Reading the editor's remarks and giving them some thought is always wise.

Form Rejection

Just because you get a form rejection doesn't necessarily mean that the manuscript has no merit. Editors, due to time restraints, may have to rely on form rejections. However, it's easy to understand why some writers question if the editor even read the manuscript when they receive vague responses. Here is an example of a form rejection:

Dear Writer:

I'm sorry, but your manuscript does not meet our needs. Please forgive this form rejection; however, due to the numerous manuscripts we receive, our time is in short supply.

Thank you for considering us.

Sincerely,

Ms. Editor

Not even form rejections are a reason to give up writing. After all, many of today's classics received their share of no's, before receiving the final yes. Thirty-eight times, publishers turned down Margaret Mitchell's *Gone with the Wind.* They knew a good story when they saw one. Or did they?

The Form/Personal Mix Rejection

The mix letter will have your name, perhaps the title of your manuscript, but all comments are so vague they could be rejecting any of a dozen manuscripts. Often, a mix rejection will come with a handwritten note at the bottom saying something along the lines of "Author shows talent but needs to work on craft." Here is an example of the mix rejection:

Dear Ms. Smith:

I've read your manuscript, TEMPTED, with interest, but I'm afraid it just didn't stand out enough for us to consider it. The number of manuscripts we receive precludes us from offering more detailed reasons for rejecting the works that land on our desks.

Thank you for allowing us to consider your work.

Sincerely,

Ms. Editor

Should you send a thank-you note to an editor for a rejection letter? While form rejections may not meet the criteria of a thank-you note, some personal rejection letters where the editor took a lot of time to make comments do seem appropriate. Plus, the more times you can get your name in front of the editor in a positive way, the more receptive she might be to read your next manuscript.

Rejection Letter Versus Revision Letter

New writers often confuse a rejection letter with a revision letter. At first glance, a revision letter can appear very much like a personal rejection letter. They may start by pointing out the positives of the writing, and then go into detail about what the editor feels was wrong with the manuscript.

Generally, in the revision letter, an editor will write: *If you would like to address these changes and resubmit the work to me, I'd be happy to review it again.* However, it's not unheard of for an editor to overlook adding that one line. Other times you might read a line such as: *As is, this manuscript will not work for us.* The "as is" basically means that if some things were changed, the book might work for them.

If you get an exceptionally detailed letter from an editor suggesting changes to your manuscript, and praising you for some aspects of your writing, you may want to write the editor a thank-you note and ask if she would consider reviewing the manuscript again after you've made the changes she recommended.

Revision letters are a good thing. When an editor makes suggestions for a book and requests the work be resubmitted, it means he or she thinks your manuscript just misses the submission requirements. While a request to review a book again is in no way a guarantee of a sale, it is a sign that you are close.

Learning from Rejection

There is a reason writing and selling your first book is compared to giving birth. They both seem to take way too long and they each involve some pain. However, in the end, when a mother holds her new baby, she will likely tell you that the end result was worth the labor pains. Writers holding their first book in their hands say the same about the pain of rejection they encountered in their struggle to get published.

One of the best pieces of advice on learning from rejection is to put the rejection away, wait until the emotional blow is over, and reread it with a clear head. Try to find the constructive criticism in the letter and then ask yourself if perhaps some changes are in order.

Being able to deal with rejection is essential to all writers. However, smart writers not only continue writing in spite of the rejection, they use it to help further their career. In other words, they learn from rejection.

While it's been pointed out in this chapter that not all rejections are a good indication of the quality of your work, if you get one or more rejections that point out the same weak areas in your story, or your writing, then it is wise to listen.

For example, if you get a couple of responses from editors saying your characters aren't sympathetic, then do a refresher course on characterization and what makes characters likeable. If pacing is mentioned in your rejections, set out to study how you can improve your pacing.

Perhaps you've only gotten one rejection, but the editor mentioned some issues that your critique partners have brought up as possibly being problematic. Or, perhaps a contest judge mentioned those same issues in her critique. Or maybe, deep down, you knew you needed to work on that area. However you may have reached the conclusion, you've come to the realization that it's time to put your pride aside and admit you need to polish your manuscript and hone your craft.

Monitor Your Reactions to Criticism

A proper reaction to feedback and criticism of your writing—be it from an editor, agent, or critique partner—is important if you are going to learn from rejection. It's human nature and not altogether a bad thing to defend yourself. That said, because writing is such a subjective business, you may want to monitor and be aware of how you react to criticism.

If you are unwilling to even consider the possibility of making changes, the problem might not only be with your manuscript, it might be with your willingness to learn as well. You may be repeating the same mistakes and may be unwilling to see the error of your ways.

Equally unproductive is the writer who, after getting feedback, immediately makes revisions without really considering them or believing in them. What happens then is that the writer no longer understands her own story and either loses enthusiasm for the work or there is a lack of continuity to the work.

FACT

While it may never be wise to refuse to comply with an editor's revisions, especially in the beginning of the working relationship, most editors understand that for revisions to work, the writer must be able to understand and believe in the suggested changes.

The best response to negative feedback is to listen and consider it before forming an opinion. You may need to put the rejection or the critique away and come back to it later. However, if the revision recommendation came from an editor, don't wait too long. You don't want that editor to lose enthusiasm over your work—or even worse, to have left the publishing house.

When It's Not the Writing

Often, rejections may be so vague that the reasons your work had been returned aren't even clear. It will be up to you to read between the lines. Being creative people, many writers start inventing all sorts of problems. "I can't plot." "I'm terrible at characterization." Or even, "I shouldn't be allowed to write a grocery list." Before you start tearing yourself apart, remember there are many reasons a manuscript could have been rejected that have nothing to do with your skills as a writer.

It might not be your writing. It could be your marketing.

While most writers only want to write, to create wonderful stories, if you don't have an agent, you will need to hone your skills as a market specialist.

Good Book, Wrong Publisher

If you've received a rejection or several rejections from the same or similar publishing houses stating, *Sorry, this book isn't right for us,* perhaps this isn't just an easy way of saying no. Maybe you have targeted the wrong publisher, or type of publisher, for your book. Editors say that one of the most common reasons for rejection is that the work simply doesn't meet their guidelines.

Make sure the type of book you are submitting fits the publisher's requirements. For example, if you are writing historicals, make sure that this publisher buys manuscripts in your time period.

Good Book, Wrong Editor

If you read your personal rejections carefully, you may learn which editors seem to like your voice and the type of plots you write. You will also be able to tell which editors aren't so crazy about your voice. Once you find an editor who likes your style, don't hesitate to submit your next book to her. Finding an editor who likes your writing voice is half the battle of getting published.

Never throw away your rejection letters. Not only will you want to refer back to them to see what an editor said about your writing, you will need them for the IRS, to prove you are pursuing writing as a business and not a hobby.

Many writers have been rejected numerous times by the same editor before selling. The writer continued to submit to that particular editor because of the positive comments on prior works.

Good Writing, Wrong Genre

Editors will often point out if your writing voice, style, or the particular focus of this story doesn't fall into the genre you are targeting. For example an editor may write: *This reads more like a straight mystery instead of a romance.* At times, the focus can easily be shifted to meet the requirements of the genre.

However if too many rejections come back pointing out the lack of tone or style needed for that particular genre, perhaps you should consider writing in a different genre.

Accepting the Subjectivity of the Writing Business

A big part of dealing with the whole rejection issue is accepting the subjectivity of the business. Not everyone will love your writing—some will even dislike your writing. It's not about you personally, it's about the personal likes and dislikes of your critic. It could be about the market, or another book they just purchased that is similar to the one you submitted. It could be that the publisher is overstocked and isn't buying any new work.

It is also wise to remember that the lesson of subjectivity in writing doesn't end after you sell a book. Published writers are constantly being told by readers which of their books are good, which book they disliked and even hated. Every book you write will be someone's favorite . . . and someone else's least favorite.

It's Not Always You; It Could Be Them

There are all sorts of books, for all sorts of readers, for all sorts of publishers and editors. Don't believe it? Have you fallen madly in love with every book you've ever read?

Probably not.

Have you read some that you couldn't fathom how they made it to the bookstore?

Probably, yes.

And in spite of how wise you are about what is and isn't great fiction, there was a writer, an editor, and an entire publishing team who thought the book you disliked was good enough to make it.

Books are like ice-cream. Some readers and editors love only vanilla; others want double chocolate fudge. Accepting that it's not always you, that it could just be the editor's tastes, can help you persevere.

Don't Get Mad; Get Published

Getting mad or allowing the rejection to eat at you isn't healthy, and it can possibly stifle your creativity. Instead, turn the whole rejection issue into a challenge. Some writers have even found ways to let rejection motivate them.

Christie Craig, one of the authors of this book, is the proud owner of more than 10,000 rejection letters resulting from both her freelance and novel career. While she started selling her work after receiving only forty rejections, the no's continued to come in. Instead of viewing rejection as something standing in her way, she viewed it as something nudging her forward. She became determined to prove to each and every editor who rejected her that they were wrong.

Rewarding Rejection

Some critique groups, and even RWA chapters, actually reward each other for rejections. And why not? A rejection is a sign that you are working toward publication. The Internal Revenue Service will generally ask for one of two things to prove you are a writer: proof of income, or a rejection letter. If you never submit, never chance getting a rejection, you'll also never be accepted. Rejection is not only a stepping stone toward accomplishing your dream; it is evidence that you are a real writer.

CHAPTER 22

The Writer's Life

There is more to being a successful—and well-published—romance novelist than just honing your craft. Writing is a business, and as with any business, you need to know how to market and sell yourself. You'll need to know how to march through the slumps to arrive at a place of success. You'll need to know the tricks of the trade, as well as a few tips for avoiding the pitfalls. So, turn the page and prepare to take those final steps to publication.

Stay Motivated

Because the main entrée of writing automatically comes with a side dish of rejection, it's important that you work at staying positive, staying motivated.

This may mean ridding yourself of the negativity demon that lurks within most people. You know that demon, don't you? It's the one that whispers in your ear that you're wasting your time writing. The one that tells you you shouldn't even be allowed to write a grocery list. Well, it's time to send that demon packing!

Start the exorcism of pessimistic thinking by changing all the negative thoughts that imply you can't do something, to ones that say you can accomplish anything. Remove all the *can'ts* and *shouldn'ts* from your internal thoughts. To paraphrase and take creative licenses with the old adage: "If you think you can write and believe you'll sell soon, you are right. If you think you can't write and will never publish, you are probably also right."

Start believing in yourself and you might be surprised how other people will believe in you as well.

Get Rid of Negative People

While generally, you will be your own worst enemy, there are some people who are just inherently negative—people who make you doubt yourself and question your sanity for even wanting to become a writer. If possible, eliminate these people from your life.

When eliminating a negative person isn't an option—for example, when the person is a part of your immediate family—explain to him that you need to focus on the positive. Ask for his support.

ALERT!

If you are constantly leaving critique meetings feeling beaten up and uninspired, maybe it's time to question if the partnership is working. Finding the right critique partner can take time and several attempts. Don't be afraid to remove yourself graciously from a bad situation.

Unfortunately, the negative people can be the very people you turn to in hopes they will help you succeed at writing. Critique partners should always point out the mistakes in your manuscripts. And it's true, it can be hard to have your mistakes brought to your attention, but pointing out flaws shouldn't cause irreparable harm to your self-confidence. In the end, a critique is about improving and should be empowering not depressing.

Surround Yourself with the Positive

Removing the negative influences from your life will leave you with some room—room for the optimistic influences. Positive people, people who believe in you, can be essential to your outlook and long-term success. This is why a lot of authors find attending writers' meetings and visiting with other authors to be so helpful. Sometimes, only another writer will truly understand your woes about this career.

ESSENTIAL

Many Olympic Gold Medal winners have attributed accomplishing their dream, in part, to the art of visualization. Take a few minutes each day to visualize yourself receiving the call or signing books at your very first autographing.

Items that send positive messages can also help motivate you. Keep those items, such as a good note from a critique partner, a great contest score sheet, or a finalist certificate, out in the open so you can see them. Some writers have found that pet rocks or paperweights with positive statements such as "Make It Happen" or "Dare to Dream" can help get them through a rough spot.

Write It Down

Getting published involves a lot of small steps. Each step is another goal completed. Write down these goals. Make sure your goals include both the larger and the smaller steps. Large, as in finishing a book. Small, as in finishing a scene or polishing a chapter.

Don't forget to celebrate each success. It may be a long haul before you sell your first book, but the journey will be much sweeter if you learn to reward yourself for each accomplishment.

Never Stop Learning

Feed the brain; nourish the soul.

Something amazing happens to your spirit when you are learning. Knowledge offers a sense of empowerment. Feeling empowered, you are able to overcome hurdles, make wiser decisions, and persevere. With the numerous online writing classes and the amazing amount of how-to books available for purchase, you don't even have to leave the comfort of your own home to learn.

Imagine a doctor who went to medical school in the early 1990s. Where would she be if she refused to learn anything new? Where would an interior designer be if he refused to keep up with new trends? Both professionals would be hard-pressed to find work without updated skills. Writing is no different. Never stop learning. Never stop attempting to improve your craft. This rule stands not only for the nearly published, but for the multipublished, as well. Learning not only keeps you feeling empowered; it is job security.

Dedicated Versus Obsessed

Every writer who made it to the bookshelves will tell you that it took serious dedication to get there—giving up some lunches with the work colleagues, staying home to write while the rest of the family goes to the latest blockbuster movie. Being dedicated to your career goals is a must in the writing business. However, sometimes there's a fine line between dedication and obsession.

FACT

A great book that will help you stay dedicated to your career without losing your focus on what's really important is *The Seven Habits of Highly Effective People,* by Stephen R. Covey. Covey offers tips on accomplishing your career goals without losing sight of real life.

Obsession is when everything else in your life, your relationships, as well as your passions and hobbies, suddenly are no longer important. While obsession may seem like a quicker route to publication, it generally leads straight to burnout.

Writers write about life. If you stop living, sooner or later your well of creativity will run dry. While chances are, sacrifices will have to be made to fit the writing in, never forget that you must maintain a proper balance of the emotional, spiritual, social, and mental aspects of your life. Keep the joy of writing alive by maintaining a full and a healthy lifestyle.

Hurdles and Pitfalls Along the Writer's Path

As glamorous as the life of a romance novelist may appear, it's partially a mirage. Yes, writing remains a dream job with tons of advantages—no one will deny that—but this doesn't mean you won't discover hurdles or face difficulties along the way.

Like roses that come with thorns, the writing career comes with its own downside. What's hard to believe is those pitfalls don't disappear when you sell your first book. It is wise to be prepared for the possible challenges your chosen career path may present.

Tossing Away the Measuring Stick

You can't measure yourself against other writers. Just because someone writes twenty pages a day, or sells their first manuscript, doesn't mean you can or ever will be able to write that fast or sell that soon. Every writer has to follow her own path to success. Instead of spending your time and energy measuring and comparing yourself to other writers, focus on what you can do to help yourself meet your own goals.

The Green-Eyed Beast

Jealousy is an ugly emotion. Yes, it's human nature to feel envy, but a full-blown case of jealousy is simply bad for the soul. In other words, it's okay to wish you could arrive at the same place as your more successful peers, but it's not okay to wish they hadn't gotten there.

Don't let the green-eyed beast eat at your sanity. Celebrate the success of others and find motivation in their accomplishments. They very well may be blazing the trail that you will soon follow.

The Writer's Vacuum

This is when you stop reading, stop attending writers' meetings, stop learning, and stop living because you feel the only thing you must do is write the book. And yes, writing the book is the number-one goal, but when you shut yourself down in all the other areas, you are unable to be objective about your own work. Balance is always the key.

Rewrite-itis

Rewrite-itis can be a severe condition that affects both published and unpublished writers. Basically, it means you are unable to ever call a book, a chapter, or even a scene finished. Behind the fancy name of rewrite-itis lies one of two fears: fear of failure or fear of success. The signs of this condition include:

- Rewriting the same scene, chapter, or book more than ten times
- Never finishing a book because you keep going back to polish the first chapters
- Constantly having someone read your work, hoping they'll give you some revisions to do
- Taking your packaged manuscript to the post office to mail to the editor or agent, only to decide the book isn't ready and then rushing home to revise again (Yes, it has happened.)

The best way to treat rewrite-itis is to set goals and deadlines and stick to them. This isn't to say you should ever send a manuscript out before it's polished, but your manuscripts are like your children. Sooner or later, you have to turn them loose on the world.

Research-itis

Some people love to do the research; some people loathe it. But some of the people who claim to love it are just doing it to avoid writing. True, research is crucial to all manuscripts, especially to historicals where facts and details will be scrutinized by your history-buff readers. However, every writer must be aware of research-itis and know when it's time to say, "Enough is enough."

The Faux Writer Syndrome

Even the most committed author is susceptible to this condition. Signs of the faux writer syndrome are easily recognized. You get so involved in the writing life that you suddenly realize that you're doing it all: talking writing, attending writer's meetings and workshops, volunteering for writing organizations, e-mailing writing buddies, and reading books about writing. You're doing it all. Well, all, that is, except actually writing.

Don't get so caught up in the writer's life that you forget the one thing that really makes you a writer: You write.

The Importance of Final Cold Reads

Consider this: You've got that finished manuscript in your hand, you've done your polishes, and it has gone through your critique group. Are you ready to send your baby out into the world? Maybe you are . . . and maybe it's time for a final cold read.

FACT

It is wise to have several writers, outside your critique group, that you can turn to for cold reads. Remember, when you ask them to read, you must be willing to reciprocate. Writing is very much a "you scratch my back, I'll scratch yours" kind of business. The alternative is paying professional book doctors or editorial services, which most new writers can't afford.

It's not rewrite-itis to have one last full read by a fellow writer or experienced critiquer before you mail out the manuscript. Preferably, this person will not have read the manuscript or heard you talk about the plot or characters. You want the read to be cold—cold, meaning the person will be picking up the manuscript without knowing anything about the story. She will be reading it just as an editor or agent will read it.

The reason a cold read is needed is that you may have explained things to your fellow critiquers but the information may not always be in the manuscript. Or, you may have changed something and unintentionally left out some important information, but because your fellow readers know this information, they fail to realize that it isn't in the manuscript. A fresh pair of eyes can discover things that you and your fellow critiquers can miss.

Get Ready for Success

Writing isn't called a business without good reason. You'll need to present yourself in a businesslike manner in person, on paper, and in cyberspace. This means you'll need to know how to talk to agents, editors, and fans. You'll need to know how to dress for success, as well as when to pitch to an editor/agent and when not to pitch. Plus, it may be time for you to start thinking about marketing tools (writing blogs) and to come up with a plan to sell yourself. And for sure, you'll need to write a resume.

Lots to learn, lots to think about, but don't worry, the next few pages will cover almost everything you need to know to start your climb to stardom.

The Writing Resume

A writing resume is not the same type of resume you would send out to get a traditional job. Most writing resumes will be condensed into one or two paragraphs at the end of your query letter. (For more about writing query letters, see Chapter 20.)

Understanding Its Purpose

So, what goes into those paragraphs? Anything that involves your writing credits or the story you are pitching. For sure, include the information if you've published anything in the past. (Short stories, articles, or even newsletter articles count.) Contest wins and placements are useful. Be sure to include any affiliations or positions you may have held for writing organizations, such as RWA.

If you are a lawyer or a brain surgeon and your story isn't about one of the two professions, then more than a mention of your day job is considered too much. If your day job were in public relations, or sales, and you feel your experience will help you promote yourself or your book, this would be pertinent information. Basically, an editor or agent won't care what you do outside your writing life unless it will affect your writing career or your ability to write your particular story.

How to Build Your Resume

Just because you don't have any publishing credits or contest finals doesn't mean your query will be rejected, however. The quality of your writing and the marketability of your story will impress an editor/agent. However, if you have credits, they sure can't hurt. Some book doctors/publishing experts insist that time is well spent attaining credits outside the genre just to prove you can write. If you're in the beginning of your career, start thinking of how you can build your resume with small publishing credits.

Dress to Impress

Okay . . . at home you can wear your PJs all day if you want. But for most writers' conferences, where you meet editors and agents, you should wear casual business to dressy business attire, depending on the event. If you have a nice suit to wear, wear it on the day you have an appointment with an editor/agent. However, whatever wardrobe you choose, make sure you feel good in it, and it makes you feel successful. There is some truth to the adage, "Clothes make the person."

ESSENTIAL

A picture says a thousand words. How you dress will be the way editors, peers, and future fans picture you. Many writers try to create an image with their wardrobe, by adding something that's not too over-the-top, but makes them stand out in a crowd—for example, a hat or unique jewelry. A lot of authors even attempt to match their wardrobe to the tone of their writing voice.

When attending regular writers' meetings, some authors choose to dress down; others choose to wear casual business attire.

When to Pitch and When Not to Pitch

Most writing conferences will set up appointments for you to speak with editors and agents if you request them. If you get stuck in an elevator, or find yourself sitting next to an agent/editor during lunch, you should only pitch to her if the conversation leads to your book. Be professional, outgoing, but courteous and never pushy.

Rather than think of the chance meeting as an opportunity to pitch your novel, think of it as a chance to make a good impression. Strike up a conversation; be yourself. Treat the agent/editor as you would any other person you've met for the first time. Then, when you write the agent or editor later and pitch your novel, you can add, "We met in the elevator. I'm the woman with the two Boston terriers who gave you advice about your new puppy."

Start Thinking about Your Brand

What is it about your writing that stands out? Are you funny and sassy? Dark and suspenseful? Most writers come up with a branding phrase that describes their writing voice and the tone of their books. *New York Times* bestselling author Nina Bangs's branding phrase is "Hot, Funny & Deliciously Different."

Some authors who write in different genres will have a branding phrase for the different types of books they write. For example, Christina Dodd's branding phrase for her romantic suspense is "Cool suspense. Hot romance."

QUESTION?

Do I need a Web site before I get published?
Some authors do post Web sites before they make that first sale. An interested editor or agent may log on to investigate the author. However, a Web site doesn't really become a needed tool until a few months before your book is to be released. Keep in consideration, however, that it does take a while to get a Web site up and running.

Choose your branding phrase carefully, because it will be attached to you for a while. Make sure it not only reflects your writing voice, but the genre in which you are writing.

Finding Time to Write

If you're like most people, you work, have a family, and a whole life outside writing. You are probably struggling to find the time to put those words down on paper. The truth is that making time to write is going to be hard, and probably requires a lot of juggling of schedules, and finagling of time. Ultimately, you may have to give up some other hobby, or learn to do without an hour or so of sleep.

You might imagine that other writers don't have day jobs. But you would be wrong. Very few romance authors in the beginning of their careers have the luxury of being able to write full-time. Many worked a full-time job outside of writing and some still do.

FACT

New York Times bestselling author Nina Bangs worked full-time for more than three years after selling her first romance novel. All three years, plus the five years before she sold, Nina woke up at 3 A.M. every morning so she could have two good hours of writing time before rushing off to her teaching job.

Below are some tips on how you may be able to squeeze a few minutes, even a few hours, out of your day to give to your writing.

- Do a time diary for a week to find out where all your time is going. Can you see what you might be able to cut back on?
- A recent survey stated that Americans spend as much as 120 hours a month watching television. Limit your TV time. Spend it writing.
- Always carry a notepad with you and when you are in lines, or on hold on the phone, jot down notes for future scenes. These small notes can jumpstart your imagination when you do sit down to write.

- Take a laptop or a notebook to work with you and spend your breaks and lunchtime writing.
- Get up early, or go to bed an hour later, to get in precious writing time.
- If young children are keeping you from writing, join a babysitting co-op where you swap childcare time.
- Ask for support from family members. Suggest they take turns doing the dishes or straightening the house, so you can spend that time writing.
- If you have a long commute to work, buy a tape recorder and learn to talk your scenes.

Writing a novel is a big dream. And like any dream, you must be committed to making it come true. If you truly want to be a writer, you will find a way to eke out the needed time to make your dream a reality.

So, what are you waiting for? Start writing!

Glossary of Terms

The following are frequently used terms in the romance genre.

ABA:
American Booksellers Association, a trade organization for independent booksellers.

Acquisitions Editor:
An editor at a publishing house who has the authority to acquire manuscripts for publication.

Advance:
Payment offered by a publisher at the signing of a contract, also known as an advance against royalties.

Agent:
Also known as a *literary agent,* the author's representative when dealing with publishing companies.

ARC:
Advanced Reading Copy, a bound galley copy of your book distributed to reviewers and booksellers in advance of publication for review purposes and to promote pre-sales.

Backlist:
The author's previously published work that is still available for purchase in a retail market.

Blurbs:
Also known as a *cover blurb,* a short endorsement by a respected reviewer/magazine/writer that is placed on the cover of a new author's work to increase sales.

Boilerplate:
Refers to the publishing company's standard contract.

BookExpo America:
Also known as *BEA,* this is the annual trade show for the ABA. Romance publishers will often schedule signings for authors with upcoming books as a promotion tool.

Book Videos:
Short videos made to promote a book's release to booksellers, librarians, and readers.

Category Romance:
See Series Romance.

CE:
See Copyeditor.

Chicklit:
A type of mainstream novel generally written in first person from the heroine's POV that may or may not include a romance.

Climax:
In a romance novel, the moment when the main plotlines are resolved; i.e., the hero and heroine resolve their emotional conflicts.

Colonial:
Historical romance set during Colonial America.

Comedy of Manners:
Lighthearted historical romance set in the Regency time period. (See Regency romances.)

Conflict:
The obstacles, both internal and external, that the hero and heroine must overcome on their path to true love.

Contemporary Romance:
Romance novel set in the present.

Copyeditor:
The editor at the publishing house who proofreads the romance manuscript for typographical errors, grammar missteps, etc., prior to publication.

Copyright:
The author's legal right to ownership of her work under federal copyright laws.

Critique:
An assessment of the editorial strengths and weaknesses of a romance novel usually performed by an author's peers as part of a critique group.

Critique Group:
A group of writers who read and critique each other's work in a supportive environment.

Dark Moment:
The moment in a novel when all seems lost; e.g., the hero and heroine have been torn apart by their internal conflicts and no resolution seems possible. (Also known as the *Black Moment*.)

Dialogue:
The conversations characters have with each other on the pages of a romance novel.

Distributor:
The third-party company that purchases the romance novels from the publisher and ships them to the bookstores and other retail outlets.

Due Date:
The date listed in a publishing contract on which the publisher requires the submission of the completed manuscript.

E-Book:
An electronic copy of a novel sold for download. They can be read on a computer or other handheld electronic device.

E-Publishers:
Electronic publishers or publishers whose books are released for download rather than in print copy. (Some e-publishers also release print editions, just as some traditional publishers release e-book versions.)

Earn-out:
The total amount of money earned by an author on a romance novel.

Editor:
The author's chief source of contact with a publishing company; the person who usually buys, edits, and oversees the publication of the novel.

Epilogue:
A scene sometimes added after the last chapter of a romance novel that provides additional information about what happened to the hero and heroine.

Erotica:
A novel, either contemporary or historical, with a high level of graphic, explicit sex between the main characters. While a romance may exist between the main characters, the romantic relationship is not the primary focus of erotica.

Erotic Romance:
A romance novel, either contemporary or historical, with a high level of graphic, explicit sex between the hero and heroine. The romantic relationship is a primary focus of the novel.

Excerpt:
A short scene from a published book, usually no more than 1–5 pages but could be as long as the first chapter.

Foreign Rights:
The clause in a publishing contract that governs the sale and distribution of foreign copies of the romance novel.

Full:
Refers to a request by an editor or agent for the complete manuscript; e.g., "Please send me a full" means the agent or editor wants to read the complete manuscript.

Futuristic:
Romance novel set in the future, usually on other planets.

Galleys:
The print layout copy of the book provided for final proofing by a publisher. (Also known as *page proofs*.)

Glitz and Glamour:
Subgenre of single-title contemporary romances set against a jetsetter, "larger than life" backdrop.

Golden Heart:
The highest award given to an unpublished romance novel by Romance Writers of America.

Gothic:
A subgenre of historical romantic suspense, usually set in a spooky old house filled with secret passageways and dark family secrets. May include paranormal elements and level of sensuality can vary.

H/H:
Hero and Heroine; the main characters of your romance novel.

HEA:
Happily Ever After, the requisite ending of every romance novel, as in, "And they lived happily ever after."

Hand Sell:
A term used to describe what happens when a bookseller "talks up" a romance novel to a customer.

Hard Cover:
A cloth-bound copy of a novel.

Hard/Soft
In a publishing contract, refers to a book being released first in hard cover, then in a mass market paperback.

Head Hopping:
Refers to an awkward POV shift, wherein the reader feels as though she is "hopping" from one character's head to the other.

Hero:
The male protagonist/main character of a romance novel.

Heroine:
The female protagonist/main character of a romance novel.

House Style Guide:
The publisher's in-house guidelines for style and manuscript formatting, which are usually provided to an author after the signing of a publishing contract.

ISBN:
International Standard Book Number; a unique number assigned to every published novel by the RR Bowker Company. It's used by booksellers to order books.

List Price:
The retail price printed on the cover of a published romance novel.

Literary Agent:
See Agent.

Mainstream:
In the romance genre, these are women's fiction novels with a strong romance element.

Manuscript:
A romance novel that has not yet been accepted for publication.

Mass Market:
A paperback edition of a romance novel usually sold in all major retail outlets, as well as drugstores, airports, and grocery stores.

Mid-List:
Romance novels by established authors that aren't on the bestseller lists.

Narrative:
The words in a novel that are not part of dialogue, such as internal thoughts, descriptions, and action.

Novella:
A short novel of between 20,000 and 40,000 words, usually published as part of an anthology of three or four such titles.

Option Clause:
A clause in a publishing contract that guarantees the publisher first look at your next manuscript.

Outline:
See Synopsis.

P&L Statement:
The Profit and Loss Statement prepared by an editor in advance of offering a publishing contract. It analyzes the various costs associated with producing the book against the anticipated sales, so the editor can arrive at a figure for the advance.

PAN:
Published Author Network. In Romance Writers of America, PAN comprises the segment of authors published by RWA-eligible publishers in novel-length romance.

POV:
Point of View. The viewpoint or perspective from which the scene is told. In a romantic suspense, POV is usually limited to the hero, the heroine, and the villain, although major secondary characters can have their own POVs in longer books.

PRO:
Professional Authors Network. In Romance Writers of America, PRO comprises the segment of unpublished authors who have successfully completed a romance manuscript and submitted same to an editor or agent.

Partial:
The first three chapters and a synopsis of a romance manuscript.

Plot:
The main storyline of a novel. In a romance, this would be the romantic relationship between the hero and heroine.

Point of View:
See POV.

Pre-sale Numbers:
Orders placed by booksellers in advance of a novel's publication.

Press Kit:
Also known as a Media Kit, this contains information on the author and her books, such as a bio, photograph, cover flats, etc.

Price Point:
The retail price printed on the spine of a romance novel.

Print Run:
The number of copies of a romance novel printed by a publisher.

Prologue
A scene added before the first chapter that contains information about an event that happened prior to the story's opening that set the story in motion.

Pub Date:
The publication date, or release date, for a romance novel.

Publicist:
The marketing or PR person who is responsible for promoting the novel; could be an individual employed by the author or an employee of the publishing company.

Publisher:
The person or company responsible for publishing the romance novel.

Query:
Also known as the *query letter*. A one-page letter outlining the basic plot of the romance novel and publishing history sent to an editor or agent prior to submitting manuscript pages.

RT:
See Romantic Times BOOKreviews magazine.

RWA:
See Romance Writers of America.

Regency:
Historical romance set during the Regency period (1800–1820.) These books vary in tone and sexual explicitness. (Also known as *comedy of manners.*)

Remaindered:
Extra copies of an unsold book sold at a huge discount.

Request:
An invitation from an editor or agent to submit part or all of a manuscript.

Resolution:
Tying up of all loose ends in a romance novel, usually the time for unveiling the HEA.

Returns:
Copies of a romance novel returned by a bookseller to a distributor for credit.

Review:
A critical evaluation of a romance novel, such as the ones offered by *Publishers Weekly, Romantic Times BOOKreviews* magazine, and others.

Revision Letter:
A letter from an editor or agent detailing the requested editorial changes to a manuscript, usually prior to an offer of publication.

Rita:
Highest award given to a published romance novel by Romance Writers of America; named for RWA cofounder Rita Gallagher.

Romance Writers of America:
The leading organization for professional and aspiring romance novelists.

Romantic Times BOOKreviews magazine:
The leading online and monthly print publication for lovers of fiction of all genres, including romance.

Royalties:
The agreed-upon percentage paid to an author for the sale of each copy of her book. Different media forms (e.g., e-book, mass market paperback) have different royalty rates.

SASE:
Self-Addressed Stamped Envelope. An envelope, addressed by the author to herself with proper postage attached that is included with query letters and submissions for a reply.

Second Printing:
When a publisher prints additional copies of a novel.

Secondary Characters:
The supporting characters of a novel who often have their own parallel stories.

Self-Publish:
When the author hires a printer and publishes her own novel.

Sensual Romance:
Contemporary or Historical romance, with explicit sexual content between the hero and heroine.

Sequel:
A book that continues the story began in the first.

Series Romance:
Also known as the category romance, romance novels released as part of an established line. Each line has its own unique style and word count, and the publisher releases the same number of titles for each line each month.

Slush Pile:
Romance novels submitted for consideration by an author without a specific request from either the editor or agent.

Small Press:
Smaller publishers, often located outside New York City, that have smaller distributions, offer smaller advances, and cater to a specialized, niche market.

Subgenre:
The specific subcategories of romance, such as Paranormal or Romantic Suspense.

Subplot:
A secondary plot in a romance novel, possibly involving secondary characters. The subplot should support the main plot in some way.

Subsidiary Rights:
A variety of additional licensing rights, such as audio and foreign sales, outside the retail sales agreement.

Sweet Romance:
Contains little if any sex or sexual situations. When referring to contemporaries, is also known as traditional romance.

Synopsis:
A written summary of the novel, usually 3–10 pages in length, that details the internal and external conflicts, major plot points, and resolution.

Tone:
The style or "feel" of a novel, such as light-hearted or dramatic.

Trade Paperback:
A larger-format paperback novel originally used for literary fiction but now commonly found for erotic romances, mainstream, or chicklit titles.

Turning Point:
Any moment in the romance novel that makes the main characters choose a different course of action.

Uncorrected Page Proofs:
The uncorrected first-run printout from a publisher, often bound and submitted to reviewers.

Vanity Press:
A "publishing" company that agrees to "publish" an author's work for a specified fee. The author assumes all costs and is responsible for marketing and sales.

Villain:
The antagonist or "bad guy" of a romance novel, especially in a romantic suspense.

Voice:
The author's specific use of language, including tone, that sets her work apart from the work of other authors.

Word of Mouth:
The PR buzz generated by readers telling other readers about a romance novel they loved.

Young Adult:
In the romance genre, refers to novels written for the preteen and teenager market. Levels of sensuality can vary from the very sweet to the sexually explicit for older readers.

Romance Markets

The romance market is in a constant state of change as new subgenres arise, publishers cease publishing, and new imprints rise up to replace those no longer in business. Please refer to the Web site of each publisher for its current, specific submission requirements. Also, as previously mentioned, for an up-to-the-minute list of current publishers, consult the latest edition of Writers Market (*www.writersmarket.com*) or the Members section of Romance Writers of America (*www.rwanational.org*).

Major Markets

The following are the major publishers of romance fiction. Submission guidelines can be obtained at their Web sites, if available.

Avon Books
HarperCollins
10 E. 53rd Street
New York, NY 10022
✐*www.avonbooks.com*

Ballantine Publishing Group
Ballantine/Ivy
1745 Broadway, 18th Floor
New York, NY 10019
✐*www.ballantinebooks.com*

The Bantam/Doubleday/Dell Group
1745 Broadway
New York, NY 10019
✐*www.randomhouse.com/bantamdell*

The Berkley Publishing Group
Penguin Putnam, Inc.
345 Hudson Street
New York, NY 10014
✐*www.penguinputnam.com*

Dorchester Publishing Company
200 Madison Avenue, Suite 2000
New York, NY 10016
✐*www.dorchesterpub.com*

Grand Central Publishing
237 Park Avenue
New York, NY 10017
✐*www.hachettebookgroupusa.com*

Harlequin Mills & Boon, Ltd.
Harlequin Enterprises, Ltd.
Eton House
18-24 Paradise Road
Richmond, Surrey TW9 1SR
United Kingdom
✐*www.millsandboon.co.uk*

Harlequin Books – New York
233 Broadway, Suite 1001
New York, NY 10279
✐*www.eharlequin.com*

Harlequin Books – Toronto
225 Duncan Mill Road
Don Mills, Ontario M3B 3K9
Canada
✐*www.eharlequin.com*

HQN Books
Harlequin Enterprises
233 Broadway, Suite 1001
New York, NY 10279
✐*www.eharlequin.com*

Kensington Publishing Corp.
850 Third Avenue, 16th Floor
New York, NY 10022
✐*www.kensingtonbooks.com*

New American Library
Penguin Putnam, Inc.
375 Hudson Street
New York, NY 10014
✐*www.penguinputnam.com*

Pocket Books
1230 Avenue of the Americas
New York, NY 10020
✐*www.simonsays.com*

Silhouette Books
233 Broadway, Suite 1001
New York, NY 10279
✐*www.eharlequin.com*

St. Martins Press
175 Fifth Avenue
New York, NY 10010
✐*www.stmartins.com*

Tor/Forge
Tom Doherty Associates LLC
175 Fifth Avenue
New York, NY 10010
✐*www.tor-forge.com*

Small Presses

The following publishers are considered small presses—smaller, independent publishers, most of whom are outside New York City—that publish romance fiction. Their submission guidelines, if available, are located at their Web sites.

ArcheBooks Publishing Inc.
9101 W. Sahara Avenue
Suite 105-112
Las Vegas, NV 89117
✐*www.archebooks.com*

Avalon Books
160 Madison Avenue
New York, NY 10016
✐*www.avalonbooks.com*

Baycrest Books
P.O. Box 2009
Monroe, MI 48161
✍*www.baycrestbooks.com*

Koenisha Publications
3196 53rd Street
Hamilton, MI 49419-9626
✍*www.koenisha.com*

Loon in Balloon Inc.
133 Weber Street North, Suite #3-513
Waterloo, ON N2J 3G9
Canada
✍*www.looninballoon.com*

Medallion Press
26609 Castleview Way
Wesley Chapel, FL 33543
✍*www.medallionpress.com*

Ooligan Press
P.O. Box 751
Portland, OR 97207-0751
✍*www.publishing.pdx.edu*

Premium Press America
2606 Eugenia Avenue, Suite C
Nashville, TN 37211-2177
✍*www.premiumpressamerica.com*

Vintage Romance Publishing
107 Clearview Circle
Goose Creek, SC 29445
✍*www.vrpublishing.com*

Whitaker House Publishers
1030 Hunt Valley Circle
New Kensington, PA 15068
✍*www.whitakerhouse.com*

White Stone Books
2761 E. Skelly Drive, Suite 700-8
Tulsa, OK 74105
✍*www.whitestonebooks.com*

WindRiver Publishing, Inc.
72 N. WindRiver Road
Silverton, ID 83867-0446
✍*www.windriverpublishing*

Specialty Markets

The following publishers are known as specialty markets, meaning they publish romances geared to a specific market. As with other publishers, refer to their Web sites for submission guidelines.

Active Bladder
Publishes: Punk rock romances
P.O. Box 24607
Philadelphia, PA 19111
✍*www.activebladder.com*

Arrow Publications, LLC
Publishes: Romances in graphic novel format
9112 Paytley Bridge Lane
Potomac, MD 20854-4432
www.arrowpub.com

Barbour Publishing, Inc.
Publishes: Christian romances for mass market audience
P.O. Box 719
Uhrichsville, OH 44683
www.barbourpublishing.com

BelleBooks
Publishes: Southern themes
P.O. Box 67
Smyrna, GA 30081
www.bellebooks.com

Borealis Press, Ltd.
Publishes: Romances considered "Canadian in content and tone"
8 Mohawk Crescent
Napean, ON K2H 7G6
Canada
www.borealispress.com

Cellar Door Publishing, LLC
Publishes: Romances in graphic novel format
3439 NE Sandy Boulevard, Suite 309
Portland, OR 97232-1959
www.cellardoorpublishing.com

Cook Communications Ministries
Publishes: Christian romances
RiverOak Fiction
4050 Lee Vance View
Colorado Springs, CO 80918

Covenant Communications, Inc.
Publishes: Inspirational romances for the LDS market
Box 416
American Fork, UT 84003-0416
www.covenant-lds.com

Genesis Press, Inc.
Publishes: Multicultural romances
P.O. Box 101
Columbus, MS 39701
www.genesis-press.com

Hatala Geroproducts
Publishes: Romances for the 60+ market
P.O. Box 42
Greentop, MO 63546
www.geroproducts.com

Howard Books (a division of Simon & Schuster)
Publishes: Inspirational romances
3117 North 7th Street
West Monroe, LA 71291
www.howardpublishing.com

Kimani Press
Publishes: African-American and Multicultural romances
BET Books
850 Third Avenue, 16th Floor
New York, NY 10022
www.eharequin.com

Manor House Publishing, Inc.
Publishes: Romances for a Canadian audience
452 Cottingham Crescent
Ancaster, ON L9G 3V6
Canada
www.manor-house.biz

New Victoria Publishers
Publishes: Lesbian romances
P.O. Box 27
Norwich, VT 05055-0027
www.newvictoria.com

Onstage Publishing
Publishes: Young adult
190 Lime Quarry Road, Suite 106K
Madison, AL 35758
www.onstagebooks.com

Red Sage Publishing
Publishes: Anthologies, erotic romance
P.O. Box 4844
Seminole, FL 33775
www.redsagepub.com

Steeple Hill Books
Publishes: Inspirational romances
Harlequin Enterprises
233 Broadway, Suite 1001
New York, NY 10279
www.eharlequin.com

Torquere Press
Publishes: Gay/Lesbian romance
P.O. Box 2545
Round Rock, TX 78680
www.torquerepress.com

WaterBrook Multnomah Publishers
Publishes: Christian romances
12265 Oracle Boulevard, Suite 200
Colorado Springs, CO 80921
www.mpbooks.com

E-Book Publishers

The following publishers primarily produce romance novels in e-book format, although many will follow with print copies following e-book release. Refer to the Web sites for each publisher for specific editorial guidelines and submission requirements.

Black Velvet Seductions Publishing
1350-C W. Southport
Box 249
Indianapolis, IN 46217
www.blackvelvetseductions.com

Diskus Publishing
P.O. Box 43
Albany, IN 47320
✍*www.diskuspublishing.com*

E-Digital Books, LLC
1155 S. Havana Street, #11-364
Aurora, CO 80012
✍*www.edigitalbookstore.com*

Ellora's Cave Publishing, Inc.
1337 Commerce Drive, #13
Stow, OH 44224
✍*www.ellorascave.com*

Lionhearted Publishing, Inc.
P.O. Box 618
Zephyr Cove, NV 89448-0618
✍*www.lionhearted.com*

Samhain Publishing, Ltd.
512 Forest Lake Drive
Warner Robins, GA 31093
✍*www.samhainpublishing.com*

APPENDIX C

Additional Resources

The following list contains resources mentioned in this book that can help you along the path to publication of your romance novel.

Bibliography

Bickham, Jack M. *Scene & Structure—Elements of Fiction Writing.* (Cincinnati, OH: Writer's Digest Books, 1993).

Campbell, Joseph. *The Hero with a Thousand Faces.* (Princeton, NJ: Princeton University Press, 1972).

Covey, Stephen R. *The Seven Habits of Highly Effective People.* (New York, NY: Simon and Schuster, 1989).

Dixon, Debra. *Goal, Motivation and Conflict: The Building Blocks of Good Fiction.* (Memphis, TN: Gryphon Books for Writers, 1999).

Hargrave, Jan. *Let Me See Your Body Talk.* (Dubuque, IA: Kendall/Hunt Publishing, 1995).

Hughes, Faye. *Can't Fight the Feeling.* (New York, NY: Bantam Loveswept, 1995).

Kent, Allison. *The Complete Idiot's Guide to Writing Erotic Romance.* (New York, NY: Alpha Books, 2006).

Maas, Donald. *Writing the Breakout Novel.* (Cincinnati, OH: Writer's Digest Books, 2002).

Michaels, Leigh. *Creating Romantic Characters: Bringing Life to Your Romance Novel.* (Ottumwa, IA: PBL, Ltd., 2004).

Noble, William. *Conflict, Action and Suspense: Elements of Fiction Writing.* (Cincinnati, OH: Writer's Digest Books, 1999).

Obstfeld, Raymond and Franz Neumann. *Careers for Your Characters: A Writer's Guide to 101 Professions from Architect to Zookeeper.* (Cincinnati, OH: Writer's Digest Books, 2002).

Penn, William. *Some Fruits of Solitude: Wise Sayings in the Conduct of Human Life;* edited by Eric K. Taylor. (Scottsdale, PA: Herald Press, 2003).

Pressfield, Steven. *The War of Art: Break Through the Blocks and Win Your Inner Creative Battles.* (New York, NY: Grand Central Publishing, 2003).

Roth, Martin. *The Fiction Writer's Silent Partner.* (Cincinnati, OH: Writer's Digest Books, 1991).

Stein, Sol. *How to Grow a Novel: The Most Common Mistakes Writers Make and How to Overcome Them.* (New York, NY: St. Martin's Press, 1999).

Stein, Sol. *Stein on Writing: A Master Editor of Some of the Most Successful Writers of Our Century Shares His Craft Techniques and Strategies.* (New York, NY: St. Martin's Press, 1995).

Thurman, Susan and Larry Shea. *The Only Grammar Book You'll Ever Need.* (Avon, MA: Adams Media Corporation, 2003).

Vogler, Christopher. *The Writer's Journey: Mythic Structure for Writers,* Third Edition. (Studio City, CA: Michael Wiese Productions, 2007).

Resources on the Web

Agent Query
www.agentquery.com
This site provides information on literary agents.

Amazon Booksellers
www.amazon.com
This site is one of the leading online retailers of books.

BabyNames.Com
www.babynames.com
This site offers millions of names, their ethnic origins, and their meaning.

Contest Divas
http://contestdivas.blogspot.com
This site offers writing contest information.

Humanmetrics: The Jung Typology Test
www.humanmetrics.com/cgi-win/JTypes2.asp

This site offers an online version of the Myers-Briggs typology test for characterization.

iStock Photo
www.istockphoto.com
This site offers thousands of royalty-free photographs and videos.

Merriam-Webster Dictionary
www.m-w.com
This is the online home of Merriam-Webster, which contains their free dictionary.

Publishers Marketplace
www.publishersmarketplace.com
This Web site provides industry news, publishing deals, and contact information for publishing professionals.

Romantic Times BOOKreviews magazine
www.romantictimes.com
This is the Web site for the leading monthly publication for fiction lovers of all genres, including romance.

Show Me the Money
www.brendahiatt.com/id2.html
This is the Web site of romance author Brenda Hiatt, who maintains a database of romance publisher advances and earn-outs.

World Wide Learn
www.worldwidelearn.com/online-courses/ writing-courses.htm?s=ypi
This Web site offers online training classes in a variety of subjects, including writing.

Write With Us

✎www.writewithus.net

This is the Web site for coauthors Christie Craig and Faye Hughes; it provides information about their upcoming workshops, online classes, and writing tips.

WritingClasses.Com

✎www.writingclasses.com

This Web site sponsored by Gotham Writers Workshops offers online writing classes in a variety of genres.

Organizations

Association of Authors' Representatives

✎www.aar-online.org

This is the Web site for AAR, the not-for-profit organization of literary agents.

Romance Writers of America

✎www.rwanational.org

This is the site for the largest group of professional writers of romance fiction in the world.

INDEX

THE EVERYTHING SERIES!

BUSINESS & PERSONAL FINANCE

Everything® Accounting Book
Everything® Budgeting Book, 2nd Ed.
Everything® Business Planning Book
Everything® Coaching and Mentoring Book, 2nd Ed.
Everything® Fundraising Book
Everything® Get Out of Debt Book
Everything® Grant Writing Book, 2nd Ed.
Everything® Guide to Buying Foreclosures
Everything® Guide to Fundraising $15.95
Everything® Guide to Mortgages
Everything® Guide to Personal Finance for Single Mothers
Everything® Home-Based Business Book, 2nd Ed.
Everything® Homebuying Book, 3rd Ed. $15.95
Everything® Homeselling Book, 2nd Ed.
Everything® Human Resource Management Book
Everything® Improve Your Credit Book
Everything® Investing Book, 2nd Ed.
Everything® Landlording Book
Everything® Leadership Book, 2nd Ed.
Everything® Managing People Book, 2nd Ed.
Everything® Negotiating Book
Everything® Online Auctions Book
Everything® Online Business Book
Everything® Personal Finance Book
Everything® Personal Finance in Your 20s & 30s Book, 2nd Ed.
Everything® Personal Finance in Your 40s & 50s Book $15.95
Everything® Project Management Book, 2nd Ed.
Everything® Real Estate Investing Book
Everything® Retirement Planning Book
Everything® Robert's Rules Book, $7.95
Everything® Selling Book
Everything® Start Your Own Business Book, 2nd Ed.
Everything® Wills & Estate Planning Book

COOKING

Everything® Barbecue Cookbook
Everything® Bartender's Book, 2nd Ed., $9.95
Everything® Calorie Counting Cookbook
Everything® Cheese Book
Everything® Chinese Cookbook
Everything® Classic Recipes Book
Everything® Cocktail Parties & Drinks Book
Everything® College Cookbook
Everything® Cooking for Baby and Toddler Book
Everything® Diabetes Cookbook
Everything® Easy Gourmet Cookbook
Everything® Fondue Cookbook
Everything® Food Allergy Cookbook $15.95
Everything® Fondue Party Book
Everything® Gluten-Free Cookbook
Everything® Glycemic Index Cookbook
Everything® Grilling Cookbook
Everything® Healthy Cooking for Parties Book $15.95
Everything® Healthy Meals in Minutes Cookbook
Everything® Holiday Cookbook
Everything® Indian Cookbook
Everything® Lactose-Free Cookbook

Everything® Low-Cholesterol Cookbook
Everything® Low-Fat High-Flavor Cookbook, 2nd Ed.
Everything® Low-Salt Cookbook
Everything® Meals for a Month Cookbook
Everything® Meals on a Budget Cookbook
Everything® Mediterranean Cookbook
Everything® Mexican Cookbook
Everything® No Trans Fat Cookbook
Everything® One-Pot Cookbook, 2nd Ed.
Everything® Organic Cooking for Baby & Toddler Book $15.95
Everything® Pizza Cookbook
Everything® Quick Meals Cookbook, 2nd Ed. $15.95
Everything® Slow Cooker Cookbook
Everything® Slow Cooking for a Crowd Cookbook
Everything® Soup Cookbook
Everything® Stir-Fry Cookbook
Everything® Sugar-Free Cookbook
Everything® Tapas and Small Plates Cookbook
Everything® Tex-Mex Cookbook
Everything® Thai Cookbook
Everything® Vegetarian Cookbook
Everything® Whole-Grain, High-Fiber Cookbook
Everything® Wild Game Cookbook
Everything® Wine Book, 2nd Ed.

GAMES

Everything® 15-Minute Sudoku Book, $9.95
Everything® 30-Minute Sudoku Book, $9.95
Everything® Bible Crosswords Book, $9.95
Everything® Blackjack Strategy Book
Everything® Brain Strain Book, $9.95
Everything® Bridge Book
Everything® Card Games Book
Everything® Card Tricks Book, $9.95
Everything® Casino Gambling Book, 2nd Ed.
Everything® Chess Basics Book
Everything® Christmas Crosswords Book $9.95
Everything® Craps Strategy Book
Everything® Crossword and Puzzle Book
Everything® Crosswords and Puzzles for Quote Lovers Book $9.95
Everything® Crossword Challenge Book
Everything® Crosswords for the Beach Book, $9.95
Everything® Cryptic Crosswords Book, $9.95
Everything® Cryptograms Book, $9.95
Everything® Easy Crosswords Book
Everything® Easy Kakuro Book, $9.95
Everything® Easy Large-Print Crosswords Book
Everything® Games Book, 2nd Ed.
Everything® Giant Book of Crosswords
Everything® Giant Sudoku Book, $9.95
Everything® Giant Word Search Book
Everything® Kakuro Challenge Book, $9.95
Everything® Large-Print Crossword Challenge Book
Everything® Large-Print Crosswords Book
Everything® Large-Print Travel Crosswords Book
Everything® Lateral Thinking Puzzles Book, $9.95
Everything® Literary Crosswords Book, $9.95
Everything® Mazes Book
Everything® Memory Booster Puzzles Book, $9.95

Everything® Movie Crosswords Book, $9.95
Everything® Music Crosswords Book, $9.95
Everything® Online Poker Book
Everything® Pencil Puzzles Book, $9.95
Everything® Poker Strategy Book
Everything® Pool & Billiards Book
Everything® Puzzles for Commuters Book, $9.95
Everything® Puzzles for Dog Lovers Book, $9.95
Everything® Sports Crosswords Book, $9.95
Everything® Test Your IQ Book, $9.95
Everything® Texas Hold 'Em Book, $9.95
Everything® Travel Crosswords Book, $9.95
Everything® Travel Mazes Book $9.95
Everything® Travel Word Search Book $9.95
Everything® TV Crosswords Book, $9.95
Everything® Word Games Challenge Book
Everything® Word Scramble Book
Everything® Word Search Book

HEALTH

Everything® Alzheimer's Book
Everything® Diabetes Book
Everything® First Aid Book, $9.95
Everything® Green Living Book
Everything® Health Guide to Addiction and Recovery
Everything® Health Guide to Adult Bipolar Disorder
Everything® Health Guide to Arthritis
Everything® Health Guide to Controlling Anxiety
Everything® Health Guide to Depression
Everything® Health Guide to Diabetes, 2nd Ed.
Everything® Health Guide to Fibromyalgia
Everything® Health Guide to Menopause, 2nd Ed.
Everything® Health Guide to Migraines
Everything® Health Guide to Multiple Sclerosis
Everything® Health Guide to OCD
Everything® Health Guide to PMS
Everything® Health Guide to Postpartum Care
Everything® Health Guide to Thyroid Disease
Everything® Hypnosis Book
Everything® Low Cholesterol Book
Everything® Menopause Book
Everything® Nutrition Book
Everything® Reflexology Book
Everything® Stress Management Book
Everything® Superfoods Book $15.95

HISTORY

Everything® American Government Book
Everything® American History Book, 2nd Ed.
Everything® American Revolution Book $15.95
Everything® Civil War Book
Everything® Freemasons Book
Everything® Irish History & Heritage Book
Everything® World War II Book, 2nd Ed.

HOBBIES

Everything® Candlemaking Book
Everything® Cartooning Book
Everything® Coin Collecting Book
Everything® Digital Photography Book, 2nd Ed.

Everything® Drawing Book
Everything® Family Tree Book, 2nd Ed.
Everything® Guide to Online Genealogy $15.95
Everything® Knitting Book
Everything® Knots Book
Everything® Photography Book
Everything® Quilting Book
Everything® Sewing Book
Everything® Soapmaking Book, 2nd Ed.
Everything® Woodworking Book

HOME IMPROVEMENT

Everything® Feng Shui Book
Everything® Feng Shui Decluttering Book, $9.95
Everything® Fix-It Book
Everything® Green Living Book
Everything® Home Decorating Book
Everything® Home Storage Solutions Book
Everything® Homebuilding Book
Everything® Organize Your Home Book, 2nd Ed.

KIDS' BOOKS

All titles are $7.95
Everything® Fairy Tales Book, $14.95
Everything® Kids' Animal Puzzle & Activity Book
Everything® Kids' Astronomy Book
Everything® Kids' Baseball Book, 5th Ed.
Everything® Kids' Bible Trivia Book
Everything® Kids' Bugs Book
Everything® Kids' Cars and Trucks Puzzle and Activity Book
Everything® Kids' Christmas Puzzle & Activity Book
Everything® Kids' Connect the Dots
    Puzzle and Activity Book
Everything® Kids' Cookbook
Everything® Kids' Crazy Puzzles Book
Everything® Kids' Dinosaurs Book
Everything® Kids' Dragons Puzzle and Activity Book
Everything® Kids' Environment Book $7.95
Everything® Kids' Fairies Puzzle and Activity Book
Everything® Kids' First Spanish Puzzle and Activity Book
Everything® Kids' Football Book
Everything® Kids' Geography Book
Everything® Kids' Gross Cookbook
Everything® Kids' Gross Hidden Pictures Book
Everything® Kids' Gross Jokes Book
Everything® Kids' Gross Mazes Book
Everything® Kids' Gross Puzzle & Activity Book
Everything® Kids' Halloween Puzzle & Activity Book
Everything® Kids' Hanukkah Puzzle and Activity Book
Everything® Kids' Hidden Pictures Book
Everything® Kids' Horses Book
Everything® Kids' Joke Book
Everything® Kids' Knock Knock Book
Everything® Kids' Learning French Book
Everything® Kids' Learning Spanish Book
Everything® Kids' Magical Science Experiments Book
Everything® Kids' Math Puzzles Book
Everything® Kids' Mazes Book
Everything® Kids' Money Book, 2nd Ed.
**Everything® Kids' Mummies, Pharoah's, and Pyramids
    Puzzle and Activity Book**
Everything® Kids' Nature Book
Everything® Kids' Pirates Puzzle and Activity Book
Everything® Kids' Presidents Book
Everything® Kids' Princess Puzzle and Activity Book
Everything® Kids' Puzzle Book

Everything® Kids' Racecars Puzzle and Activity Book
Everything® Kids' Riddles & Brain Teasers Book
Everything® Kids' Science Experiments Book
Everything® Kids' Sharks Book
Everything® Kids' Soccer Book
Everything® Kids' Spelling Book
Everything® Kids' Spies Puzzle and Activity Book
Everything® Kids' States Book
Everything® Kids' Travel Activity Book
Everything® Kids' Word Search Puzzle and Activity Book

LANGUAGE

Everything® Conversational Japanese Book with CD, $19.95
Everything® French Grammar Book
Everything® French Phrase Book, $9.95
Everything® French Verb Book, $9.95
Everything® German Phrase Book $9.95
Everything® German Practice Book with CD, $19.95
Everything® Inglés Book
Everything® Intermediate Spanish Book with CD, $19.95
Everything® Italian Phrase Book $9.95
Everything® Italian Practice Book with CD, $19.95
Everything® Learning Brazilian Portuguese Book with CD, $19.95
Everything® Learning French Book with CD, 2nd Ed., $19.95
Everything® Learning German Book
Everything® Learning Italian Book
Everything® Learning Latin Book
Everything® Learning Russian Book with CD, $19.95
Everything® Learning Spanish Book
Everything® Learning Spanish Book with CD, 2nd Ed., $19.95
Everything® Russian Practice Book with CD, $19.95
Everything® Sign Language Book $15.95
Everything® Spanish Grammar Book
Everything® Spanish Phrase Book, $9.95
Everything® Spanish Practice Book with CD, $19.95
Everything® Spanish Verb Book, $9.95
Everything® Speaking Mandarin Chinese Book with CD, $19.95

MUSIC

Everything® Bass Guitar Book with CD, $19.95
Everything® Drums Book with CD, $19.95
Everything® Guitar Book with CD, 2nd Ed., $19.95
Everything® Guitar Chords Book with CD, $19.95
Everything® Guitar Scales Book with CD $19.95
Everything® Harmonica Book with CD, $15.95
Everything® Home Recording Book
Everything® Music Theory Book with CD, $19.95
Everything® Reading Music Book with CD, $19.95
Everything® Rock & Blues Guitar Book with CD, $19.95
Everything® Rock & Blues Piano Book with CD, $19.95
Everything® Rock Drums Book with CD $19.95
Everything® Singing Book with CD $19.95
Everything® Songwriting Book

NEW AGE

Everything® Astrology Book, 2nd Ed.
Everything® Birthday Personology Book
Everything® Celtic Wisdom Book $15.95
Everything® Dreams Book, 2nd Ed.
Everything® Law of Attraction Book $15.95
Everything® Love Signs Book, $9.95
Everything® Love Spells Book, $9.95
Everything® Paganism Book
Everything® Palmistry Book
Everything® Psychic Book

Everything® Reiki Book
Everything® Sex Signs Book, $9.95
Everything® Spells & Charms Book, 2nd Ed.
Everything® Tarot Book, 2nd Ed.
Everything® Toltec Wisdom Book
Everything® Wicca & Witchcraft Book, 2nd Ed.

PARENTING

Everything® Baby Names Book, 2nd Ed.
Everything® Baby Shower Book, 2nd Ed.
Everything® Baby Sign Language Book with DVD
Everything® Baby's First Year Book
Everything® Birthing Book
Everything® Breastfeeding Book
Everything® Father-to-Be Book
Everything® Father's First Year Book
Everything® Get Ready for Baby Book, 2nd Ed.
Everything® Get Your Baby to Sleep Book, $9.95
Everything® Getting Pregnant Book
Everything® Guide to Pregnancy Over 35
Everything® Guide to Raising a One-Year-Old
Everything® Guide to Raising a Two-Year-Old
Everything® Guide to Raising Adolescent Boys
Everything® Guide to Raising Adolescent Girls
Everything® Mother's First Year Book
Everything® Parent's Guide to Childhood Illnesses
Everything® Parent's Guide to Children and Divorce
Everything® Parent's Guide to Children with ADD/ADHD
Everything® Parent's Guide to Children with Asperger's
    Syndrome
Everything® Parent's Guide to Children with Anxiety
Everything® Parent's Guide to Children with Asthma
Everything® Parent's Guide to Children with Autism
Everything® Parent's Guide to Children with Bipolar Disorder
Everything® Parent's Guide to Children with Depression
Everything® Parent's Guide to Children with Dyslexia
Everything® Parent's Guide to Children with Juvenile Diabetes
Everything® Parent's Guide to Children with OCD
Everything® Parent's Guide to Positive Discipline
**Everything® Parent's Guide to Raising Your
    Adopted Child**
Everything® Parent's Guide to Raising a Successful Child
Everything® Parent's Guide to Raising Boys
Everything® Parent's Guide to Raising Girls
Everything® Parent's Guide to Raising Siblings
Everything® Parent's Guide to Sensory Integration Disorder
Everything® Parent's Guide to Tantrums
Everything® Parent's Guide to the Strong-Willed Child
Everything® Parenting a Teenager Book
Everything® Potty Training Book, $9.95
Everything® Pregnancy Book, 3rd Ed.
Everything® Pregnancy Fitness Book
Everything® Pregnancy Nutrition Book
Everything® Pregnancy Organizer, 2nd Ed., $16.95
Everything® Toddler Activities Book
Everything® Toddler Book
Everything® Tween Book
Everything® Twins, Triplets, and More Book

PETS

Everything® Aquarium Book
Everything® Boxer Book
Everything® Cat Book, 2nd Ed.
Everything® Chihuahua Book
Everything® Cooking for Dogs Book
Everything® Dachshund Book

Everything® Dog Book, 2nd Ed.
Everything® Dog Grooming Book
Everything® Dog Obedience Book
Everything® Dog Owner's Organizer, $16.95
Everything® Dog Training and Tricks Book
Everything® German Shepherd Book
Everything® Golden Retriever Book
Everything® Horse Book $15.95
Everything® Horse Care Book
Everything® Horseback Riding Book
Everything® Labrador Retriever Book
Everything® Poodle Book
Everything® Pug Book
Everything® Puppy Book
Everything® Rottweiler Book
Everything® Small Dogs Book
Everything® Tropical Fish Book
Everything® Yorkshire Terrier Book

REFERENCE

Everything® American Presidents Book
Everything® Blogging Book
Everything® Build Your Vocabulary Book, $9.95
Everything® Car Care Book
Everything® Classical Mythology Book
Everything® Da Vinci Book
Everything® Einstein Book
Everything® Enneagram Book
Everything® Etiquette Book, 2nd Ed.
Everything® Family Christmas Book $15.95
Everything® Guide to C. S. Lewis & Narnia
Everything® Guide to Divorce, 2nd Ed. $15.95
Everything® Guide to Edgar Allan Poe
Everything® Guide to Understanding Philosophy
Everything® Inventions and Patents Book
Everything® Jacqueline Kennedy Onassis Book
Everything® John F. Kennedy Book
Everything® Mafia Book
Everything® Martin Luther King Jr. Book
Everything® Philosophy Book
Everything® Pirates Book
Everything® Private Investigation Book
Everything® Psychology Book
Everything® Public Speaking Book, $9.95
Everything® Shakespeare Book, 2nd Ed.

RELIGION

Everything® Angels Book
Everything® Bible Book
Everything® Bible Study Book with CD, $19.95
Everything® Buddhism Book
Everything® Catholicism Book
Everything® Christianity Book
Everything® Gnostic Gospels Book
Everything® Hinduism Book $15.95
Everything® History of the Bible Book
Everything® Jesus Book
Everything® Jewish History & Heritage Book
Everything® Judaism Book
Everything® Kabbalah Book

Everything® Koran Book
Everything® Mary Book
Everything® Mary Magdalene Book
Everything® Prayer Book
Everything® Saints Book, 2nd Ed.
Everything® Torah Book
Everything® Understanding Islam Book
Everything® Women of the Bible Book
Everything® World's Religions Book

SCHOOL & CAREERS

Everything® Career Tests Book
Everything® College Major Test Book
Everything® College Survival Book, 2nd Ed.
Everything® Cover Letter Book, 2nd Ed.
Everything® Filmmaking Book
Everything® Get-a-Job Book, 2nd Ed.
Everything® Guide to Being a Paralegal
Everything® Guide to Being a Personal Trainer
Everything® Guide to Being a Real Estate Agent
Everything® Guide to Being a Sales Rep
Everything® Guide to Being an Event Planner
Everything® Guide to Careers in Health Care
Everything® Guide to Careers in Law Enforcement
Everything® Guide to Government Jobs
Everything® Guide to Starting and Running a Catering
    Business
Everything® Guide to Starting and Running a Restaurant
Everything® Guide to Starting and Running
    a Retail Store
Everything® Job Interview Book, 2nd Ed.
Everything® New Nurse Book
Everything® New Teacher Book
Everything® Paying for College Book
Everything® Practice Interview Book
Everything® Resume Book, 3rd Ed.
Everything® Study Book

SELF-HELP

Everything® Body Language Book
Everything® Dating Book, 2nd Ed.
Everything® Great Sex Book
Everything® Guide to Caring for Aging Parents $15.95
Everything® Self-Esteem Book
Everything® Self-Hypnosis Book $9.95
Everything® Tantric Sex Book

SPORTS & FITNESS

Everything® Easy Fitness Book
Everything® Fishing Book
Everything® Guide to Weight Training $15.95
Everything® Krav Maga for Fitness Book
Everything® Running Book, 2nd Ed.
Everything® Triathlon Training Book $15.95

TRAVEL

Everything® Family Guide to Coastal Florida
Everything® Family Guide to Cruise Vacations
Everything® Family Guide to Hawaii

Everything® Family Guide to Las Vegas, 2nd Ed.
Everything® Family Guide to Mexico
Everything® Family Guide to New England, 2nd Ed.
Everything® Family Guide to New York City, 3rd Ed.
Everything® Family Guide to Northern California
    and Lake Tahoe
Everything® Family Guide to RV Travel & Campgrounds
Everything® Family Guide to the Caribbean
Everything® Family Guide to the Disneyland® Resort, California
    Adventure®, Universal Studios®, and the Anaheim
    Area, 2nd Ed.
Everything® Family Guide to the Walt Disney World Resort®,
    Universal Studios®, and Greater Orlando, 5th Ed.
Everything® Family Guide to Timeshares
Everything® Family Guide to Washington D.C., 2nd Ed.

WEDDINGS

Everything® Bachelorette Party Book, $9.95
Everything® Bridesmaid Book, $9.95
Everything® Destination Wedding Book
Everything® Father of the Bride Book, $9.95
Everything® Green Wedding Book, $15.95
Everything® Groom Book, $9.95
Everything® Jewish Wedding Book, 2nd Ed., $15.95
Everything® Mother of the Bride Book, $9.95
Everything® Outdoor Wedding Book
Everything® Wedding Book, 3rd Ed.
Everything® Wedding Checklist, $9.95
Everything® Wedding Etiquette Book, $9.95
Everything® Wedding Organizer, 2nd Ed., $16.95
Everything® Wedding Shower Book, $9.95
Everything® Wedding Vows Book, 3rd Ed., $9.95
Everything® Wedding Workout Book
Everything® Weddings on a Budget Book, 2nd Ed., $9.95

WRITING

Everything® Creative Writing Book
Everything® Get Published Book, 2nd Ed.
Everything® Grammar and Style Book, 2nd Ed.
Everything® Guide to Magazine Writing
Everything® Guide to Writing a Book Proposal
Everything® Guide to Writing a Novel
Everything® Guide to Writing Children's Books
Everything® Guide to Writing Copy
Everything® Guide to Writing Graphic Novels
Everything® Guide to Writing Research Papers
Everything® Guide to Writing a Romance Novel $15.95
Everything® Improve Your Writing Book, 2nd Ed.
Everything® Writing Poetry Book